San Francisco

Cities of the Imagination

Cities of the Imagination

San Francisco

A cultural and literary history

Mick Sinclair

Signal

Signal Books
Oxford

First published in 2004 by
Signal Books Limited
36 Minster Road
Oxford OX4 1LY
www.signalbooks.co.uk

A catalogue record for this book is available from the British Library

ISBN 1-902669-64-9 Cloth
ISBN 1-902669-65-7 Paper

Drawings by Nicki Averill

Cover Design: Baseline Arts
Typesetting: Devdan Sen
Cover Images: James Davis Travel Photography; Mary Evans Picture Library;
Redferns Music Picture Library

Printed and bound in Canada by Webcom

Contents

Foreword

A city is how we encounter it—both in terms of our lives in it and how we come to know it. Mick Sinclair's take on San Francisco is revelatory for someone who thought he knew the city well.

Such an effect this small city has on the world. Compared to the longevity of European towns, San Francisco is a child. Compared to the vast acreage of New York, Chicago, and Los Angeles, San Francisco's geography is that of a small town. Yet its intellectual life reflects a polis of the mind in great scope. The blending of architecture and the natural landscape is unexcelled. It's the inspiration of songs, yet there is also the grim—"all made out of ticky-tacky and they all look just the same"—sung of the hillside housing in southern San Francisco.

I've been inspired by San Francisco's place and history as a port city, where novel ideas are born, where writers and explorers bring their own visions to a welcoming place. I started a radio cultural talk and performance show to bring these voices to a larger world, because I found the sensibility of San Francisco to be distinct in the US. Its élan and worldliness feels European, yet it has an economic boisterousness that George Babbitt would bathe in with glee.

San Francisco is a favorite city of travelers, according to many Chamber-of-Commerce-driven polls. I find this amusing given that the liberal politics and libidinous behavior of our citizens lead to invective and jokes made on late-night talk shows: "Only in San Francisco!" Yet, as Mick Sinclair astutely sets forth in his engaging account of this disparity between the conventional "other" of our land and the desired ways of life as practiced by San Franciscans, we've touched the subconscious imaginations of Americans as well as the rest of the world since the 1840s.

So how did this place, San Francisco, a city of realities, as well as imagination, come to be what it is? This guide has answers both for visitors and for residents. "United Nations" gives some discomforting insight to our self-illusioned liberality, and "Turning America on Its Head" depicts the seduction and maturation of Free Love. What a *frisson* to come across Richard Brautigan's 1968 ode to "mutual programming harmony" as computers and humans find their way back to nature hand-in-keyboard. Mind-blowing, to coin a phrase.

San Francisco looks north and south for comforting comparisons: Seattle dwellers for years felt like second stringers to the City by the Bay, Angelenos travel north for bookstores and cleaner air... but we do nurture our own little sibling envy of New York. What does it mean that the largest readership of the *New Yorker* magazine and the *New York Times* outside New York is in the Bay Area? There is a vision, a self-appreciation of the residents that we are in the know, as we put others in the know, and want to read about ourselves in the most national of organs. Yet with this narcissism comes both arrogance and insecurity.

Herb Caen, our city's Sam Pepys, claimed that the phrase "the more things change the more they stay the same" sounds better in English than in the original French. I'm reminded of this phrase when I read Mick Sinclair's depiction of the mayors who are marked as honorable and visionary, and those who were as mendacious rapscallions. Sex can be (and will be) straight or gay, or both. The where's and who's of it are here, through the decades, as an important part of the city's history. We've been a violent place, a sensual place, and also a place of imagination and fervent desires to preserve the beauty of it. Along the way, we've not treated immigrants well. I cringe to read that history, because it clashes with my imagined city.

Our history is similar to those other rambunctious and wealth-infused Western towns that went through booms and busts, fires and fancies of new wealth: Seattle, Skagway, Dawson City. San Francisco is still a town of the Wild West.

For too long San Francisco was known, even in the media business, as where you'd go in a freezing East Coast February to do a story on the "fruits and nuts." I wanted the world to know that San Francisco is more than its kooks and freaks, that thoughtful people live here, in a harmony born of the acceptance of others. As this history shows, San Francisco has overcome early isolation, to become a mediating influence in the world. Filmmakers including Francis Ford Coppola make this city their production center as a way to protect the integrity of their art from their tawdrier cousins in Hollywood.

San Francisco's history includes the voiceless struggling to speak, often in great conflict with recalcitrant legal and social conventions. Sinclair offers again the voices of the immigrants, ethnic, sexual, and racial, who populate this landscape. The early Miwok are remembered, as is fitting, with the few words that Ishi and his antecedents gave us, remnants of a culture resident more than 5,000 years in the Bay Area. When Sinclair gets to the sixties and seventies, we discover the Haight-Ashbury. His experience interviewing pop stars gives perspective, and the "you-are-thereness" of the voices he finds, like Ralph J. Gleason, who vividly recreates an era marked by brio, wit, and drugs.

How strange, too, to be part of what is now history in the account of this city. Our production offices were forced out by the quintupling rents during the dotcommification, yet one enterprise, now defunct, backed our radio tour to report on surfers in Antarctica.

What visitors and residents alike don't see is the sadness of much of the history of San Francisco. The place seems such a playground—with cable cars and ferry boasts, grand views and intimate cafés and wine bars. Yet its suicide rate is high, in part, some speculate, because the nadir of a personal life fails to reach the zenith of the imagined.

Each week I begin my broadcast with the phrase, "from the city known for its hills, its restaurants, and its arbitrary parking laws." As the world has changed, and I've traveled, I've seen many places fit those descriptors... or at least one of them. Wheeled vehicles—skateboards, bicycles, cars, buses and trucks—pose imminent threats to the walker and bystander. The last Friday of each month, cyclists gather en Critical Masse to slow cars, sometimes hindered, sometimes aided by the police. The relationship between authority and expressive citizens gives rich material to Sinclair's chapter "Turning America on Its Head."

San Francisco—the name itself sounds like a ready-made lyric to a song, a place of left hearts, as well as luggage, a place of gates golden and social opening and closing, a place to dance, and a place to walk. San Francisco is still young, yet has led many lives. The history is accumulating, day by day. You are a part of it by being here, moving here, living here, loving here, leaving here. Give this place time and it will show you life.

Sedge Thomson

Preface

San Francisco can please in many ways. The way it pleased me most on my first visit—some time between the Loma Preita earthquake and the Oakland hills fires—was by being much smaller than I expected and much smaller than its immense reputation would suggest. For the writer on a research mission, a small city of great renown is a welcome thing: no time-consuming journeys between points of interest and no awkward writing later on when concocting a sentence to link together two places that might logically be regarded as neighbors despite having many miles of urban nothingness (hello Los Angeles!) between them.

And, having previously been exposed in a professional capacity to some of Europe's oldest parts and consequently called upon to compress several thousand years of human civilization into a few snappily-written pages, the fact that San Francisco effectively began with the gold rush, making it a young city even by American standards, made me confident that I might actually get somewhere close to telling its story adequately.

San Francisco revealed itself—on that first and through many subsequent stays—as a city (or simply and assertively as *"the City"*, as it has been known in northern California since the gold rush) that has not grown up nor settled down, but one that stays true to its origins as a place where anything and everything seems possible. This is a rare part of the US where eccentricity is more prized than conformity, where "liberal" is not a dirty word, and from where off-center literary, cultural and political movements have evolved and resonated around the world.

Throughout its brief existence San Francisco has followed a script of such madcap twists and turns that nobody has accurately predicted exactly what might happen next. The likelihood of another major earthquake is inescapable but the city could equally be changed beyond recognition by an overdose of "Manhattanization", gentrification, privatization, or any of the other economy-based phenomena that threaten on a daily basis. Alternatively, given the local habit of turning to the past whenever the future looks ugly, it could be the first city to die of nostalgia.

Journalists, travelers, historians, and other chroniclers have created an enormous factual archive on the curious case of San Francisco, yet the city has inspired comparatively little fiction (put down those sticks! I said *comparatively* little). Because where is the novelist who would dare to invent Joshua Norton, a self-proclaimed emperor officially recognized as such by the city; Lillie Coit's tower and her obsession with fires; the Co-existence Bagel Shop; the breasts of Carol Doda; the money-less shops of The Diggers; Herb Caen, a newspaper columnist worshipped as a deity; the Sydney Ducks; the Grateful Dead; or a cyber-age attempt to recreate the Great Library of Alexandria in a former Spanish garrison?

Hopefully this book explains how all of these things, and many more no less extraordinary, fit together to make San Francisco a place where truth really can be stranger than fiction.

Could *you* make it up?

Mick Sinclair
London, 2003

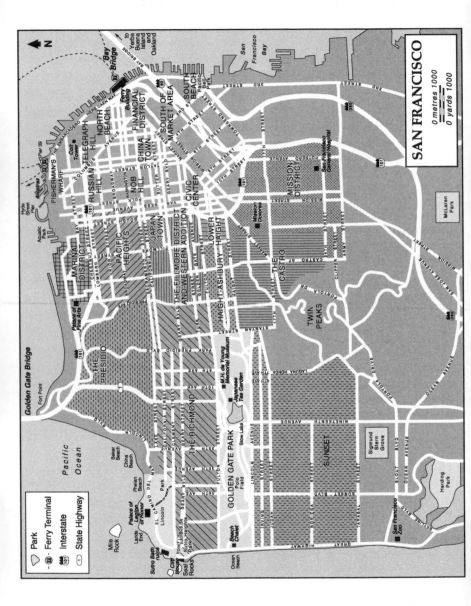

SAN FRANCISCO

INTRODUCTION

Navigating San Francisco

San Francisco occupies the seven-mile-wide northern tip of the San Francisco peninsula. Without room to expand, the city is characterized by a compact patchwork of neighborhoods set around hills, valleys, and flatlands, and occupied by a population never able to grow much beyond 750,000.

Historical Geography

Around 10,000 Native Americans are thought to have inhabited the peninsula immediately prior to the eighteenth-century Spanish arrival although few are believed to have occupied the site of the future San Francisco, then an unprepossessing mixture of rugged hills and sand dunes.

The Spanish established a *presidio*, or garrison, overlooking the Golden Gate on the peninsula's northwest corner. The site, and the surrounding 1,500 acres, are still known today as the Presidio and form a largely wooded area that served for many years as a US military base. The mission that the original *presidio* ostensibly protected was located inland, three miles south, its chapel the only surviving element in the area now known as the Mission District. The Mission District's growth was not triggered by the mission—both it and the Presidio became neglected after the collapse of the Spanish empire—but by the much later westward expansion of what became San Francisco.

The city grew from Yerba Buena, a small trading post sited on San Francisco Bay (from which Yerba Buena would take a new name) on the eastern side of the peninsula. Through the crucial years of the 1848-52 gold rush when San Francisco's population exploded beyond the wildest dreams of its early settlers, the crescent-shaped shoreline of Yerba Buena was filled-in, creating land that evolved into a commercial center and seeded the present Financial District. From this point, and from the former social hub of Portsmouth Square just north, the American city (California switched from Mexican to US ownership in 1848) began to grow, expanding north and south, and west across the peninsula towards the Pacific Ocean.

Growth was far from steady, however, characterized by economic booms and busts and occasional earthquakes, notably the 1906 earthquake and fire that left much of the city in ruins and erased most evidence of the nineteenth century from areas adjacent to the bay.

The Modern City

Easily spotted by its high-rise offices—including the unmistakable Transamerica Pyramid—the Financial District forms a major part of what is commonly referred to as "Downtown". Although no hard and fast boundaries exist, Downtown is generally regarded as including the area around the Ferry Building, on the eastern waterfront, Union Square, traditionally a prime area for shopping and tourist hotels, as well as, from the 1990s, the adjacent area immediately south of Market Street (see next page). To the west, Downtown touches the tawdry but improving Tenderloin area, beyond which lies UN Plaza and the resplendent City Hall.

Within the shadow of the Financial District's towers lies Chinatown whose northern boundaries have pressed into the once predominately Italian area of North Beach. Despite many cafés and restaurants of Italian origin (or affection), North Beach lost its distinctive ethnic population as it had earlier lost its beach, consumed by landfill as the city pushed its northern waterfront out to what is now Fisherman's Wharf. Once genuinely populated by a working fishing fleet, Fisherman's Wharf is the only section of San Francisco where tourists and tourists services are more prevalent than locals, although the dockside does provide the ferry service to Alcatraz Island, a one-time military installation that found great infamy as a prison, easily spotted from most high vantage points.

Rising between North Beach and Fisherman's Wharf, Telegraph Hill is cloaked by expensive homes and topped by the distinctive concrete erection of Coit Tower. On the other side of North Beach, west of Columbus Avenue, lies Russian Hill while, further west beyond the broad thoroughfare of Van Ness Avenue, are the serial humps of expensive Pacific Heights. Another landfill episode created the flatlands north of Pacific Heights initially to hold the 1915 Panama-Pacific Exposition but since consumed by the affluent Marina District which retains the landmark Expo relic, the Palace of Fine Arts.

Previously the site of the city's most extravagant private homes, Nob Hill forms a steep western wall to Chinatown, and beyond it lie areas that were created as separate entities from the city proper but which became engulfed by San Francisco's relentless expansion. They include the strongly African-American Western Addition (within which is the Fillmore District) and Haight-Ashbury, the cradle of 1960s hippiedom, both with many of their original Victorian and Edwardian homes intact. Further west are younger neighborhoods, such as the Richmond, south of the Presidio and north of Golden Gate Park (a three-mile long, one-mile-wide green rectangle reaching almost to the ocean), which retain a sense of suburban serenity despite their closeness (by the standards of most urban areas) to the heart of the city.

Increasingly taking overspill from the Financial District and, during the 1990s, the hub of the city's mushrooming cyberspace economy, the area immediately south of Market Street and close to the bay has been known since the 1980s as "SoMa" (an informal abbreviation derived from SOuth of MArket Street or, as some suggest, an acronym for "South of Market Area"). Within SoMa, its wide blocks originally providing jobs and housing for a blue collar workforce, is the growing modern cultural complex of Yerba Buena Center and the much less celebrated loft apartments that attracted non-San Franciscan dotcom beneficiaries, much to the disgust and detriment of the established community.

Parallel to Market Street, Mission Street is SoMa's prime east-west route, which, in a rare link with pre-US times, follows the course of the original Mission trail that linked the declining Mission Dolores with Yerba Buena. The Mission District is a changing but long Latino-dominated area, its continuity threatened like neighboring SoMa as the 1990s dotcom explosion made landlords and property speculators hungry for bigger profits. As Mission Street swings south, the land to the west is consumed by the predominantly gay Castro area, divided by a series of hills from Haight-Ashbury, immediately north.

Up and Down in San Francisco

Two-dimensional maps do little to prepare first-timers for San Francisco's harshest reality: the city's 43 (some say 44) hills and the fact that streets often pass right over them. A 1970s airline advertising campaign offered: "When you are tired of walking around San Francisco you can always lean against it." What looks like an easily-walked route on paper can involve a strength-sapping gradient, the most severe being a Russian Hill section of Filbert Street which reaches a 31.5-degree angle. The most photographed slope, however, is another part of Russian Hill where zigzagging herbaceous borders were added to a part of Lombard Street during the 1920s, causing traffic to weave slowly along its course while descending towards North Beach.

Maritime Navigation

As essential to San Francisco's character as neighborhoods and hills are the offshore areas, of which there are three. To the east is the broad and placid San Francisco Bay, fed by fresh water rivers from California's mountains. Providing safe anchorage for ocean-going vessels, the sheltered bay—on the east side of which lie Oakland and the university community of Berkeley—enabled the trading post of Yerba Buena to take root.

To reach Yerba Buena, ships passed through the Golden Gate, the strait defining the northern waterfront of the city and from which the famous bridge takes its name. Despite what many assume, the strait itself was named in 1846, before the discovery of California's gold. Unlike the bay, the Golden Gate's waters are deep and choppy and its span usually assaulted by strong winds. The Golden Gate gives access to the Pacific Ocean, filling the gap between San Francisco and Asia and providing the kind of sunsets that conclude romantic comedies and add several thousand dollars to the value of ocean-view properties in San Francisco's most westerly reaches.

PART ONE

The Instant City

In January 1847, when the population of the United States was approaching 23 million and the city of New York held almost 500,000 people, a few hundred souls living on the tip of a hilly, windswept peninsula on the California coast decided to change their settlement's name from Yerba Buena to San Francisco. They hoped to benefit from the good reputation among seafarers, particularly whalers who knew it as a supply stop, of San Francisco Bay on which the settlement sat.

Whatever its name, prospects seemed limited for a place settled by long-departed Spanish, governed for decades without interest by Mexico, and recently described by a local rancher, Rincón de la Salinas, as "having a population of less than 400, with no commerce, no wealth, no power and without a name, save as a small trading post and mission."

What nobody could have predicted was the discovery of California gold in January 1848 (the same year that California came under US control), which triggered the biggest population movement the world had ever seen to a place, San Francisco, very few had previously heard of. The remote settlement, where tents outnumbered buildings and streets were rutted tracks, would be transformed at unprecedented pace into the US's tenth biggest city by 1870 and gain commercial importance as a conduit for gold rush fortunes and the country's major Pacific port.

A Great and Magnificent Port
Spanish navigators discovered Alta California (today's state of California) in 1542, believing the coastline to be that of a peninsula or island. At a site thought to be today's Point Reyes, the British seafarer Sir Francis Drake berthed in 1579 to make repairs to his ship, the *Golden Hind*. Yet there were no attempts to settle California until 1769,

when the Spanish launched the Sacred Expedition, commanded by Gaspar de Portolá and under the religious leadership of Junípero Serra. Traveling overland, the expedition's main base was at San Diego, where the first of what, by 1823, would be 21 California missions (and several branch missions) reaching over 400 miles north to Sonoma, was built.

The excellent natural harborage afforded by San Francisco Bay had been missed in the 1542 voyage as its entrance, the Golden Gate, was concealed by cliffs and difficult to spot from the ocean. Instead, the bay was accidentally discovered in 1769 by the Portolá party seeking a route to Monterey. The leading missionary of the party, Juan Crespi, observed: "without any doubt this is a very great and magnificent port."

Not until March 1775 did another overland party, led by Juan Bautista de Anza, reach the area, planting a cross at the northern tip of the San Francisco peninsula to mark the future site of a *presidio*, a defensive fortification above the Golden Gate. Three miles south in a more sheltered location, the mission of San Francisco de Asís (later known as Mission Dolores) was founded. In August of that year, Juan Manuel de Ayala captained the first ship to pass through the Golden Gate and into the bay, mapping the region and giving its features their enduring Spanish names. Chaplain and cartographer on the Anza expedition was Pedro Font, whose diaries, written in 1777 and published in 1930, record: "although in all my travels I saw very good sites and beautiful country, I saw none which pleased me as much as this. And I think that if it could be well settled... there would not be anything more beautiful in the world."

Extending and supposedly strengthening the Spanish empire (though California's remoteness and lack of obvious material wealth caused many Spaniards to regard it as an unnecessary burden), the mission system forcibly housed natives on mission compounds, converted them to Catholicism, and exploited their labor. Isolated from other settlements, each mission had to be largely self-sufficient and, to this end, natives might be trained in masonry, milling, shoemaking, saddlery, pottery, and weaving. The harsh working conditions and a lack of immunity to European diseases would devastate California's native population and destroy its cultures.

Despite the arrival of a British ship under George Vancouver in 1792 and, from 1812, the establishment of a Russian fur trapping settlement sixty miles north of San Francisco, anticipated encroachments from rival European powers failed to materialize. Instead, the Spanish empire itself collapsed and in 1822 control of California passed to the newly independent nation of Mexico.

With scant interest in and little ability to exploit the distant and barely populated region, the Mexican government permitted large sections of California to pass into the ownership of the Californios (California-born of Spanish or Mexican descent) and rewarded foreigners who wished to settle with large land grants. The fertile valleys and mild climate proved ideal for raising cattle and crops. In *The Beginnings of San Francisco*, Zoeth Skinner Eldredge described the outlook around San Francisco Bay in 1835 as: "a vast solitude through whose bordering groves ranged the red deer, the elk, and the antelope, while bears, and panthers, and other ferocious beasts frequented the hills and often descended upon the scattered farm yards."

A bay-side settlement on the eastern side of the San Francisco peninsula developed as a trading post for hides and tallow, and for servicing whaling ships taking advantage of the sheltered anchorage to stock up on supplies. The post was named Yerba Buena (or "good herb") for the wild mint-flavored plant that grew there. Settlers typically took Mexican citizenship, adopted Catholicism, and married into the local population. One who followed this path was English whaler William A. Richardson (1795-1858) who left his ship in San Francisco Bay, married the daughter of the Presidio's *comandante*, and in 1835 erected what would be regarded as Yerba Buena's first house (see pp.23-4).

Numbering a few hundred, Yerba Buena's population was an ethnic mixture that included English, Scots, French, Spanish, Dutch, German, Pacific Islanders, and what would be a growing number of arrivals from the US. One of the latter was Massachusetts-born William Sturges Hinckley (1807-46), who arrived in California in 1829, adopted Mexican citizenship and in 1844 was appointed Yerba Buena's *alcalde* (a civic leadership role that combined the duties of mayor, sheriff, and judge). Among Hinckley's achievements was overseeing the construction of a small bridge crossing a saltwater lagoon that filled with the incoming tide and made travel through the settlement difficult. Such was its success that another settler, William Heath Davis, recalled "people came from far and near to look at and admire it, especially the native Californians, who arrived from the mission and elsewhere, with their wives and children, to contemplate the remarkable structure."

Californios were renowned for their horse skills and hospitality but displayed little appetite for business or the economic development of the region. California trade became dominated by foreigners, particularly the entrepreneurial Americans who would buy hides from the Californios to manufacture leather goods that would then be sold back to the Californios.

Advised to spend time outdoors to improve his eyesight which had been damaged by measles, a Harvard student, Richard Henry Dana, spent 16 months at sea working on a ship trading between the US and California. Published in 1840, his *Two Years Before the Mast* provided a detailed account of his time and became an important source of knowledge of the Californio era. In one section he describes "the remote and almost unknown coast of California" along which his ship sailed to enter the Golden Gate in the winter of 1835–6:

> *[The ship] floated into the vast solitude of the Bay of San Francisco. All around was the stillness of nature. One vessel, a Russian, lay at anchor there, but during our whole stay not a sail came or went. Our trade was with remote Missions, which sent hides to us in launches manned by their Indians. Our anchorage was between a small island, called Yerba Buena, and a gravel beach in a little bight or cove of the same name, formed by two small, projecting points. Beyond, to the westward of the landing-place, were dreary sand-hills, with little grass to be seen, and few trees, and beyond them higher hills, steep and barren, their sides gullied by the rains. Some five or six miles beyond the landing-place, to the right, was a ruinous Presidio, and some three or four miles to the left was the Mission of Dolores, as ruinous as the Presidio, almost deserted, with but few Indians attached to it, and but little property in cattle. Over a region far beyond our sight there were no other human habitations, except that an enterprising Yankee, years in advance of his time, had put up, on the rising ground above the landing, a shanty of rough boards, where he carried on a very small retail trade between the hide ships and the Indians.*

The doctrine of Manifest Destiny, driving the expansion of the US, brought uncertainty over the future of California, even after Mexico rejected the US's offer in 1835 of $500,000 for San Francisco Bay. Looking fretfully ahead to 1846, a Yerba Buena merchant commented: "I am afraid we shall see a great deal of trouble in California this year. There are 7 or 8,000 emigrants from the USA expected."

The US-Mexico War that began in 1846 saw the brief creation of the independent Bear Flag Republic (the origin of the bear on California's state flag) and the arrival of a US warship, the *Portsmouth*, in San Francisco Bay. After several days at anchor, US troops rowed ashore on July 9, 1846, and hoisted the Stars and Stripes above Yerba Buena's central plaza as the ship's band played *Yankee Doodle Dandy*. Martial law was declared and the plaza was re-named Portsmouth Square. Born in Hawaii to a Bostonian father and a Polynesian mother, William Heath Davis (1822-1909) had married into one of the major land-owning Californio families. He would later be remembered for his valuable memoirs, *Seventy Five Years in California*, a section of which recalled the less-than-tense martial law period:

> *We were out on a visit one evening, and were crossing Portsmouth Square, on the way home, about eleven o'clock, when we were hailed by the guard on duty: 'Halt! who goes there?'. 'Friends,' we answered. 'Advance and give the countersign!' commanded the sentry. We advanced, but both Howard and myself had forgotten it. We explained our position. The guard said he was obliged to take us to the guardhouse, which he accordingly did, armed with his musket, one of us on each side of him. Fortunately, Captain Watson was still up, and, on seeing us approach under arrest, burst out laughing.*

The US-Mexico War ended with the Treaty of Guadalupe Hidalgo, under which Mexico accepted a payment of $15 million from the US in return for Texas, New Mexico, and California. As a US city renamed San Francisco, the former Yerba Buena could expect slow and uneventful growth in trade as a minor Pacific port. Gertrude Atherton wrote: "the only excitement was the arrival of mail from the East, and an occasional fight or fandango."

Any prospect of sudden wealth was stymied by the isolation and distance from the eastern US. Travel overland entailed a covered wagon trek of six months across mountain passes liable to become blocked by snow (the grisly fate of the Donner Party, of which 40 out of 87 trapped travelers died and survivors resorted to cannibalism, was a recent memory). The alternative was a ship via Cape Horn, a 17,000-mi journey from New York that might take eight months and involve poor food, terrible weather, rough seas, and unpredictable captains. The more adventurous might shorten the journey by crossing the isthmus of Panama, an arduous horseback journey through malarial rainforest (the Panama Canal would not open until 1915) followed by a struggle to find a ship continuing to San Francisco.

Gold: Half the Size of a Pea
On January 28, 1848, John Marshall, a wheelwright from New Jersey who had traveled west, was building a sawmill on John Sutter's ranch, near the site of present-day Sacramento, when something a foot deep in the clear water of the American River caught his eye: "I reached my hand down and picked it up; it made my heart thump, for I was certain it was gold. The piece was about half the size and shape of a pea. Then I saw another."

That night, Marshall and Sutter (1803-80, a German-born settler who had acquired 48,000 acres and had dreams of a vast agricultural empire reaching to the Pacific coast), with the aid of *Encyclopedia Americana*, conducted tests on the metal and concluded it was indeed gold. Sutter hoped to keep the discovery quiet to ensure his work force would remain and his land would not be overrun. But as word spread among Sutter's workers, it reached the ears of Sam Brannan, a larger-than-life figure who was a supply store partner and proprietor of the *California Star* newspaper. In San Francisco, news of the discovery was largely dismissed (as were earlier extravagant claims, such as the discovery of California coal) until May 12, when Sam Brannan, allegedly having equipped his supply store with all the pre-requisites of gold prospecting, marched through Portsmouth Square holding aloft a gold-filled quinine bottle yelling "Gold! Gold in the American River!"

Almost immediately San Francisco's stores were divested of lamps, pickaxes, shovels, food and clothing as its population (like those of other California settlements) headed toward what became known as the "diggings". By the end of May, there were two thousand men "scratching like hens in the sand and gravel of the Sacramento Valley" and they were soon joined by many more from Mexico and Central and South America. On May 29, 1848, the San Francisco-based journal, *The Californian*, carried the following:

> *The whole country from San Francisco to Los Angeles, and from the sea shore to the base of the Sierra Nevada, resounds with the sordid cry of gold! GOLD!! GOLD!!!—while the field is left half planted, the house half built, and every thing neglected but the manufacture of shovels and pickaxes, and the means of transportation to the spot where one man obtained one hundred and twenty-eight dollars' worth of the real stuff in one day's washing, and the average for all concerned is twenty dollars per diem!*

That would be the last issue of the paper for some months. The next day its entire staff departed for the diggings. According to Gertrude Atherton: "Even the editor was on the highroad, a pick over one shoulder, a shovel over the other, and a pan under his arm."

On the US East Coast, where the population was used to wild claims from the frontier lands, there was widespread skepticism over the validity of the discovery. This changed in December 1848 when President Polk announced the claim was true and put 230 ounces of California gold on display. The *New York Tribune* trumpeted: "Fortune lies upon the surface of the earth as plentiful as the mud in our streets." And with that, the gold rush began.

The World Rushes in

The mass exodus from San Francisco during May 1848 raised doubts about the city's very survival as land values briefly plummeted and demand for services fell. As California's major port, however, San Francisco was the gateway to the diggings and during 1849 its population rocketed from 812 to 20,000.

As a plot of land costing $16 in 1847 sold for $45,000 eighteen months later, fears of economic collapse quickly disappeared and prices, compared with the rest of the US, reached astronomical heights.

With fresh fruit and farm produce in heavy demand, apples sold for $5 each; eggs reached $50 a dozen, and a loaf of bread would cost ten or twenty times its New York equivalent. Of tools, a shovel could be $25, a metal pan $5; while a decent blanket could cost $40 and a strong pair of boots $100, the same price as a gallon of whisky.

Accommodation was similarly expensive. A hotel room might be infested with rats, lice, and fleas but human occupants could still be charged $150 for a week's stay; a cheaper option was a bunk on the outside porch of a house for $20. Profits made by shopkeepers were offset by spiraling rents: a small shop cost perhaps $4,000 a month; the annual rent for a popular gambling venue, the El Dorado, was $40,000, and that was just a canvas tent.

At a time when the average national wage for unskilled labor was a dollar a day, even menial jobs in San Francisco became lucrative. Domestic servants could command $200 a month, almost matching the $8 per day paid to members of Congress. Zoeth Skinner Eldredge described how: "Sailors, cooks, or day laborers, frequently became heads of profitable establishments, while doctors, lawyers, and other professional men, worked for wages, even as waiters and shoeblacks." Van Wyck Brockes's *In the Times of Melville and Whitman* portrayed a socially chaotic San Francisco: "There were ex-doctors sweeping the streets, ex-ministers who were gamblers, bankers and Sicilian bandits who were waiters in cafés, lawyers washing the decks of ships and penniless counts and marquises who were lightermen or fishermen or porters."

With only around 2,000 women in a city of almost 30,000 people, traditionally female occupations such as washing, ironing and cooking, too, became highly paid. Some miners realized they could save money by shipping their clothing to China or Hawaii to be cleaned; others simply wore what they had until it disintegrated, then bought new. Women were such a rare sight that an auction house on Montgomery Street would suspend trading when a female was spotted, allowing the traders to watch her pass by. Children were even rarer. In *Roughing It*, Mark Twain described dining in the post-gold rush days with a San Francisco woman who remembered a story her father told her of her arrival in the city as a small child being carried by servant:

A huge miner, bearded, belted, spurred, and bristling with deadly weapons—just down from a long campaign in the mountains, evidently—barred the way, stopped the servant, and stood gazing, with a face all alive with gratification and astonishment. Then he said, reverently: 'Well, if it ain't a child!' And then he snatched a little leather sack out of his pocket and said to the servant: 'There's a hundred and fifty dollars in dust, there, and I'll give it to you to let me kiss the child!'

Few arrivals planned to stay long in San Francisco, however, and most made for the diggings the instant they landed. As their crews deserted, ships were abandoned in the bay even before passengers and cargo had been unloaded, leaving both to the mercy of thieves. Some ships rotted, others were put to practical use: the *Niantic* was converted into a hotel; the *Euphemia* was used as a jail. Many more provided the landfill that extended San Francisco eastwards, filling-in the crescent-shaped bay of old Yerba Buena and forming the foundations of the present-day Financial District.

In *Life by Land and Sea*, Prentice Mulford recalled the scene that greeted him on his arrival in the mid-1850s and the methods of a scrap prospector called Hare:

Rows of old hulks were moored off Market street wharf, maritime relics of '49. That was "Rotten Row." One by one they fell victims to Hare.

Hare purchased them, set Chinamen to picking their bones, broke them up, put the shattered timbers in one pile, the iron bolts in another, the copper in another, the cordage in another, and so in a short time all that remained of these bluff-bowed, old-fashioned ships and brigs, that had so often doubled the stormy corner of Cape Horn or smoked their try-pots in the Arctic ocean was so many ghastly heaps of marine debris.

Mulford's schoolboy belief, shared by many in the eastern US, was of California as a "fearfully hot country and full of snakes." But the prospect of a quick and easy fortune at the diggings outweighed ignorance of the region, and tens of thousands took the chance and traveled west, as did many more from around the globe. In January 1849, the *New York Herald* reported: "Everyday men of property and means are advertising their possessions for sale on order to furnish themselves with means to reach that golden land... Poets, philosophers, lawyers, brokers, bankers, merchants, farmers, clergymen, all are feeling the impulse." Sent by the *New York Tribune* to cover the gold rush, journalist Bayard Taylor wrote: "The very air is pregnant with the magnetism of bold, spirited, unwearied action, and he who but ventures into the outer circle of the whirlpool, is spinning... in its dizzy vortex."

With a third of the gold rush population arriving from outside the US, San Francisco's small polyglot population suddenly became a large and frenzied melting pot. Taylor wrote of the city in September 1849: "Yankees of every possible variety, native Californians in sarapes and sombreros, Chileans, Sonorans, Kanaks from Hawaii, Chinese with long tails, Malays armed with their everlasting creeses, and others in whom embronzed and beared visages it was impossible to recognise any especial nationality."

For a short time, the rivers of the mother lode (as the gold bearing area became known, based on the erroneous assumption that there was a single vein of gold off which all others branched) yielded their precious cargo to anyone who stood in a river and panned for it. Early arrivals reported finding up to five pounds of gold a day. Very soon, the gold became harder to extract and the industry became dominated by well-financed companies with the means to blast rock and build mines. Work at the diggings was tough and life in the new mining camps no less so. Place names echoed the rambunctious mood: Hangtown, Rough and Ready, Whisky Bay, Brandy Gulch, Humbug Hill, Hell's Delight.

San Francisco, by contrast, promised plentiful pleasures, including what Herbert Asbury described as "the roaring temptations of the brothel, the gambling houses, and the other fascinating flesh-pots of the city" where miners "squandered their hard-earned fortunes on harlots, liquor, and games of chance; they paid hundreds of dollars for fruit, vegetables, and game out of season; they met without a murmur of protest the extraordinary expenses of common food and lodging." In addition, miners arriving in San Francisco typically indulged in elaborate personal displays, wearing huge gold rings and using diamonds to fasten their shorts; those who could stand the pain had their teeth removed and replaced with gold plates. In *Gold Dust: The California Gold Rush and the Forty-niners*, Donald Hale Jackson wrote: "San Francisco was the most exciting city in the world in the summer of 1849. Life telescoped there: a man lived a year in a month." A *New York Evening Post* correspondent on the spot reported more succinctly: "The people of San Francisco are mad, stark mad."

On the proceeds of the gold rush San Francisco was beginning to look like an American city. Tents were replaced by wooden buildings, and while fires were frequent a lawyer of the time commented: "We burn down a city in a night and rebuild it in a day. Contracts for new buildings are signed by the light that is consuming the old." In 1853, the main streets were still paved with wooden planks but they were newly illuminated at night by street lamps fueled with kerosene from whale oil.

Returning in 1859, Richard Henry Dana found a place very different from the Yerba Buena he had seen 24 years earlier:

When I awoke in the morning, and looked from my windows over the city of San Francisco, with its storehouses, towers, and steeples; its court-houses, theatres, and hospitals; its daily journals; its well-filled learned professions; its fortresses and light-houses; its wharves and harbor, with their thousand-ton clipper ships, more in number than London or Liverpool sheltered that day, itself one of the capitals of the American Republic... when I saw all these things, and reflected on what I once was and saw here, and what now surrounded me, I could scarcely keep my hold on reality at all.

Winners, Losers—and Emperor Norton

The gold rush made San Francisco a city, made California a rich and independently-minded state, and made fortunes of unimagined enormity for some individuals. The enduring riches, however, went not to those who panned or mined for gold but to the suppliers of provisions and services. Of the figures brought to prominence by the gold rush, some were loved, some were loathed, some founded octopus-like business empires whose tentacles reached into every facet of life, and some died poor and embittered. But only one was accepted on the streets of San Francisco as an emperor.

If there was one man for whom the gold rush should have earned a fortune it was John Sutter, on whose land the initial discovery was made. Sutter's holdings included 13,000 head of cattle, a flour mill, a ten-acre orchard, two acres of roses, and the large adobe structure of Sutter's Fort serving as ranch headquarters and a reception point for overland travelers which seeded the modern-day state capital, Sacramento. Sutter's dreams of an even bigger agricultural domain were ended as his laborers gave up farm work for gold panning and thousands of squatters trampled over his land, slaughtering cattle and raiding food supplies.

In an 1857 magazine article, Sutter lamented: "By this sudden discovery of the gold, all my great plans were destroyed. Had I succeeded for a few years before the gold was discovered, I would have been the richest citizen on the Pacific shore; but it had to be different. Instead of being rich, I am ruined..." Sutter acquired a pension from the state government but lost it when he sought compensation from the US government, a fight which continued to his death in 1880 and which was continued after it by his descendants. Intriguingly, Russian filmmaker Sergei Eisenstein, during his brief stay in Hollywood, hoped to make a biopic, *Sutter's Gold: An American Tragedy*, but his screenplay was rejected for its anti-capitalist sentiment.

Initially at least, one who fared better than Sutter was Sam Brannan. Brannan (1819-89) arrived in San Francisco in 1846 aboard the *Brooklyn*, part of a group of 238 Mormons seeking a new life free of the religious intolerance of the US, only to find their destination had, during the course of their voyage, become part of the US. Brannan was an unlikely Mormon (he was excommunicated from the church for diverting its funds into his own pockets, and he survived San Francisco's first jury trial for land sale irregularities) but was a perfect gold-rush millionaire. By selling prospecting equipment at extortionate prices, Brannan made $36,000 in nine weeks and became the richest person in California. His interests expanded into banking and transport, and he looked beyond San Francisco to develop the natural springs at what he named Calistoga (combining the names of California and the spa resort of Saratoga in New York State). His downfall was a high-risk investment in Mexico and a propensity for alcohol that had caused his wife to file for divorce on account of his "notorious intemperance". In 1889, Brannan died in a rural boarding house impoverished, due in part to the divorce settlement; his body lay in a vault for a year until burial costs could be raised.

A German-born tailor, Levi Strauss (1830-1902) landed in San Francisco in 1850 equipped not with gold panning utensils, but with the canvas he hoped to fashion into tents and wagon covers. Yet instead of making these, Strauss found the material suitable for making strong, loose-fitting trousers, ideal for the needs of a gold miner. In 1873, the canvas was replaced with blue denim and, thanks to the idea of a partner, its strength was increased by the use of copper rivets giving birth to the "jean" (said to derive from the use of Genoese cloth). Steadily, demand for Levi clothing spread to cowboys and lumberjacks, and anyone needing hard-wearing work clothing. Strauss died in 1902, his descendants continuing the business which evolved into today's global brand with its headquarters within the architecturally elegant 1980s Levi Plaza, not far from Strauss's original site at 99 Battery Street. Manufacturing continues from a factory in the Mission District.

Also from Germany, Claus Spreckels (1820-1908) worked his way across the US before settling in San Francisco in 1856 and opening a grocery store. Aware that the price of imported sugar supplies could be undercut by local production, Spreckels founded what became the world's largest sugar refinery in the Salinas Valley. By crafting deals with rival suppliers on the East Coast and controlling sugar cultivation in Hawaii, Spreckels gained a monopoly on California sugar. To avoid dependence on the Big Four's railroads, Spreckels constructed his own rail line and in San Francisco competed against monopolies in street lighting and power.

After his death, Spreckels' sons feuded among themselves while continuing to be a pre-eminent California family. Adolph Spreckels (1857-1924) took over the sugar business and erected the French Renaissance mansion (one of several Spreckels-family mansions nicknamed "sugar palaces"), which still overlooks Lafayette Park, before founding with his wife, Alma, the California Palace of the Legion of Honor. The eldest son, John (1853-1926), founded several newspapers, among them the *San Francisco Call*, and built a business empire in San Diego. Rudolph, the youngest son, shunned the family business and even competed against it, creating his own fortune and becoming a political reformer—most notably challenging San Francisco's corrupt administration—before losing his money in the Depression.

In terms of wealth, power and political influence, the biggest beneficiaries of the gold rush were four Sacramento merchants, Charles Crocker (1822-88), Mark Hopkins (1813-78), Collis P. Huntington (1821-1900), and Leland Stanford (1824-93). Each made a tidy fortune through gold rush supplies and each made a much larger one by pooling their resources into the Central Pacific Railroad. Based on dubiously obtained government subsidies and low-paid labor, the Central Pacific Railroad cut through the northern California mountains completing the western section of the transcontinental railroad in 1869.

The railroad gave the Big Four, as they became known, ownership of enormous tracts of land and control of transportation into and out of northern California, enabling them to decide the fates of entire communities. Already wielding influence on its workings, the Big Four cemented their grip on the state legislature in 1861 when Stanford became governor. Twenty years later, by merging their company with the Southern Pacific Railroad, the Big Four extended their power across the whole state and would dominate California life for decades.

In San Francisco, the Big Four flaunted their wealth with lavish Nob Hill mansions (see pp.29-32). These became the focus of anti-capitalist rallies in the 1870s as the economic boom expected on the railroad's completion instead became a bust, as cheaply manufactured eastern goods undercut local prices and put traders out of business. Yet despite the widespread hostility towards them, the Big Four retained their grip on power and even, in 1899, forced through a law forbidding political cartoons, displeased as they were at being caricatured in the press. The mansions disappeared with the 1906 fire by which time each of the four had died; their monopolies were broken up during the 1910s.

William Ralston (1826-75) had the business acumen of the Big Four but none of the ruthlessness and greed. His wealth financed businesses large and small throughout the Bay Area in furtherance of his dream of San Francisco becoming one of the world's greatest cities. Ralston co-founded the Bank of California and became its president, insisting on the title of "cashier". Similarly, when it was proposed to name a central California town in his honor, Ralston declined the invitation and the town instead became Modesto, the Spanish word for modest.

Ralston directed the bank's major investments into shipping and factories, using profits from mining shares in the silver-bearing comstock lode of Nevada. In San Francisco, he financed the California Theater in 1869 and later surpassed his own Grand Hotel with the even grander Palace Hotel, intended to outshine anything its rich guests might have experienced in New York or Boston, or indeed in London or Paris.

With his propensity to lend to any business, Ralston won the favor of small businessmen. In a 1937 biography, *Ralston's Ring*, George Lyman wrote "No one was ever turned away from Ralston's office who had something to contribute to California welfare or who needed help or a word of encouragement." Completing the picture of the kind-hearted capitalist, Ralston personally gave generously to widows, orphans, and beggars.

By 1875, however, San Francisco's economic downturn, which Ralston had failed to anticipate, coupled to financial uncertainties in the eastern US and losses in the comstock lode, suddenly placed a massive burden on the bank's resources. As rumors spread about the bank's predicament, "Black Friday", August 26, brought withdrawals totaling $1.4 million, draining the bank of its cash reserves and forcing its closure. That evening, having resigned as the bank's president,

Ralston took his customary after-work swim in the bay. Witnesses claimed to have seen the banker in difficulties although some regarded his drowning as a suicide. Ralston's funeral was attended by 50,000 people.

Claus Spreckels cornered the sugar market and Joshua Norton (1819-80) looked to do the same with rice. But instead of making a fortune, Norton made himself an emperor. Born in London, Norton traveled to San Francisco carrying $40,000, a legacy from his recently deceased father, arriving in 1849 to open a general store. Benefiting from the gold rush, Norton made $250,000 in four years and looked to buy up the city's rice supplies. His plan backfired when the price of rice fell and the shortage he had hoped to exploit turned out to be a glut.

After fading from public view (it is thought he suffered a nervous breakdown), Norton reappeared in September 1859 when he delivered a proclamation to the *San Francisco Bulletin*, which the paper duly printed on the following day's front page. It announced Norton as "Norton I, Emperor of the United States and Protector of Mexico", the identity by which Norton would be known throughout the remainder of his life. Far from merely being tolerated as yet another eccentric, Norton was celebrated in San Francisco. Attired in a cockaded hat, gold-plated epaulettes and carrying a ceremonial saber, Norton (always with his two dogs, Lazarus and Bummer; Mark Twain would write an obituary for the latter) became a familiar figure, dining free in restaurants that would be rewarded with the right to post a "By Appointment To His Imperial Majesty" sign; riding without payment on street cars; enjoying a complementary seat at theatrical productions (where the audience would rise to acknowledge his entry), and issuing promissory notes which were accepted by many businesses and by some banks. On the street, passers-by would bow or curtsy and police saluted, particularly after an incident in 1867 when a novice officer, unversed in San Francisco ways, detained Norton for "involuntary treatment for mental disorder". This slight led to a public apology from the police chief and the city granting Norton free board and lodging for life by way of amends.

The 1870 US census formally recorded his occupation as "emperor" and Norton lived up to his role by inspecting sewers and drains, and discussing crime statistics with police. He campaigned for civic improvements, not least a bridge that would link San Francisco with Oakland, and each week attended a different religious service to avoid any accusation of bias.

On the evening of January 8, 1880, on his way to lecture at the Academy of Sciences, Norton dropped dead on California Street. Next day, the *San Francisco Chronicle* recorded:

On the reeking pavement, in the darkness of a moonless night under the dripping rain, and surrounded by a hastily gathered crowd of wondering strangers, Norton I, by the grace of God, Emperor of the United States and Protector of Mexico, departed this life. Other sovereigns have died with no more of kindly care—other sovereigns have died as they have lived with all the pomp of earthly majesty, but death having touched them, Norton I rises up the exact peer of the haughtiest King or Kaiser that ever wore a crown.

With city flags at half-mast, a two-mile funeral cortege carried Norton to his burial watched by upwards of 10,000 mourners. In June 1934, as part of the city's program of relocating its dead to Colma, Norton was reburied, with the mayor in attendance and music from the municipal band, and a military salute from an infantry battalion. Completed two years later, the Bay Bridge, foreseen by Norton half a century earlier, bears a plaque acknowledging the emperor's "prophetic wisdom".

PART TWO

Shaping San Francisco

San Francisco had 812 residents in March 1848. By 1852, its population was 36,151 and four years later reached 56,000. With newspapers, hotels, restaurants, shops, banks, well-filled warehouses and the steady stream of ships that made it the US's "emporium of the Pacific", San Francisco was functioning as a city but could not hide its true self: a tiny trading post that had burst at the seams. Many businesses operated from tents and most domestic homes were improvised on land of which ownership was disputed. Even the shoreline changed as uprooted trees, assorted debris and abandoned ships were utilized as landfill, pushing back the waterfront to create new wharves and commercial spaces.

Among those drawn to California by the gold rush were the architects, developers and builders who failed to find a fortune at the diggings but in San Francisco found a city urgently needing to be built. As land ownership issues were resolved, San Francisco swiftly acquired a style commensurate with its size and importance. Aided by street plans which made no concessions to the city's hills, and by changing fashions in residential building fueled by consumer magazines and mechanized carpentry, a San Francisco emerged bearing some of the US's most distinctive homes: among them the Stick, Italianate and Queen Anne houses (many of which remain today) of the moderately well-off, and the over-sized and often over-bearing mansions of the rich and powerful.

The office of Wells Fargo, one of the first trusted financial institutions to appear in San Francisco during the gold rush, was the city's first brick-built structure. Through the 1860s, the Financial District became established on land created from the bay and sprouted steadily upwards with the advent of steel framed-buildings during the 1880s. Ninety years later, San Francisco's attempts to invigorate its declining economy saw the Financial District gain the vertical growth dubbed "Manhattization", a word spat as much as spoken among San Franciscans fearful of the city losing its individuality and joined in the 1990s in the local lexicon of hate by "gentrification", a process accelerated by a booming technology economy and a massive influx of high-earning dotcom employees. As established populations were uprooted and low-rent homes became luxury apartments, the cyberspace explosion threatened to change the face, and the character, of San Francisco faster than any event since the gold rush.

Rubbish and Bones

An Englishman who arrived in 1822 as first mate on a whaling ship, William A. Richardson became Yerba Buena's first recorded settler and set the tone for its early domestic architecture: his first home comprised a ship's sail stretched across wooden posts. Adopting the Catholic faith and acquiring Mexican citizenship, Richardson married the daughter of the Presidio's *comandante*, gained a 19,500-acre land grant and was appointed Captain of the Port, making him responsible for collecting duties and enforcing trade bans on behalf of the Mexican government. He graduated to a wooden house (in June 1835, cited as Yerba Buena's first building on a site in today's Grant Avenue) and a year later attained the comparative luxury of an adobe house: its thick mudbrick walls retaining heat during the winter and remaining cool during hot spells.

By the 1840s, Mission Dolores and the Presidio were in advanced states of neglect (the latter described as "little better than a heap of rubbish and bones, on which jackals, dogs, and other vultures were constantly preying") but the complex of buildings they comprised were still by far the most substantial structures in the area, which otherwise comprised a few adobe homes such as Richardson's and many more dwellings and stores occupying ramshackle wooden huts or temporary canvas shelters. These were arranged haphazardly along "streets" composed of little more than mud and frequently needing wooden boards to be laid across them to become passable. The sight of a horse-drawn cart and its owner sinking into the mire was common. Herbert Asbury states: "Several times during the rainy season of 1849-50 horses, mules, and carts were sucked down into the mud, and the animals were drowned; and many men, trying to cross the streets while drunk, narrowly escaped similar deaths."

At the request of the Mexican governor, Richardson made informal plans of Yerba Buena but there was a need for a more detailed survey to properly divide the settlement into saleable land lots. In 1839, Jean-Jacques Vioget (1799-1855), a Swiss-born former soldier and engineer who had arrived as a trader in 1837, was commissioned by Francisco de Haro, the first *alcalde*, to survey and plan the settlement. The result was an eight-block area bordered by what became Montgomery (then marking the waterfront), Sacramento, Grant and Pacific streets. While Vioget's plan suited the settlement of the time, it would later attract great derision and it was widely suggested that he got the job solely because he owned the only set of surveyor's tools in Yerba Buena. In the *Overland Monthly* of 1869, M.G. Upton mocked the urban plan:

> *To the serene Gallic (Vioget was regarded as French) mind it made but very little difference that some of the streets which he had laid out followed the lines of a dromedary's back, or that others described semi-*

circles—some up, some down—up Telegraph Hill from the eastern front
of the city—up a grade, which a goat could not travel—then down on
the other side—then up Russian Hill, and then down sloping toward the
Presidio. And this crossed with equally rigid lines, leaving grades for the
description of which pen and ink are totally inadequate.

Vioget's plan had taken account of the current level of occupation
in Yerba Buena and matched this to a Spanish-style system of parallel
streets leading out from a central plaza, the open space that became
Portsmouth Square, close to the sandy cove where ships docked. But
Vioget's "right angled" intersections were 2.5 degrees off true and the
subsequent correction caused some buildings to jut into the street.

The O'Farrell Plan

Shortly after Yerba Buena became San Francisco, the *alcalde*
commissioned Irish-born Jaspar O'Farrell (1817-75, a widely traveled
civil engineer described by Upton as "an explosive Celt, but of much
determination and skill in his profession") to improve and extend
Vioget's work. O'Farrell widened and straightened streets laid out by
Vioget and created the 120-foot-wide Market Street to form a direct
route to the mission (parallel to the extant trail that became Mission
Street) with new streets branching off to the south. To the north,
however, Vioget's streets met Market Street at a 36-degree angle.
Though O'Farrell could not have foreseen the future implications, this
fact contributed to the frustrations of San Francisco motorists, creating
intensely complicated junctions along much of the north side of
Market Street.

Like his predecessor, O'Farrell divided the new parts of the city
into lots for sale. Some, however, were "water" and "beach" lots on the
bay that were either fully underwater or at least submerged at high tide.
Using mud, sand and assorted debris as fill, these lots evolved into the
streets that pushed the waterfront east and now form the Financial
District.

One facet of both plans, and the subsequent extension of the city
by William Eddy in 1849, was their disregard for topography. Streets
either did, or subsequently would, run directly up and down hills
rather than navigating courses around them. Some of the highest

points, such as Nob Hill, remained barely populated until the cable car made their steep approach accessible, and there evolved the rule-of-thumb guide that living high equaled wealth; living low equaled poverty. The quirks of the eventual cityscape did at least provide a fruitful option for film directors, notably Peter Yates with the fabled car chase in the 1968 movie *Bullitt*, shot on the steep residential streets of Pacific Heights and Potrero Hill.

Elegant and Handsomely-furnished Homes
With proper accommodation scarce and expensive, the transient population of the gold rush did most of its sleeping on plain bunks without mattresses, or on bare planks laid across chairs, for which impromptu landlords charged a tidy sum. Inadequate sanitation contributed to an outbreak of cholera in October 1850, introduced by a steamship arriving from Panama, which killed up to 300 people.

Describing San Francisco in 1849, *The Annals of San Francisco*, published in 1885, recorded: "There was no such thing as a *home* to be found. Scarcely even a proper *house* could be seen. Both dwellings and places of business were either common canvas tents, or small rough board shanties, or frame buildings of one story. Only the great gambling saloons, the hotels, restaurants, and a few public buildings and stores had any pretensions to size, comfort or elegance." But in its records for the following year the publication gleefully notes: "The tents and shanties of last year had totally disappeared from the centre of the town, while many of the old frame buildings that had not been destroyed by fire were replaced by others of a larger and stronger kind, if not by extensive fire-proof brick structures." And by 1854, the *Annals* confidently concluded: "San Franciscans can now ask for nothing more on the score of domestic comforts. Their streets and houses are well lighted by a beautiful gas-light; they dwell in elegant and handsomely-furnished houses; their tables are largely supplied with fish, flesh, and fowl from the mountains, rivers and valleys of their teeming land..."

Due to the uncertain boundaries of Mexican land grants and the claims of squatters and others, ownership of San Francisco's increasingly valuable land was a confused issue. After many courtroom arguments, the 1860s saw the advent of homestead associations permitted to buy large sections of land, divide it into lots and sell the lots for a fee usually collected as a monthly repayment. Buyers ranged from individuals seeking a plot on which to raise their own home to developers who would purchase a large tract and build speculatively, hoping to profit from rising property values.

Among the professionals attracted to the gold rush were the architects who found San Francisco in need of their skills. Along with a ready supply of designers, developers and builders, San Francisco also had access to supplies of wood, particularly redwood, which became a favored construction material by dint of being easily worked and resistant to damp, termites and fire. Some even believed, erroneously, that wood-built homes would be sufficiently flexible to withstand earthquakes.

From the late 1860s, the family homes that arose on the tidily-arranged land lots were predominantly Italianate, a style loosely inspired by the rural architecture of northern Italy. While always bearing low-pitched protruding roofs and emphasizing the vertical, early Italianate dwellings were relatively plain-fronted. Later, the style became more ornate, with five-sided bay windows (which also boosted the amount of light reaching the interior) and front doors on raised porches framed by porticoes. The front door itself typically boasted indented rectangular wooden panels while the window frames were arched or indented and further elaborated by a prominent sill below and a shield above: the glass and its surround being carefully proportionate to the house.

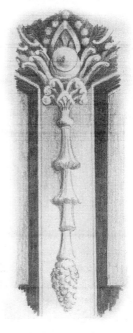

Rising levels of ornamentation evolved from the practical need for light, from the increased daring of architects, and from the advances in carpentry that enabled wood to be worked into forms previously existing only in the imaginations of the most artistically-minded carpenters. The idea of wood as a building material in its own right gave rise to the San Francisco Stick style.

Prevalent from the 1880s, this architectural fashion (so-named for the rows of identically vertically-accented homes that some thought resembled a bunch of sticks) developed the Italianate emphasis on the vertical into something close to religious devotion. Mechanized carpentry enabled long, thin strips of wood to accentuate the straight lines of the house, expressed in rigorously right-angled bay windows. The Stick style ended the tradition of making wood imitate stone and eschewed the rounded decorative features of Italianate homes. Machine chisels and lathes increased wood's viability as a decorative material and aided the advent of a form of Stick commonly referred to as Eastlake, in a misappropriation of the ideas of British design writer Charles Eastlake. With his 1865 book, *Hints on Household Taste in Furniture, Upholstery, and Other Details*, Eastlake had popularized the William Morris-led Arts and Crafts movement. In the US, however, the book was taken as a cue to overload basic designs with extraneous embellishments and decoration.

Simultaneously, building decorations were being cheaply mass produced for the first time and made available in department stores and through mail-order catalogs. Such frills were sold on the premise that what was right for the fashionable addresses of London, Paris or New York must be right (albeit in cheap imitation form and for an entirely different form of house) for San Francisco. Eastlake himself was appalled by what he discovered was bearing his name in San Francisco, commenting that the city's "Eastlakes" were "a phase of taste in architecture and industrial arts with which I can have no real sympathy and which by all accounts seems to be extravagant and bizarre."

By the late 1880s, the move away from the straight-line purity of the early Stick style toward greater elaboration was proceeding apace as Queen Anne homes sprouted in San Francisco's wealthier quarters. Marked by corner towers, turrets, witches' caps, steeply-gabled roofs, and stained glass windows, the Queen Anne style also swapped vertical accentuation for the horizontal. A particular home's diversity of features and aura of bulkiness was viewed as symbolizing the owner's wealth and social standing. Despite its name, the Queen Anne style bore little resemblance to the English architecture of that monarch's reign (1702–1714) and resulted instead from a misinterpretation of the work of English architect Richard Norman Shaw.

Never using one material where two, or preferably more, were possible, the most elaborate Queen Annes were coated with shingles, tiles and bricks, and liberally dotted with windows that might be long, short, flat or bay, with at least one being a porthole, while the roofline, made irregular by chimneys, dormers, and variable-sized gables, resembled a relief map of the Himalayas.

The Nobs of Nob Hill

San Francisco has 43 hills but since the late 1800s no single one has been more synonymous with wealth and prestige than Nob Hill, rising sharply above Chinatown and the Financial District. Elegant, expensive hotels and pricey high-rise apartments line its streets today, but previously Nob Hill held some of the most spectacular homes ever seen in California.

Proximity to the increasingly important Financial District encouraged a colony of moderately well-off merchants to settle the hill through the 1860s but it was the invention of the cable car in 1873 that made San Francisco's steepest slopes accessible. A cable car route linking the Financial District with Nob Hill's 338-ft summit was laid out along California Street in 1878, paid for by railroad baron Leland Stanford who erected the first of the neighborhood's mansions.

Stanford's extravagant Italianate abode featured the largest private dining room in the west, an Indian parlor, a Pompeiian drawing room, and twenty-five bedrooms. Within its walls, Stanford led "a life of conspicuous consumption as squire of a medieval fortress", while the house fulfilled its owner's desire to create, according to the *Daily Alta California*, "a comfortable home for himself and family for the remainder of his life, and a worthy place for the entertainment of such friends as he desires to have immediately about him."

Stanford had judiciously purchased plots of land adjacent to the cable car line that he sold to his millionaire peers eager to relocate from Rincon Hill as Nob Hill became the city's social benchmark. In 1882, Robert Louis Stevenson described Nob Hill as "the Hill of palaces... it is here that millionaires are gathered together vying with each other for display." And vie they did. Charles Crocker's $2.3-million mansion was fitted with a million-dollar art collection, a library, a billiard room, a working theater, and a 76-foot-high tower from which he could gaze smugly across the city. For sheer expense and architectural eccentricity, however, the race for the most ostentatious Nob Hill home was won by Mark Hopkins who, despite envisioning something far plainer and cheaper, spent $3 million on a forty-room home designed (one description suggests "hallucinated") by his wife in a mind-boggling pseudo-Gothic hotchpotch of towers, spires and turrets. In *The Fantastic City* socialite Amelia Ransome Neville remembers visiting the Hopkins mansion: "Within, the house was a mess of anachronisms. One entered portals of a feudal castle to pass into the court of a doge's palace, all carved Italian walnut with a gallery around the second story where murals of Venetian scenes were set between the arches."

While they might have reveled in their splendor, the Nobs of Nob Hill, already widely despised for their wealth and the questionable business practices that underpinned it, earned more opprobrium from the public as their showy mansions loomed above the city. In an act seen as typically arrogant, Charles Crocker erected a forty-foot-high "spite fence" around the modest home of a neighbor, German-born undertaker Nicholas Yung who had arrived before the cable car line and refused to sell his land to Crocker. Said Crocker: "From my tower you can survey the entire City as it washes up and down the hills just like it's one big job, and you can supervise the construction of it, and all while standing *over* the shoulders of Stanford, Hopkins, and everyone else! I would have been happier than a condor in the sky—except for that crazy undertaker Nicholas Yung."

Yung's daughter would later write: "How gloomy our house became, how sad. All we could see out our windows was the blank wood of the rich man's fury...The flowers in our garden all died, and our lawn turned brown, while inside the house everything felt perpetually damp." Eventually Yung (who Crocker called "the little weasel") transported his house to a new site in the Mission District but still refused to sell his Nob Hill land, leaving the Crocker fence enclosing an empty plot. Yung died in 1880 but the feud continued and the fence remained. Only after Crocker's death in 1888 and the sale of the mansion to a new owner was the conflict resolved.

The mansions brought little luck to their owners. Hopkins died before his was completed (his widow married the interior designer) and the death at fifteen of the son of Leland Stanford prompted the

distraught parents to found the educational institution that evolved into Stanford University. All but one of the mansions perished in the fire of 1906. Thanks to sandstone walls that withstood the flames, the sole survivor was the 1886 James Flood mansion. New York-born Flood (1826-89) had been running a city restaurant dispensing fish stew lunches to stockbrokers. Through eavesdropping and a good deal of cunning, Flood and his partners were able to manipulate stock, eventually controlling the Nevada silver mines that struck "the most stupendous treasure trove of precious metals ever to dazzle the eye of man." Flood's income rose to $250,000 a month and he "retired without delay" from the fish stew business.

With the 42-rm mansion, Flood had fortuitously chosen to reflect his origins by forsaking wood for Connecticut River Valley sandstone, the material used in the brownstone townhouses of New York. Remodeled by Willis Polk following the fire and occupied since 1911 by the exclusive Pacific Union Club, the mansion also retains some of its original ironwork fence, which cost $30,000 and for which Flood employed a full-time polisher. Amelia Ransome Neville recalled: "The beautifully wrought metal flashed for the entire length of two blocks on the square where the brownstone mansion stood, and it was the sole task of one retainer to keep it bright. Passing any hour of the day one discovered him polishing away at some section of it."

Even before 1906, there were indications of a new direction for Nob Hill. From 1902, the daughter of silver-mine beneficiary James "Bonanza Jim" Graham Fair began pouring money into the construction of what would become the 600-rm Fairmont Hotel on land owned by her father. Aided by the work of Julia Morgan, best known as the architect of William Randolph Hearst's San Simeon mansion, the hotel emerged from the destruction of the fire to set new standards in luxury. A rival appeared in 1911 when the Stanford Court Hotel opened on the site of the Stanford mansion, and another in the 1920s when the Mark Hopkins Hotel arose where once stood the Hopkins mansion. All three still provide comfortable accommodation and attentive service for those who can afford it: those who can't, can at least experience Nob Hill's height by riding the glass-fronted elevator that brings vertiginous views from the Fairmont's 22-story tower.

On the site of Charles Crocker's home is Grace Cathedral, its Episcopal services well-attended each Sunday by a congregation whose immaculate appearance suggests it might well include the modern peers of the original Nobs. Facing the cathedral, the small and pleasurable Huntington Park is bordered by the granite walls that once marked the grounds of the David Colton mansion. A junior partner of the Big Four, Colton died in 1878 and his widow used his correspondence with Collis Huntington to reveal the corruption of the railroad barons, not least their influencing of elections and bribing of politicians, in a court case that rocked California in the late 1800s.

In 1944, John Dos Passos wrote of Nob Hill for *Harper's Magazine*: "I remember it years ago when there were still gardens on it and big broken-paned mansions of brown stone, and even, if I remember right, a few wind-bleached frame houses with turrets and scalelike shingles imitating stone and scrollsaw woodwork round the porches. Now it's all hotels and apartment houses, but their massive banality is made up for by the freakishness of the terrain. At the top, in front of the last of the old General-Grant-style houses, I stop a second to get my breath and to mop the sweat off my eyebrows."

Pacific Heights

Be they Queen Anne, Italianate, imitation New York brownstone or clinker brick, Pacific Heights mansions appear in more styles and in greater numbers than in any other district of San Francisco. Like Nob Hill, Pacific Heights benefited from a cable car line making its slopes navigable. Unlike Nob Hill, however, Pacific Heights comprises much more than a single hill: streets flow over crests and sweep through valleys, promising ample land for ample homes with the most prized plots bringing scintillating views over the city and the bay.

During the 1850s, much of Pacific Heights was Cow Hollow, a place of dairy farms and laundries set around a lagoon, close to today's Union Street. The smells and sounds of cows had little appeal for rich settlers who by the 1890s had raised mansions along Van Ness Avenue and succeeded in having the animals removed and the lagoon filled in. The avenue's width, at 125 feet the widest thoroughfare in the city, made it the obvious choice for a cable car route and for dynamiting in a vain attempt to halt the 1906 fire. The mansions were lost and the street instead became, and remains, a commercial strip dominated by restaurants, shops, and offices. Mansions west of Van Ness Avenue survived 1906 and the arrival of the stucco-fronted low-rise apartment blocks which now consume seemingly every gap between them.

A rare reminder of the days of Cow Hollow is the Casebolt House, 2727 Pierce Street, its handsome Italianate style gaining a dignity that befits its age by being set back from the street, its bright white exterior peering out from behind a melange of shrubbery and two towering palms. Its original owner Henry Casebolt was a blacksmith whose skills earned him a fortune during the gold rush; the apparent grandeur obscures the fact that nothing more exotic than salvaged wood provided the main building material. Also pre-dating the 1906 fire, the 1886 Haas-Lilienthal House, 2007 Franklin Street, is one of the few Pacific Heights homes to be open to the public. An entertaining example of flamboyant Queen Anne style, the house was occupied by a descendant of its original owners until 1972. Many early fixtures and fittings remain, proudly displayed on tours organized by the Foundation for San Francisco's Architectural Heritage which now own the building.

The grandest Pacific Heights home occupies, appropriately, the highest ground, overlooking Lafayette Park and bringing (apparently) views of six counties from its second-floor windows. The 55-rm Spreckels Mansion, 2080 Washington Street, was completed in 1913 for Adolph Spreckels (son of sugar-mogul Claus) and his wife, Alma de Bretteville. Architect George Applegate impressed his benefactors sufficiently for him to be subsequently chosen to construct their art museum, the California Palace of the Legion of Honor. Twenty-four years Adolph's junior, Alma outlived her husband by forty years, becoming "a salty grand dame" of San Francisco society before dying in 1968. The white limestone mansion subsequently fell into neglect before being purchased in 1990, reputedly for $8 million, by best-selling romance author Danielle Steele.

Taming the Hills: Andrew Hallidie's Cable Cars

Invented by London-born Andrew Smith Hallidie (1836-1900), cable cars made San Francisco's steepest hills accessible and consequently shaped the city's social geography, most spectacularly so with Nob Hill. Legend has it that Hallidie was inspired to develop his revolutionary technology after seeing several horses die as they attempted to carry a load up one of the city's slopes (the more likely reason is that he intended to profit from his patent on wire rope).

Hallidie arrived in California in 1852, developed wire rope as means of transporting heavy loads in gold mining areas, and oversaw its successful use with a suspension bridge. His cable car concept became reality at 5am on August 2, 1873 (some accounts say August 1), when the first car was tested along Clay Street. As the name suggests, cable cars run by gripping a constantly moving—at 9.5mph—underground cable and stop by releasing the grip and applying a brake. All cables converge on a gigantic steel drum at the Cable Car Barn (now open as a museum) at the corner of Washington and Mason streets.

While they became an emblem of the city—and their clanging bells a feature in San Francisco-set fiction and films—and were formally recognized as a National Historical Landmark in 1964, cable cars looked likely to be phased out of operation in the early 1980s but were saved by popular demand and a two-year $60 million restoration. Where once there were eight, now only three routes operate, two between Union Square and Fisherman's Wharf and a third between the Financial District and Van Ness Avenue following California Street over the summit of Nob Hill.

Away From the Hills

A stroll through Pacific Heights might seduce the visitor into thinking that late nineteenth- and early twentieth-century San Francisco was a place where even the humblest lived as lords. In reality, of course, this was far from true. Ordinary San Franciscans lived at best modestly and worked long hours. In 1860 laborers went on strike for a reduction in their working day from twelve to ten hours. As workers organized through the following decades, employers sought to undermine their demands by importing cheap labor from the eastern US on the transcontinental railroad.

While working people occupied side streets and alleys throughout the city, a "working-class ghetto" developed amid the crowded wooden tenements raised on the flat land south of Market Street. The weakness of the ground and the flammability of the buildings caused the neighborhood to be among the worst affected by the 1906 earthquake and fire. The post-1906 rebuilding brought the factories and freight yards that helped keep the south of Market Street area a blue-collar stronghold, its militancy fueling a series of strikes during 1907 and 1908, first by electrical workers seeking a pay rise from $5 to $6 a day and subsequently by thousands demanding the eight-hour day in effect elsewhere in the US.

Of rents, the *San Francisco Chronicle* reported in 1904 that $7–17 a week was typically charged for a small three- or four-bedroom apartment, "some with, some without bathroom" where "plumbing was good but not the most modern", and found rents to be double the US average, although food was cheaper than the national norm. Deducing that it was possible for a family of four to live in San Francisco on $14 a week, the reporter nonetheless noted that she was unable to explain how.

As the city expanded to absorb areas previously considered peripheral, once affluent family homes were divided into apartments, particularly in Haight-Ashbury and the Western Addition, where houses that had been the height of middle-class domestic sophistication underwent cheap alterations and suffered decades of neglect from absentee landlords. By the 1970s, however, such homes were being snapped up at modest prices by a new breed of settler: restoration-minded owner-occupiers charmed by Victorian and Edwardian architectural styles. A prime example are the six "painted ladies" on the east side of Alamo Square which have become the most photographed row of houses in San Francisco (aided by the juxtaposition provided by the Financial District rising in the background). Built by developer Mathew Kavanagh in the mid-1890s and sold for $3,500 each, the houses today are resplendent with what seem perennially fresh coats of paint and not a blemish defacing their carpentry. Prospective buyers should expect a long wait and little change from $2 million.

San Francisco in Ruins
Despite the best efforts of architects, engineers, and city planners, the single most cityscape-defining event in San Francisco history came in 1906 and owed nothing to humans but everything to geology. On average, an earthquake strong enough to be felt occurs three times a week somewhere in California and of dozens of major fault lines, the longest is the 650-mi San Andreas which passes directly through the San Francisco peninsula. Six years before it reached San Francisco, Spain's Sacred Expedition recorded the first European experience of a California earthquake. Later the *Annals of San Francisco* noted:

In September, 1829, several very severe shocks of an earthquake were experienced in San Francisco, which forced open lock-fast doors and windows. In 1839, an equally severe earthquake took place. In 1812,

*however, a much more serious convulsion had been felt over all Califor-
nia, which shook down houses and some churches in several parts of the
country, and killed a considerable number of human beings... It may be
mentioned, when on this subject, that since these dates, no serious occur-
rences of this nature have happened at San Francisco; though almost
every year slight shocks, and occasionally smarter ones have been felt.
God help the city if any great catastrophe of this nature should ever take
place!*

In October 1865 what at the time was considered a great
catastrophe did take place. One who experienced it while walking
along Third Street and turning a corner by a frame house was Mark
Twain, who wrote in *Roughin' It*:

*I fell up against the frame house and hurt my elbow. I knew what it was,
now, and from mere reportorial instinct, nothing else, took out my watch
and noted the time of day; at that moment a third and still severer shock
came, and as I reeled about on the pavement trying to keep my footing,
I saw a sight! The entire front of a tall four-story brick building in Third
Street sprung outward like a door and fell sprawling across the street, raising a dust like a great volume of smoke! ... (A) street car had stopped, the
horses were rearing and plunging, the passengers were pouring out at
both ends, and one fat man had crashed half way through a glass
window on one side of the car, got wedged fast and was squirming and
screaming like an impaled madman.*

Three years later another large earthquake left four people dead as
chimneys toppled and fissures opened in the streets. The *San Francisco
Call* responded by offering rudimentary earthquake preparedness tips,
suggesting residents were safer indoors than rushing onto the streets
where they might be struck by falling masonry.

April 18, 1906

Shortly after 5am on Wednesday April 18, 1906, an earthquake now
estimated at 7.9 on the Richter scale struck northern California. In San
Francisco, walls fell from buildings, chimneys collapsed, cable car lines
buckled as streets contorted, windows and dishes smashed, and

residents were tossed from their beds. An eyewitness described ground that "rose and fell like an ocean at ebb tide." Built on marsh and on land reclaimed from the bay, North Beach and the Financial District were devastated by the initial quake, which lasted around a minute, while liquefaction of the ground south of Market Street caused densely-inhabited tenements to fall and catch fire. Many buildings that survived the first shock collapsed as over a hundred aftershocks followed.

The editor of the *San Francisco Examiner*, who had just left his office recalled: "I saw for an instant the big buildings in what looked like a crazy dance. Then it seemed as though my head were split with the roar that crashed into my ears. Big buildings were crumbling as one might crush a biscuit in one's hand. Great gray clouds of dust shot up with flying timbers, and storms of masonry rained into the street. Wild, high jangles of smashing glass cut a sharp note into the frightful roaring." The celebrated landscape photographer Ansel Adams, then three years old and living in the family home some miles from what was then considered the city amid the sand dunes overlooking the Golden Gate, remembered when the earthquake struck, describing in his autobiography: "Our west window gave way in a shower of glass, and the handsome brick chimney passed by the north window, slicing through the greenhouse my father had just completed." Adams's sister, Nelly, lost a chunk of her bedroom wall and awoke "to a broad view of the Golden Gate and the cold morning breeze." Shortly after, Ansel was enjoying the aftershocks in the garden when one knocked him against a brick wall and he acquired the broken septum that would be a feature of his face for the rest of his life.

Remaining upright, the St. Francis Hotel offered a free breakfast of bread, fruit and hot coffee. Wearing a fur coat over his pajamas, Enrico Caruso was among those at the hotel. The famed Italian tenor had performed as Don Jose in *Carmen* the previous evening at the Mission Opera House and had stayed at the Palace Hotel from which he allegedly fled "carrying a portrait of Theodore Roosevelt and a towel around his throat, shouting 'Give me Vesuvius!'" In his own account of the morning, Caruso described waking up and:

feeling my bed rocking as though I am in a ship on the ocean, and for a moment I think I am dreaming that I am crossing the water on my way to my beautiful country... as the rocking continues, I get up and go to the window, raise the shade and look out. And what I see makes me tremble with fear. I see the buildings toppling over, big pieces of masonry falling, and from the street below I hear the cries and screams of men and women and children. I remain speechless, thinking I am in some dreadful nightmare, and for something like forty seconds I stand there, while the buildings fall and my room still rocks like a boat on the sea.

Broken gas mains, short-circuiting electrical cables (one witness described overhead power cables snapping and hitting the ground "writhing and hissing like reptiles"), overturned stoves and lanterns, and the fact that ninety percent of the city's buildings were made of wood, enabled fires to ignite quickly around the city. Separate fires grew larger and joined together into ever bigger blazes that spread street by street. With water mains destroyed, fire-fighting potential was minimal and further hindered by the destruction of several fire stations and the fatal wounding of the chief fire officer when the dome of the California Hotel crashed into the Bush Street station.

Three major fires that blazed during the afternoon had, by evening, combined into a single firestorm raging between the waterfront and Van Ness Avenue. One account told how being in the street "was like looking in the door of a furnace. Flames and smoke rolled with the draught created by the intense heat, rolling up the street with a roar, then up hundreds of feet. It was an awful sight." Temperatures rose high enough to twist metal and melt glass; smoke carried five miles high. The mayor ordered power supplies to be switched off, imposed a dusk to dawn curfew and issued a shoot-to-kill order to army and police to prevent looting (of several apparent looters shot, some were later found to be residents seeking to retrieve their possessions). Many thousands made their way to the open spaces of Golden Gate Park or the Presidio, some crossed by ferry to the safety of Oakland or Marin County.

Of the immediate aftermath of the earthquake, an eyewitness wrote: "Each and every person I saw was temporarily insane. Laughing idiots commented on the fun they were having. Terror marked their faces, and yet their voices indicated a certain enjoyment that maniacs have when they kill and gloat over their prey. Women, hysterical to an extreme point, cried and raved for those they loved when they were standing at their elbow. Mothers searched madly for their children who had strayed, while little ones wailed for their protectors... Strong men bellowed like babies in their furor(e)." Photographer Arnold Genthe, whose home and studio on Sutter Street were destroyed in the fire and who took some of the most haunting images of the disaster, remembered calmer but no less strange scenes:

> *The streets presented a weird appearance, mother and children in their nightgowns, men in pyjamas and dinner coats, women scantily dressed with evening wraps hastily thrown over them. Many ludicrous sights met the eye: an old lady carrying a large bird cage with four kittens inside, while the original occupant, the parrot, perched on her hand; a man tenderly holding a pot of calla lilies, muttering to himself; a scrub woman, in one hand a new broom and in the other a large black hat with ostrich plumes; a man in an old-fashioned nightshirt and swallow tails, being startled when a friendly policeman spoke to him, 'Say, Mister, I guess you better put on some pants.'*

On Thursday, for the first and only time, the *Call, Chronicle,* and *Examiner* published a combined edition (using the presses of the *Oakland Herald,* their own having been destroyed) headlined: "Earthquake and Fire: San Francisco In Ruins." The report continued: "Downtown everything is in ruins. Not a business house stands. Theatres are crumpled into heaps. Factories and Commission houses lie smouldering on their former sites." And it concluded with the fatalistic assertion: "Everyone in San Francisco is prepared to leave the city. For the firm belief is that San Francisco will be totally destroyed."

Attempts by the army to halt the flames by dynamiting buildings to create a firebreak failed, the sound of constant explosions adding to the sense of unreality. Eventually it was a change in wind direction, the unusual easterly breeze that fanned the flames giving way to the more common westerly, that caused the fire to burn itself out without crossing the wide Van Ness Avenue to threaten the remainder of the city.

The official death toll was 300, but estimates subsequently put the number far higher, suggesting that 3-4,000 may have perished. Certainly 250,000 (of a population of 400,000) were left homeless, some occupying tents and later the 5,000 shed-like refugee cottages that filled the city's open spaces. For some weeks cooking was allowed only on outdoor stoves. Anticipating a food shortage, the harbor had been blockaded (and remained so until food supplies arrived by train) and several ships fully laden with food that were about to leave were boarded by police and ordered to remain, their cargo unloaded and distributed. Across ten square miles, the calamity had claimed 28,000 buildings including City Hall in which San Francisco's official records had been destroyed.

The good humor and cooperative spirit of the homeless—evinced by hand-written notices such as "Eat Drink and Be Merry for tomorrow we may have to go to Oakland"—was one response to the disaster. Less heart-warming were many re-settlement problems, not least the racism and greed that underpinned a scheme to reconstruct Chinatown on the fringes of the city (see p.156).

A city in need of rebuilding brought an economic boom: first an army of debris shifters and later 60,000 construction workers were able to charge high rates for their labor. In three years following the fire, new construction valued at $150 million was completed, many structures fitted with fire-resistant materials. The rebuilding also provided a chance to create a planned city quite unlike the entity that had grown in the frenzy of the gold rush.

The sense of a new beginning was strengthened by the anti-graft trials that ended widespread corruption in the city administration, symbolized by the imprisonment of political fixer Abe Ruef. Even an outbreak of bubonic plague in 1907 that claimed 77 lives did little to hamper the pervading upbeat mood, while the 1911 election of James "Sunny Jim" Rolph to the first of what would be five mayoral terms, found an amiable and widely-liked politician at the city's head. It was Rolph who presided over the re-shaping of the city including the monumental project that created a new City Hall at the heart of a Civic Center complex.

San Francisco's recovery from the fire (since the major damage was caused by the fire rather than the earthquake, the disaster of 1906 is officially described as a fire) was signaled to the outside world with staging of the 1915 Panama-Pacific Exposition in what became the Marina District.

All Tomorrow's Parties

Geology has no respect for rebuilt cities and earthquakes were, of course, as common a feature of San Francisco after the fire as they were before it. Increased use of fire-resistant building materials and the steady advance of earthquake-safe building technology ensured much greater stability, however, and the belief that even an earthquake of the size of 1906 would cause considerably less damage than it had then. Such belief received its severest test on October 17, 1989, when the 6.9 magnitude Loma Prieta earthquake (so-named for its epicenter, 56 miles south of San Francisco) rocked the city. The event was seen live by a nationwide TV audience, occurring as a World Series baseball game between the San Francisco Giants and Oakland A's was about to begin at Candlestick Park.

Much of the damage occurred in the Marina District, where the ground—composed of sand and debris from the bay—underwent liquefaction and apartment blocks began sinking. Meanwhile, an upper section of the double-tiered Bay Bridge collapsed onto the span beneath. Overall, deaths numbered a relatively low 65 but property damage was estimated at $6–10 billion. The temporary closure of the Bay Bridge underlined the importance of traffic arteries into and out of the city and raised general concerns over bridge safety. Little comfort came from the revised predictions of the US Geological Survey, which declared a 67 percent probability of an earthquake of magnitude 7 or higher striking the Bay Area by 2020.

The prospect of another major earthquake underpins William Gibson's future-set novels *Virtual Light* and *All Tomorrow's Parties*. After a tumultuous quake nicknamed Little Big One, the Bay Bridge is permanently closed and becomes "a world within a world" as its span is squatted by "tattoo parlours, gaming arcades, dimly-lit stalls stacked with decaying magazines, sellers of fireworks, of cut bait, betting shops, sushi bars, unlicensed pawnbrokers, herbalists, barbers, bars" and a displaced community who fashion ingenious dwellings amid the towers and cables, an "intricately suspended barrio, with its unnumbered population and zones of more private fantasy." Read with a knowledge of local history, the bridge appears as a futuristic replay of a bygone San Francisco while the rest of the city—confirming the worst fears of real life present-day San Franciscans—is rebuilt to a global corporate template, eradicating every trace of its individuality and selling its prized public assets; not least Golden Gate Park, which has been purchased by filmmaker George Lucas, walled, and renamed Skywalker Park.

Citadels of Commerce

As San Francisco grew at lightning pace from a sleepy Mexican outpost to the US's major Pacific port, an ad-hoc business quarter evolved along Montgomery Street, then adjacent to the bay and convenient for the commercial wharves. Canvas and wood were soon replaced by stone and brick as building materials, and two- and three-story offices (the few that remain line Jackson Street, their ground floors predominantly occupied by pricey antique stores) arose. Pushing the shoreline east, landfill created new streets that became and remain the city's Financial District, informally inaugurated by the opening of the Bank of California on the corner of California and Sansome streets in 1866. By the 1880s, San Francisco was at its peak as a port, with its wharves servicing over 500 vessels annually, creating a salty dog's dream vista of schooners, square riggers, clippers, and steamers. Gaining its first outlet on the Pacific enabled the US to sharply increase its trade with Asia, but equally salient was the fact that New York was no further from San Francisco by ship than was Europe. The latter became a major market for grain from northern California's farms, while incoming cargo typically included food and manufactured goods. The city also became an important whaling center, providing access to the Arctic Ocean hunting grounds at a time when whale oil was in high demand for lamps and whale bone a prerequisite of ladies' corsetry.

While the view over the bay may have revealed ships, masts, and constant maritime activity, the city's skyline was dominated by church spires and factory chimneys until the Chicago architectural firm of Daniel Burnham and John Root created a ten-story home for the *San Francisco Chronicle* on the junction of Market and Kearney streets in 1889 and two years later completed the Mills Building at 220 Montgomery Street. Both structures used the new steel-frame construction method and pneumatic elevators to carry people between floors.

The 1906 earthquake and fire razed the Financial District's masonry structures but, while stripped of their skin, many steel-framed buildings survived and some remained strong enough to be rebuilt. The reconstruction typically saw steel skeletons being covered with lightweight terra cotta (valued for its decorative and fire-retardant qualities) rather than brick, creating a commercial neighborhood of remarkable aesthetic cohesion. A major influence on the new look was the Beaux Arts-inspired City Beautiful movement, encouraged particularly by Daniel Burnham and Willis Polk and popularized by the 1893 World's Columbian Exposition in Chicago.

Yet the movement had, it was true, been pre-empted in San Francisco by Albert Pissis, who completed the landmark Hibernia Bank, at the junction of Jones and Market streets, in 1892. The bank's granite facade and rows of columns imposed a sense of harmony and order into a haphazard streetscape of brick and wood while inviting customers to be awestruck as they passed through the two-story, copper-domed entrance. Despite the acclaim heaped upon the bank and its designer, Pissis had fallen from favor by the time of his death in

1962 but the bank remained and is now again acknowledged as a rare gem on Market Street, despite its fall into disuse and disrepair.

Willis Polk: Architect, Visionary, Drunkard

When Willis Polk (1865-1924) described the Hibernia Bank as the most beautiful building in San Francisco it was praise indeed. Polk is remembered for his many architectural contributions to the city but during his life was equally renowned for his acerbic criticism of buildings and their builders, much of which was published in the weekly magazine *The Wave*. The 1898 City Hall, for example, was dismissed as representing "the last degenerate epoch of architecture", while Polk's outspoken style helped make him a prominent member of Russian Hill bohemia.

Born in Illinois, Polk had worked as an eight-year-old carrying tools and nails to roofers on new constructions and by the age of thirteen had become an architect's apprentice. After a string of jobs with architects across the US (including with Daniel Burnham in Chicago), Polk arrived in San Francisco in 1889. Through the next decade he made a mark with ingenious mixings and re-workings of traditional styles, best revealed by the fusing of medieval, Mediterranean and classical ideas brought to several shingle-fronted homes on Vallejo and Florence streets. Through the 1900s Polk increasingly designed classically-inspired commercial buildings, including the Merchants Exchange Building at 465 California Street. In creating a new home for the exchange, where ship-owners, warehousemen and traders would all gather awaiting news of arriving ships to be announced by a rooftop look-out with a view over the bay, Polk employed a doubled-column entrance and a sky-lit atrium to create a suitably portentous approach to the Grain Trading Hall, the building's hub, where San Francisco's prominent place in Pacific trade was emphasized by William Coulter's epic maritime paintings.

From 1905 Polk headed the San Francisco office of Burnham & Root, overseeing post-fire rebuilding and assisting with the plans for a grand Civic Center complex. After 1910 he reverted to working for himself and in 1917 unveiled the landmark Hallidie Building (130-150 Sutter Street). The use of a curtain wall suspended in front of a building's exterior had become widespread in San Francisco following

Polk's deployment of the feature in the Merchant's Exchange Building. But where most curtains were disguised as masonry walls, Polk gave the Hallidie Building the world's first glass curtain, boldly hung several feet in front of the building's reinforced concrete wall.

Despite his achievement with the Hallidie Building, Polk's commissions declined and his architectural practice frequently faced bankruptcy. Polk's one-time apprentice, Addison Mizner, later to create the millionaires' Florida playground of Palm Beach, was made a partner to avoid paying him wages. Some attributed the lack of money to Polk's efforts to keep pace with San Francisco high society and his appetite for strong drink. Payment for the Filoli mansion, William Bourn's sumptuous country retreat (used during the 1980s as the setting for TV's *Dynasty*) was made as a stipend to Polk's wife, apparently out of fear that the architect would drink the proceeds. Between the Hallidie Building and his death in 1924, Polk's only construction of note was the 1921 Beach Chalet on the western edge of Golden Gate Park. Unoccupied and neglected for many years until re-opening in the 1990s with a restaurant on the upper level and a park visitor center on the ground floor, the Beach Chalet is lined by Lucien Labaudt's evocative 1930s murals of San Franciscans at play.

Perhaps the strongest testament to Polk came from Bernard Maybeck, to whom Polk, overseeing the 1915 Panama-Pacific Exposition, had passed the commission for the Palace of Fine Arts: "You have put up a monument to your ideals through me and made a sacrifice for them... there is in you a yearning for the highest ideals."

Polk's Merchant Exchange Building defined the Financial District's style until the mid-1920s, when San Francisco acquired several landmark buildings whose cutbacks, vertical accentuation and art deco terra-cotta decoration echoed the office towers of New York and Chicago. Inspired by Eliel Saarinen's design for Chicago's Tribune Tower, Thomas Pflueger's 1924 Pacific Telephone Building at 140 New Montgomery Street gave San Francisco its first skyscraper, which still rises with graceful aplomb above the low-rise south of Market Street (SoMa) area. Soon after, the Financial District gained George Kelham's Russ Building (235 Montgomery Street), its heavily Gothic ornamentation suggestive of a European cathedral and its 32 stories making it the tallest building in the city until 1964. By contrast, Pflueger brought a Mayan influence to bear on the terra cotta-clad 450 Sutter Street.

Manhattanization and Urban Renewal

Economic depression, world war, and a post-war slump all contributed to a lack of major new commercial building in San Francisco between the early 1930s and the mid-1960s. By the time large-scale construction recommenced, the city's building regulations were outdated and unable to exert control over the new breed of high-rises. The result was San Francisco's first experience of what would be a lasting terror: "Manhattanization". The term was inspired by a June 1968 issue of the *Bay Guardian* whose front page yelled "Manhattan Madness" and predicted "San Francisco will duplicate the crushing problems... that have made Manhattan Island virtually unlivable."

San Francisco had already been experiencing several years of "urban renewal", controversial initiatives that razed established and predominately low-income neighborhoods to create new commercial space, notably the Fillmore District which had been the heart of African-American San Francisco. By the early 1970s, city authorities had devised the Urban Design Plan, a complex set of regulations intended to placate public protest while giving a conditional green light to high-rise developers. Their hope was that San Francisco could solve its economic problems (the city had long since lost its commercial prominence in California as power shifted to the south of the state) by becoming a regional hub for banking and financial firms, staffed by an army of Bay Area commuters carried to work aboard BART. This was the Bay Area Rapid Transit, a then state-of-the-art rail-based underground public transport system linking San Francisco with other Bay Area communities, including a section beneath San Francisco Bay reaching Berkeley and Oakland, the first part of which opened in 1972.

Completed in 1969, the Bank of America World Headquarters (now Bank of America Center) at 555 California Street carried 52 floors to a height of 779 feet and suggested that high-rise architecture could bring something more aesthetically appealing than mere office space to San Francisco. Partly a reference to Pflueger's 450 Sutter Street, the California Street building's zigzagged exterior of dark red carnelian granite reacts with sunlight in different ways throughout the day, at times making the potentially overbearing structure seem almost transparent—though never almost transparent enough to those San Franciscans who failed to warm to it. Shortly after, the Transamerica Pyramid was an initially despised but subsequently admired addition. As if to bless the new-look San Francisco, the four 190-foot-high hyperbolic paraboloids of St. Mary's Cathedral appeared on a Geary Street hill in 1971.

The Ultimate High Rise

Despite individual architectural successes, the argument that commuting office workers would contribute significantly to the city's economy was undermined by *The Ultimate High Rise*, a detailed study carried out by the *Bay Guardian*. Its findings included: "Demographic impact-high-rise office growth in the city has driven 100,000 middle class residents to the suburbs, caused the loss of 14,000 blue collar jobs, and tripled welfare costs. New jobs in high-rises go to suburbanites, while jobs lost were held by city residents... Environmental impact-high-rise office growth causes air and water pollution that cost the city $1 billion to clean up, and imposed an additional $5 billion in region-wide costs to alleviate traffic congestion."

By 1985, however, Paul Goldberger, writing in the *New York Times* of San Francisco's new and more stringent Downtown Plan, suggested that the city enjoyed "the finest downtown plan in the nation", one that "tames the madness of overbuilding (more) than any other city has even come close to doing."

Yerba Buena Center

When the $60-million San Francisco Museum of Modern Art (SFMoMA) opened its doors in 1995, it gave the city its first purpose-built art museum of significant size and became a major component in the development of an 87-acre South of Market Street culture-and-commerce plot known as Yerba Buena Center.

Thirty years in the making, Yerba Buena Center was initially conceived as a sports venue that it was hoped would stimulate the regeneration of a declining neighborhood dominated by run-down hotels and industrial spaces within walking distance of Downtown's shops, offices and tourist accommodation. The Moscone Convention Center opened between Third and Fourth streets in 1981 and, subject to the ups and downs of local and national economies (nearly all projects depended on private financing), the scheme took shape through the 1990s, gaining impetus by the demolition of the Embarcadero Freeway, damaged beyond reasonable repair by the 1989 Loma Prieta earthquake.

Yerba Buena Center is announced by SFMoMA's immense black-and-white truncated cylinder emerging periscope-like from a red brick exterior. The privately funded, Mario Botta-designed museum carries San Francisco's dreams of joining the top ranks of art-exhibiting cities. Across Third Street, the Center for the Arts provides a publicly financed home for smaller-scale avant-garde theater, dance and visual arts, described by the *Washington Post* as having "the look of a elegant, precision-tuned factory... just right for a building devoted to experimental art." Both buildings sit alongside the five-acre green splash of The Esplanade, an amiable if sleep-inducing rendition of an urban park with benches and whimsical sculptures: a bronze businessman here, a sinking ship there. Off the walkway, a waterfall-in-a-grotto serves as a tribute to Martin Luther King with selected quotes from the civil rights leader inscribed onto twelve glass-and-granite panels behind a twenty-foot-high cascade.

Amid Yerba Buena Center's post-post-modern architecture is the unlikely sight of a 1916 carousel. Previously a feature of Playland-At-The-Beach, an amusement park close to the Cliff House that closed in the early 1970s, the carousel forms a low-tech approach to the Children's Block. At the core of the Children's Block the high-tech Zeum (the name was picked from a kid-tested short-list, with rejected possibilities including the Rolling Hamster Studio), is a $56-million educational center packed with computers, multimedia, video and other things—not least workshops on underwater film-making— intended to encourage the use of "technology as a creative tool".

To conventioneers, Financial District workers, and tourists reticent to venture far beyond their hotels, Yerba Buena Center promises to deliver the cream of San Francisco culture in one handy dollop. As a result, during the 1990s, seemingly every cultural institution in the city strived to find a new home within its confines: the Jewish Museum, the Mexican Museum, the Cartoon Art Museum, and the California Historical Society among them. Ironically in 2001, escalating rents forced the Ansel Adams Center for Photography, based here for many years, to close. Reflecting the area's rising profile, several international chain hotels loom, or are intending to loom, over the district, while Fourth Street holds the block-long, five-story-high gray box of the Metreon, a shopping, dining and leisure complex owned by the Sony corporation. To lessen public protest, Sony rents some ground floor space to local independent retailers.

Possibly the only local building still serving its original purpose is the 1872 St. Patrick's Church, its once dominant tower barely registering on the new skyline. Erected to serve SoMa's then substantial Irish population, the church adapted to the changing ethnic nature of its congregation and by the early 1960s was probably one of the world's few churches to be bedecked with the colors of the Irish tricolor while conducting Mass in Tagalog.

One effect of the development of Yerba Buena Center was to make SoMa a very popular place to live. During the 1980s, some of the neighborhood's disused warehouses were converted to "live-work" spaces under city initiatives intended to enable artists, already drawn to the spacious, well-lit interiors, to stay in the district. By the 1990s, however, landlords were happy to see the artists priced out in favor of high-earning multimedia and dotcom professionals, many employed in local firms or reverse commuting to jobs in Silicon Valley. New loft-style apartments tailored to the needs of the young and affluent appeared and by the late 1990s, SoMa was being targeted by New York-based developers and investors looking to create residential towers for high-rise living.

Another contributor to soaring property values was the development of China Basin and South Beach, former industrial districts on SoMa's southeastern edge. After controversies over funding and the forcible removal of local homeless, the area evolved into what the city planning department described with fearless blandness as: "vibrant mixed use residential and commercial neighborhoods." The most prominent feature, Pacific Bell Park, is a $255-million, 41,000-seat new home for baseball's San Francisco Giants which opened in 2000 with the promise that impecunious fans could watch at least part of the matches for free from standing-room only pens accessed from the Waterfront Promenade on the stadium's east side.

An anniversary issue of the *Bay Guardian* warned in October 1998: "in a few short years San Francisco will be the first fully gentrified city in American history... It will be a nasty little place, filled with frustrated wealthy people who once thought it would be hip to live in a city that now no longer can offer the cutting edges of culture that brought them here. It will be a parody of itself, a wax museum that once had the chance to define the future of urban civilization... if we don't take emergency steps, now, today, there won't be much left to save of San Francisco tomorrow." That San Francisco has not yet become a "nasty little place" might be largely due to the dotcom crash of 2000 and the subsequent wider economic downturn, putting many new developments on hold and forcing previously high-spending residents to re-think their priorities—and in some cases look for a new job or leave the city.

The future shape of San Francisco is uncertain: as it always has been.

PART THREE

Crime and Culture, Punishment and Pleasure

Gold rush San Francisco was a place of excitement and opportunity, a boom town like no other that offered people of sufficient guile and daring a multitude of ways—by fair means or foul—to get very rich very fast. With a police force barely worthy of the name, crime flourished and much of it was organized by gangs acting with the connivance of politicians, most of whom acquired their civil roles with a view to lining their own pockets. Such a cauldron of corruption prompted legitimate businessmen to twice take matters into their own hands, forming vigilance committees to dispense populist justice with the aid of a hangman's noose, and overseeing an armed volunteer militia—in itself completely illegal—to patrol the city's streets.

With little else to pass the time, gambling became San Francisco's most popular and lucrative form of entertainment, a magnet for gold-bearing miners arriving from the diggings. Hundreds of drinking dens, legal and otherwise, also flourished as did a multinational population of prostitutes. By the 1860s, such vices had coalesced into the Barbary Coast, a section of the waterfront that charted new lows in debauchery and in which a customer, assuming he was not simply murdered or robbed, risked being knocked unconscious and ferried out to a waiting ship to become an unwilling crew member, the process that became known as Shanghaiing.

From such origins emerged more "respectable" forms of entertainment and a series of grand theaters catering to post-gold rush audiences increasingly composed of working-class families as well as the upper social strata of bankers, financiers, and prosperous merchants. These venues provided a steady diet of quality drama, dance, and opera, including the US's first full-length performance of *Swan Lake* and its first complete *Nutcracker*, on which San Francisco came to pride itself. The city also established a reputation for making stars of those regarded too daring, such as the provocative Adah Menken and spider-dancing Lola Montez, to be fully embraced elsewhere.

Drawn west by the frenzy of the gold rush were the writers and would-be writers who helped San Francisco become the center of literary life in the American West. The region's first periodicals carried work by the soon-to-be celebrated Mark Twain and the celebrated-then-forgotten Bret Harte. By the 1890s, Russian Hill had developed into the West's first bohemia, a grouping of writers, artists and intellectuals whose influence would not be matched until the 1950s and the San Francisco Poetry Renaissance, the birth of the Beat Generation, which centered on the new bohemia of North Beach.

The topsy-turvy life of San Francisco was documented by a wealth of newspapers, the owner/editors of which were as likely to make the news—most spectacularly by shooting, or being shot by, their rivals—as report it. Larger-than-life William Randolph Hearst would alter the course of American journalism with the *San Francisco Examiner*, but of more lasting local prominence were the De Young brothers who founded the *San Francisco Chronicle* and one of whom provided the core collections of what became the M. H. De Young Memorial Museum. The De Youngs also formed one side of the city's longest-running and most celebrated feud: their conflict with the Spreckels family extended not just to rival newspapers but also to rival art museums (the latter founding the California Palace of the Legion of Honor) and, typically for the lawless times, an assassination attempt.

Fires, Ducks, Hounds, and Hangings

San Francisco promised rich pickings, not only to gold prospectors and their suppliers but to criminals able to operate virtually at will in a city too chaotic and too new to have an effective system of law and order. Between 1847 and 1850, San Francisco's population grew from a few hundred to 20,000. In this time the police force doubled in size: from six men to twelve. Even in the unlikely event of a felon being apprehended, the city lacked, as the first mayor elected under US rule, John W. Geary, put it, "the means of confining a prisoner for an hour".

What police there were, were poorly paid and often in league with criminals. Judges were easily swayed and often corrupt, jurors were likely to be dishonest, witnesses unreliable, and lawyers operated with scant knowledge of the law. Bail was offered in nearly all cases and once it was granted the accused rarely returned to face trial. Complicating matters was California's three-year transition from Mexican to US rule, made slower by being overseen by military rather than civil authorities, and the fact that anyone possessing sufficient acumen to organize the city would sooner be seeking their fortune at the diggings.

The fires that repeatedly raged through San Francisco's tightly packed and often tinder-dry wooden buildings were frequently the result of arson. The threat of fire enabled criminals to demand protection money from businesses; actual blazes promised easy looting from unattended shops and warehouses as their proprietors dashed out to stop the flames spreading. Arson, protection rackets, and other forms of crime were orchestrated by the Sydney Ducks, a gang of British-born ex-convicts who had served time in Australian penal colonies. "The Sydney Ducks are cackling in the pond" became a much-used comment in the aftermath of any violent crime. It was also noted that the wind direction on the days of the biggest fires was usually from the east and north, blowing the flames away from Sydney Town, the waterfront area around Broadway and Portsmouth Street that the Ducks occupied. Notorious as "a veritable cesspool of corruption", Sydney Town set the tone for an area that, by the 1860s, would later be even more ill-famed as the Barbary Coast.

Sometimes in league with the Ducks were the Hounds, originating from a group of volunteer soldiers recruited in New York City to fight in the US-Mexico War who had promised, in the drive to encourage westward settlement, to stay in California once hostilities were ended. The Hounds occupied a tent on Montgomery Street nicknamed Tammany Hall after the corrupt New York City administration. Often parading through the city with a pipe and drum band, the Hounds insisted they were making San Francisco safe for Americans by continually harassing Spanish-speaking groups, particularly Mexicans, Peruvians, and Chileans. The latter endured a vicious attack in July 1849 described in *The Annals of San Francisco*:

These [the Chileans' tents] *they violently tore down, plundering them of money and valuables, which they carried away, and totally destroying on the spot such articles as they did not think it worth while to seize. Without provocation, and in cold blood, they barbarously beat with sticks and stones, and cuffed and kicked the unoffending foreigners. Not content with that, they repeatedly and wantonly fired among the injured people, and amid the shrieks of terrified women and groans of wounded men, recklessly continued their terrible course in different quarters, wherever in fact malice or thirst for plunder led them. This was in broad daylight; but there were no individuals brave or foolhardy enough to resist the progress of such a savage mob, whose exact force was unknown, but who were believed to be both numerous and desperate.*

While there were some who secretly supported the Hounds, the attack on the Chileans galvanized the general populace. A mass meeting at Portsmouth Square on the day following the assault saw 230 volunteer policemen sworn-in. Armed with muskets, the force arrested those thought responsible who were then tried before the *alcalde* and a group of elected judges. With the impromptu court passing sentences of up to ten years hard labor, the immediate problem of the Hounds abated but the wider problem of law and order remained. Murders and robberies were regular events and continued to go unpunished. In a taste of what would follow, a crowd of 5,000 assembled in February 1851, calling for the immediate hanging of two Sydney Ducks after they molested a leading merchant.

By early May 1851, as San Francisco was approaching the first anniversary of one of its biggest fires, rumors spread that the Sydney Ducks were planning to mark the date with an even bigger blaze, hoping to destroy the city in retaliation for the imprisonment, awaiting execution, of one of their number for shooting a sheriff. Late on May 3, a Sydney Duck was seen running from a paint shop, which shortly afterwards was ablaze. The city was quickly engulfed in its most destructive fire to date. Two thousand buildings were destroyed in ten hours and the damage put at $12 million. The flames had been visible as far away as Monterey.

Mindful of the success of the makeshift militia organized against the Hounds, the *Alta California* reflected the public mood by campaigning for the formation of a citizens' safety committee. The result was the Committee of Vigilance, its constitution signed by 103 citizens on June 10. Almost immediately, the committee was called to action when a Sydney Duck, John Jenkins, was caught stealing a safe. The Vigilance Committee sat in judgment on Jenkins, found him guilty, and sentenced him to be hanged. He was marched to Portsmouth Square and hanged just after 2am. The *Alta California* reported:

> *The crowd, which numbered upwards of a thousand, were perfectly quiescent, or only applauded by look, gesture, and subdued voice the action of the committee. Before the prisoner had reached the building, a score of persons seized the loose end of the rope and ran backwards, dragging the wretch along the ground and raising him to the beam. Thus they held him till he was dead. Nor did they let the body go until some hours afterwards, new volunteers relieving those who were tired holding the rope. Little noise or confusion took place. Muttered whispers among the spectators guided their movements or betrayed their feelings. The prisoner had not spoken a word, either upon the march or during the rapid preparations for his execution. At the end he was perhaps strung up almost before he was aware of what was so immediately coming. He was a strong-built, healthy man, and his struggles, when hanging, were very violent for a few minutes.*

Another Duck was hanged on July 11, as subsequently were two others, despite attempts to intervene by the governor of California and his sheriffs who raided the committee's offices and moved two men held there awaiting execution to jail. The vigilantes, however, stormed the jail and the hangings were duly carried out.

Although tensions rose between San Francisco and the state government, the effect on the Sydney Ducks was the required one. Crime fell dramatically as many either kept a very low profile or left the city, some returning to Australia where another gold rush was underway. In September, with some of its members elected to state and local government positions, the Vigilance Committee disbanded.

A Low Set of Politicians

San Francisco enjoyed several relatively crime- and fire-free years until the mid-1850s, which brought a gradual return of criminals and an economic depression as the end of the gold rush curtailed migration to San Francisco, reduced demand for services, and led to a sharp decline in land and property values. In New York, it was reported that two-thirds of the 489 murders committed in California during 1855 were in San Francisco where none had been punished. *The Annals of San Francisco* quotes an anonymous writer saying of the city: "Masked men appeared openly in the streets and garrotted citizens, apparently defying law or resistance; the rough element had apparently banded together for the purpose of preying upon the wealth held by honest hands... Politics was in fact accountable for this chaotic condition of city affairs."

Politics in San Francisco at this time did indeed have much in common with crime. It had become, according to the memoirs of General William T. Sherman, a military leader who for a time ran a San Francisco bank, "a regular and profitable business... [wherein] the better classes avoided the elections and dodged jury-duty, so that the affairs of the city government necessarily passed into the hands of a low set of professional politicians."

With bribery and corruption rife, the city administration was controlled by one man, David Broderick (1820-59). While Broderick did much to improve the city and the lot of the ordinary man, he was a scion of New York's corrupt Tammany Hall regime and offered political posts in return for financial favors. He reputedly made several hundred thousand dollars a year by doing this as well as gaining unparalleled influence in city and state affairs and furthering his ambition of becoming a US senator. Broderick's scam of minting coins worth less than their face value was but one of many that came to light during the troubled period. Another was perpetrated by assistant alderman Henry Meiggs, who used forged city warrants to embezzle $800,000 from investors before fleeing to South America. By 1855, despite the gold rush fortune that had flowed through it, San Francisco was almost $2 million in debt.

Virulent anti-corruption editorials and exposés were run by the media, particularly by the *San Francisco Bulletin* under the editorship of James King of William (1822-56). (Born plain James King, he added his father's forename to his own to distinguish himself from other James Kings.) King's editorials took a high moral tone, hitting out against dishonesty and the city's lack of law and order (this was partly due to personal experience; as a banker, he had made a fortune but lost it through a dishonest employee). Capturing the mood of the city, King wrote: "The best man in San Francisco may be shot down tomorrow by some ruffian who does not like what he has said or done; yet the chances are an hundred to one that that ruffian will escape punishment."

On 14 May, 1856, a long-running feud between King and James P. Casey, an elected member of the Board of Supervisors who had been found to be an ex-convict suspected of vote rigging, culminated with Casey shooting King in broad daylight near the corner of Montgomery and Washington streets. News of the shooting quickly spread and within two hours a large crowd had gathered at the county jail where Casey was held. The shooting also prompted the immediate formation of a second Committee of Vigilance. Their proclamation railed against a state of affairs in which

Organized gangs of bad men, of all political parties, or who assumed any particular creed from mercenary and corrupt motives, have parcelled out our offices among themselves, or sold them to the highest bidders; Have provided themselves with convenient tools to obey their nod, as Clerks, Inspectors and Judges of election;

Have employed bullies and professional fighters to destroy tally-lists by force, and prevent peaceable citizens from ascertaining, in a lawful manner, the true number of votes polled at our elections;

And have used cunningly contrived ballot boxes with false sides and bottoms, so prepared that by means of a spring or slide, spurious tickets, concealed there previous to the election, could be mingled with genuine votes.

Two days later, 3,000 men who had volunteered for service with the committee took up arms and marched on the county jail, successfully demanding that Casey be handed over to them for trial by the Vigilance Committee.

As King was being buried on May 22, Casey (along with Charles Cora who had killed a US Marshal) was hung in front of the Committee of Vigilance's office on Sacramento Street (no. 41, in what was a liquor warehouse). Several thousand who had formed a funeral cortège for King now raced to get a glimpse of the execution. By the time the inert bodies were cut down, an estimated 20,000 onlookers had gazed at the corpses.

After buying or seizing all the arms in the city, the Committee of Vigilance militia patrolled San Francisco with the support of most of its people but enraging politicians who saw the committee as a threat to their own survival and who demanded that the governor of California intervene. The law-and-order group (many found the title ironic) was formed to oppose the committee's power but ultimately even the state authorities were unable to mount a challenge to the unofficial militia. The Vigilance Committee declared: "the people have no faith in the officers of the law" and on June 9 issued the proclamation: "All political, religious, and sectional differences and issues have given way to the paramount necessity of a thorough and fundamental reform and purification of the social and political body." After a few more hangings and the creation of the People Party, which many of its members joined, the second Vigilance Committee considered its point had been made and voted to disband itself.

David Broderick had sought to remain aloof from the conflict, aware that taking sides might damage his chance of becoming a US senator, a post he duly attained in 1857. Two years later, however, Broderick died after a pistol duel with David S. Terry, a former Chief Justice in the California Supreme Court, ostensibly over Broderick's opposition to slavery. Despite his underhand dealings to control San Francisco politics, Broderick's unprecedented rise from humble origins to the US Senate allowed him to die a hero.

Pandemonium Let Loose

Other than lawlessness, first impressions for anyone setting foot in San Francisco during the early years of the gold rush were of a place almost entirely devoted to gambling. The very kernel of the city, Portsmouth Square, had gambling saloons along three sides that operated around the clock seven days a week, and often had punters standing three or four deep around the tables. Gold and silver chippings were commonly staked, as was gold dust, accepted as regular currency. Popular games included roulette, *vingt-et-un*, and faro, although poker (except as dice poker) was rare, its slow pace unsuited to the hell-for-leather mood. Typically, miners were indifferent to their losses, believing that another visit to the diggings would soon replenish their pockets.

Gambling was not solely the preserve of miners. Judges, doctors, and lawyers were all regularly seen at the tables, as were the clergy. In *The Beginnings of San Francisco*, Zoeth Skinner Eldredge describes a Methodist's minister's visit: "On arriving at San Francisco in September 1849, Brother Taylor asked a person who came on board the ship if there were any ministers of the gospel in San Francisco. 'Yes,' he said, 'we have one preacher, but preaching won't pay here, so he quit preaching and went to gambling'." Another arrival, quoted in Herbert Asbury's *The Barbary Coast*, said: "It was a scene I shall never forget. On all sides of you were gambling houses, each with its band of music in full blast. Crowds were going in and coming out; fortunes were being lost and won; terrible imprecations and blasphemies rose amid the horrid wail, and it seemed to me pandemonium was let loose."

Some venues had a daily take of $200,000, despite stakes that were usually around 50 cents and rarely more than $10. Incidents of high stakes and high losses quickly passed into city folklore. One drunken miner wagered $20,000 on the turn of a card and another lost $89,000 over a three-day session. Aside from the gambling houses, substantial profits were made by professional gamblers who preyed on the cash-rich, usually inebriated, miners.

Within a few years of the start of the gold rush, San Francisco held perhaps a thousand gambling venues. One of the earliest, the El Dorado, like most initially operating from a canvas tent, evolved into a wooden building and sought to attract clients, for whom competition was increasingly intense, with paintings of "nude women in various abandoned postures". Some gambling venues offered live entertainment, including one boasting a French woman playing the violin—a service for which she was paid two ounces of gold dust.

Gambling's proliferation was encouraged by an absence of regulation. Efforts to impose legal controls either failed or were simply ignored, and for decades gambling became an integral part of the city, with most drinking places and theaters having a section devoted to its pursuit. Gambling at least provided a way to pass the time in a city where alternative forms of diversion, other than drinking and visiting prostitutes, was rare.

The earliest recorded public entertainments included a circus held during the spring of 1849 on a plot of land near the junction of Kearny and Clay streets, an appearance of the Philadelphia Minstrels in October 1849, and the city's first theatrical performance in January 1850 at Washington Hall: "a flimsy board structure on Portsmouth Square which later became the town's most elegant brothel." Melodeons (sometimes written "melodeans" and in other variations), a type of music hall so-named for having an melodeon (a keyboard instrument) on the premises, quickly appeared, offering performances that might range on any given night from Shakespearean drama to acrobats and performing bears. Among them was the Bella Union, at Washington and Kearny streets, which developed from a gambling venue into something billing itself as "the Melodeon of the people... Unapproachable and Beyond Competition". It included Big Bertha, "a sprightly lass of two hundred and eighty pounds who sang sentimental ballads in a squeaky soprano," among its most popular turns. Like all the city's early entertainment venues, the Bella Union was regularly burned to the ground and perished for good during the 1906 earthquake and fire.

A cut above the melodeons, which generally catered to all-male audiences, were the larger and usually ornately decorated theaters where mixed-sex audiences and the city's social elite could enjoy refined evenings of drama and opera. Christmas 1853 saw the opening of the Metropolitan Theater on Washington Street, presenting the twin attractions of Edwin Booth in *Richard the Third* and gas lamps, the first city theater to be so lit. In 1869, the even grander California Theater opened on Bush Street, financed by banker William Ralston and presided over by actor Lawrence Barrett. The opening night was recorded by Amelia Ransom Neville in *The Fantastic City*.

The city's wealth, beauty, and fashion were all there, the ladies in light silks with flittering fans and their hair done in the new mode with long 'Follow-me-lad' curls over one shoulder—an audience of 'carriage folk.' Those who did not own clarence or barouche commandeered public hacks for the evening, and they rolled up Bush Street from Kearney, the horses' hoofs clattering on cobble-stones. The lobby with its mirrors fairly glittered with elated people assembling, long silk skirts sweeping the tessellated marble floor; and the elegant Barrett, in full evening regalia, stood smiling like a host welcoming his guests.

Another venue where San Francisco audiences could slake their seemingly insatiable thirst for opera came with the opening of the Tivoli Beer Garden in 1875, an establishment that steadily acquired sufficient gravitas to become the Tivoli Opera House and occupy a series of increasingly splendid venues. Regularly joined by internationally known stars, the Tivoli's resident company performed nightly, making over 4,000 appearances until succumbing to the 1906 disaster.

Tom Maguire: Napoleon of the Stage

An illiterate settler from New York who had previously driven horse-drawn cabs and tended theater bars for a living, Tom Maguire (1820-96) owned Porter's Hall, a saloon and gambling venue on Portsmouth Square, and in 1850 opened the Jenny Lind Theatre on an upper floor (despite its name, singer Jenny Lind never appeared at the theater nor had any connection with it). In 1851, in one of the city's calamitous fires, the building burned to the ground as, nine days after its opening, did its replacement. A third Jenny Lind Theatre arose on the same site, this time built of stone with an interior elaborated with fancy cupolas and frescoes, and a stage curtain carrying a depiction of the Grand Canal of Venice. In its entries for 1851, *The Annals of San Francisco* records:

> *OCTOBER 4th.—Opening of the new Jenny Lind Theatre on the Plaza. This was a large and handsome house. The interior was fitted up with exquisite taste; and altogether in size, beauty and comfort, it rivalled the most noted theatres in the Atlantic States. It could seat comfortably upwards of two thousand persons. The opening night presented a brilliant display of beauty and fashion, and every part of the immense building was crowded to excess... A new era in theatricals was now begun in San Francisco; and since that period the city has never wanted one or two first class theatres and excellent stock companies, among which "stars" of the first magnitude annually make their appearance. Before this date there had been various dramatic companies in San Francisco, but not before had there been so magnificent a stage for their performances.*

Despite the acclaim accorded to the new theater, Maguire's financial problems caused him to exploit his political connections in the city's corrupt Broderick administration to arrange to sell the building for $200,000 for conversion into a new City Hall. Variously described as the "Jenny Lind swindle" and the "Jenny Lind juggle", the affair occupied the city's newspapers for months and contributed to the downfall of Broderick and his cronies. Ironically, despite the immense cost of its purchase and the refitting of the interior to make it suitable for civic purposes, the building performed much better than expected as a city hall, its demise in that role only due to the fast growth of the city itself. For his part in the deal, Maguire was banished from San Francisco but ignored this order and, having established a theater monopoly in several California towns, returned to San Francisco to open the Maguire Opera House on Washington Street in 1856 and the Maguire Academy of Music on Pine Street eight years later.

A penchant for lavish productions whose costs exceeded takings, a libel suit from the prominent De Young family, and a disregard for the formalities of making royalty payments to playwrights, led to Maguire's downfall and, in 1880, his imprisonment in New York. On his release, Maguire's remaining years were spent in poverty, despite being remembered as "the Napoleon of the San Francisco stage", the title of a biography of Maguire published during the Depression.

Although described by newspaper columnist Walter Thompson as "a man totally lacking in taste and good dramatic judgement", Maguire brought many of the leading actors of the era, among them Edwin Booth and Edwin Forrest, to San Francisco and for a time employed David Belasco as a manager. Destined to become one of the US's most noted playwrights and producers, Belasco emerged from an impoverished upbringing in a south of Market Street home to earn a living as what he would later describe as a "theatrical vagabond". An early indication of the breadth of his talents was displayed at 22 Geary Street in 1878, where a store front was converted into the "Egyptian Hall", a setting for a series of one-act plays and farces which Belasco wrote and appeared in. Moving to New York, Belasco eventually acquired a theater he renamed the Belasco in 1910, using it for a series of hit plays with which he pioneered naturalistic acting and realistic sets. Following his death in 1931, Belasco's coffin lay in state in San Francisco's City Hall.

The Mesmerizing Adah Menken

As the cream of the nation's theatrical talent began appearing in San Francisco, their rapturous receptions were, in part, a response to the fact that they had made the effort, their journey to San Francisco involving a long voyage around Cape Horn. Top performers were rewarded not only by ovations, but also by high fees and some established lasting links with the city's affections, sometimes as much for their personal style as their stage gifts.

In 1863, Tom Maguire paid a reputed $1,500 a week (other sources suggest $500) to bring Adah Isaacs Menken to his new Opera House. Menken (1835-68) had stunned puritanical New York audiences with her appearance in the equestrian melodrama *Mazeppa*. Traditionally, the title role had been played by a man and the final scene, involving a bareback horse ride by the completely nude lead character, had been taken by a stuffed dummy. Menken, however, not only played the role but insisted that, in the interests of dramatic realism, she play the final scene herself wearing a flesh-colored body stocking. With the *New York Tribune* demanding she be banned from the stage, Menken responded to her critics with: "I'll go to the one place where the audience demands real art; I'll go to San Francisco." Maguire advertised her San Francisco appearances as "Miss Menken, stripped by her captors, will ride a fiery steed at furious gallop onto and across the stage and into the distance."

In *Mazeppa*, Menken thrilled San Francisco. In *The Fantastic City*, Amelia Ransome Neville recalled that Menken "was the toast of the town in the sixties. An indifferent actress, she had a lovely face, with masses of red-gold hair, and the figure of a Greek dancer... Audiences went wild over her, and thrilled young ladies who rarely met people of the theatre would ask more privileged men friends, 'What is she like off the stage?' She was a gentle young adventuress, it appeared, given to writing poetry." Indeed, some of Menken's poetry was published in the *Golden Era*, and her San Francisco social group included literary figures such as Bret Harte, Joaquin Miller and Charles Warren Stoddard. Cashing in on her fame by offering "private entertainment" for silver mining tycoons, Menken ensured she would not be accepted in more conventional social circles. Meanwhile, her short and apparently violent marriage to California-born boxing champion John Heenan, one of four marriages in seven years, did nothing to diminish her passionate reputation, something that guaranteed a steady supply of male admirers.

Menken left San Francisco to take *Mazeppa* to London (where her fans included Charles Dickens who, of a slim volume of Menken's poetry, observed, "She is a sensitive poet who, unfortunately, cannot write") and later Paris, where she died in 1868, aged an improbably young 33. San Francisco journalist Samuel Dickson wrote of Menken's time in the city: "She was adored by its gay blades, and even to this day you may find very old gentlemen who, when you praise this or that actress, will look at you with pained surprise and say, 'Young man, you and your generation have not lived. You should have known Adah Menken. You should have seen her in *Mazeppa.*'"

Even Menken's horse is accorded a footnote in *The Fantastic City*: "The white horse, named Mazeppa, Adah Menken left to one of our bachelor friends when she departed California. He rode it daily to his office in Sansome Street until one day it disappeared—stolen from the hitching-post. It was traced to a ship that had sailed for Australia that morning, and there was nothing to be done about it after that."

Spider-Dancing Lola Montez

Another taboo-busting woman to make an impression on San Francisco was Lola Montez (1818-61), who had arriving in 1853 preceded by a racy reputation based on her erotic Spider Dance and a life of the kind most fiction writers would reject for being beyond belief. Claiming to be the daughter of a Spanish matador, and with some biographical accounts suggesting her mother was "a Spanish beauty", Montez was actually born Eliza Gilbert in Limerick, Ireland, to an Irish mother and a father who was an army captain in India, where she spent her early years. Marrying young in England to avoid her mother's choice of suitor, Montez quickly separated from her husband and traveled to Spain where she acquired a new name and basic skills in flamenco dancing.

As "Lola Montez, the Spanish dancer", she debuted on the London stage in a performance that included what would variously be termed "La Tarantula", the "Spanish Tarantula", "El Zapateado", and the "Neapolitan", but would become better known as the Spider Dance.

Originally intended as a bridge between formal dances, the spider dance involved Montez steadily divesting herself of clothing while apparently seeking to remove a spider from her person.

While Montez's dance skills were questionable, her charismatic and erotic appeal to male audiences was not. From London she traveled to Poland where she accidentally scarred the Tsar of Russia for life with her riding crop. In Bavaria, she stormed the king's palace after the Bavarian State Theater refused to allow her to perform. Through the king's affections, she not only performed but acquired the titles Baroness of Rosenthal and Countess of Lansfield, and an influence on Bavarian affairs that resulted in her banishment, the king fearing her presence would trigger a revolution.

Arriving in New York in 1851, Montez was "throwing tantrums and striking men with her whip at the slightest provocation" while a stage manager remarked that she "danced through a certain routine of steps, without regard to time, music or anything else." A female audience member quoted in the *Nevada Journal* described Montez as having "flounced about like a stuck pig, and clenched her short clothes, raising them nearly to her waist, while with a thin, scrawny leg she keeps up a constant thumping upon the stage, as if she was in a slight spasm."

In San Francisco, of course, Montez was perfectly at home. First appearing in the city in 1853, she entertained guests at her hotel suite with caviar and champagne and very soon married a local journalist, Patrick Hull, in a wedding ceremony held at Mission Dolores and attended by the mayor. Amelia Ransome Neville wrote:

> We heard much light gossip of her; there had been no scandals in her San Francisco days. Every one who had seen her spoke of her startling beauty; a perfect figure, smooth brown hair, magnolia skin, and large gray eyes filled with expression. She would promenade Montgomery Street in a short black velvet jacket over a flaring skirt of silk, a broad hat with black lace falling over the brim. Word would go down the street, 'Lola Montez,' and every one stared in the most discreet manner possible. It was known that she had once struck her riding-whip across the face of a man too bold in his admiration.

And of a benefit performance for the city's firemen, who tossed their caps onto the stage:

> *She ignored them at first, dancing gracefully while keeping time with the castanets, now slowly flitting across the stage, then rapidly whirling away and shaking out the spiders from her skirts. But as the climax to the dance drew near, Montez transformed one of the caps into a spidery sex object. After pirouetting around and over it petticoats, spread to their outmost, she poised herself with a foot on either side, and dipped her body down till there was almost contact. She sprang angrily to her feet, stamped upon and crushed it to the floor, ending the dance...*

Montez entered what was described by some as a semi-retirement in the California mining town of Grass Valley. Admittedly it was a quiet period, disturbed only by the local parson describing her as a "shameless devil in the guise of a beautiful and fascinating dancer" and her whip attack on the editor of the *Grass Valley Telegraph*. At home, Montez studied ESP and astrology, and kept a pet bear. A few years later, she left the US for a disappointing tour of Australia (although some accounts describe her shows as receiving rapturous ovations). The reality of her final days—she died in New York in 1861—divided biographers as much as the details of the rest of her life. Some have her "lecturing on free love and selling rejuvenation cream", others walking penniless through the streets until she died, another suggests she embraced religion and was cared for to the end by a kindly priest.

While providing a lively episode to its theatrical history, Montez was never the toast of San Francisco in the way that Menken was. She did, however, make a major contribution to the city's cultural life by giving dance lessons to a young Grass Valley neighbor: the eight-year-old Lotta Crabtree.

Lotta Crabtree's Beautiful Ankle

Published in 1928, Constance Rourke's *Troupers of the Gold Coast, or the rise of Lotta Crabtree*, writes of Montez and Crabtree: "Lola taught her to dance; and though that imperious spirit would never have admitted it, Lotta had a far truer sense of rhythm than Lola herself ever had. Lotta's tiny feet learned the intricacies of a few ballet steps. Liking innovation, Lola had picked up fandangos and highland flings; these too she taught Lotta in sudden gusts of pleasure... In a blacksmith's shop... Lola stood the child on an anvil, clapped her hands, had her dance before a little crowd, and declared that she must go to Paris."

Rather than Paris, Lotta Crabtree (1847-1924) moved with her mother to San Francisco in 1856, part of the continuing search for her father who had left the family home in New York to join the gold rush. Failing to find her husband and without any source of income, Mrs. Crabtree made use of her daughter's theatrical talents. The 12-year-old Lotta quickly thrilled San Francisco as she had the gold rush camps with:

Jigs, flings, wild polkas, breakdowns, the whole range of soft-shoe danc-ing: in her five or six years of traveling in the mines or playing to small audiences in San Francisco she had picked up every bold and lively changing step which could provoke a sudden cheer, and danced them with a delicate sprightliness or a rough and romping humor... She danced as Topsy, as a wild Irish boy, as a Cockney with a Cockney song. She had a Scotch fling, and came out as an American sailor with horn-pipe.

In 1859 she was billed as "Miss Lotta, the San Francisco favorite" and by the age of 16 she had toured the US and become a star in New York, the start of a career that would make her the highest paid actress in the US. Ascribed with having the "face of a beautiful doll and the ways of a playful kitten", even in middle age, Crabtree was given youthful roles and credited with possessing "the most beautiful ankle in the world". Her lack of a husband, meanwhile, stimulated endless debate on her private life, including a front page of the *New York Times* speculating on "The Loves of Lotta".

Still in her early twenties, Lotta returned to San Francisco in 1869 on the new transcontinental railroad to be honored at a civic reception. Retiring from the stage in 1891 to an estate in New Jersey, Lotta traveled again to San Francisco in 1915 to make her final performance on Lotta Crabtree Day, part of the Panama-Pacific International Exposition.

Aside from memories, another reminder of Crabtree in San Francisco is Lotta's Fountain at the junction of Market and Kearny

Streets, given by Lotta to the city and its people in 1875 but now largely ignored by the pedestrian and vehicular traffic moving in a constant swirl around it. Ben Adams' *San Francisco: an Informal Guide* describes "a tall rather commonplace cast-iron fountain... [but] to old timers Lotta's Fountain, set on a granite base with ornamental lion heads and weather-beaten brass medallions depicting California scenes, evokes sentimental anecdotes and a torrent of great names." Other than supplying drinking water to people and horses (the troughs for the latter long since removed), the fountain provided a vantage point to watch fires and a rallying point during the earthquake and fire of 1906. On Christmas Eve 1910, however, it provided perhaps its most spectacular civic role, hosting a free performance from Italian opera star Luisa Tetrazzini.

An estimated 250,000 San Franciscans made their way to Lotta's Fountain that night to listen to the renowned singer, a coloratura soprano who appeared wearing a white gown, white gloves and a white ostrich boa. She sang *The Last Rose of Summer* and *I Would Linger In This Dream* before an unexpected rendition of *Auld Lang Syne* with the joyous crowd joining in. Amelia Ransome Neville described the occasion in *The Fantastic City*: "The converging streets were black with people and the windows of near-by buildings were all filled. Those who heard her said her silver voice seemed to rise to the stars through the still night; and the utter silence of the great crowd in the dark streets was curiously thrilling. The singing was Tetrazzini's Christmas gift to the city which had first welcomed her to America."

The appearance resulted from Tetrazzini's contractual dispute with producer Oscar Hammerstein. With the New York impresario seeking to prevent the soprano from appearing anywhere in the US except under his auspices, Tetrazzini declared: "I will sing in San Francisco if I have to sing there in the streets, for I knew the streets of San Francisco are free. I never thought I would be a street singer but I want to do this thing for San Francisco, because this is the first place in the United States where I sang, and because I like San Francisco. San Francisco is my country."

If anything was certain to win adulation from San Franciscans and bring them to the streets, it was such remarks. Not given to false modesty, the singer would later recount the event over two pages in her autobiography, describing it as "the greatest concert San Francisco or the world had ever seen." A bas-relief on the fountain puts things more simply: "Here in 1910, Tetrazzini sang for the citizens of San Francisco."

Isadora Duncan: The California Faun

While Lotta and Luisa may have professed their love for San Francisco, one of the performing arts' greatest figures was born in the city but could not wait to leave it. In a long-since demolished house at 501 Taylor Street, Isadora Duncan (1878-1927) became one of four children born to an arts-loving cashier of the Bank of California, Joseph Duncan, and his wife, Mary Dora. In the year following Isadora's birth, Joseph declared his affection for a Russian Hill spinster, the poet and literary godmother Ina Donna Coolbrith, and a divorce soon followed. The outraged Mary Dora took the Duncan children to a modest home in Oakland and a life of little money but many stories about the scandalous behavior of their wicked father: "a demon in human garb".

As Isadora grew, she voraciously read books from the Oakland Public Library, her tastes in literature developed by its librarian, the same Ina Donna Coolbrith. Meeting her father for the first time, Isadora was amazed to discover him a gentle and charming man, with artistic sensibilities similar to her own. The confusion between the reality and her mother's description was enough to make the twelve-year-old Isadora vow never to marry, the acrimony between her parents fueling her later declaration: "Marriage is an absurd and enslaving institution, leading—especially with artists—inevitably to the divorce courts, and preposterous and vulgar lawsuits."

To earn money for the family, Isadora and her older sister Elisabeth gave dance lessons, first in Oakland and then in San Francisco where, according to journalist Samuel Dickson, "they taught the young hopefuls of San Francisco society forms of the dance that were fifty years ahead of their time." Persuading her mother to travel east, Isadora appeared in Chicago as "the California faun" and in stage plays in New York. But her brilliant and innovative dance style was not properly recognized until 1899 in London, where her free-flowing, gestural movements were widely admired, as they were subsequently across Europe.

Isadora had a short and eventful life (her Russian husband committed suicide when the relationship ended; her children were both killed in a driving accident; and her own death in 1927, resulting from her shawl becoming entwined around the wheel of her sports car, became the stuff of tragic legend). In that time she returned to San Francisco only once, making a tour of her childhood haunts in 1922.

San Francisco would not forget having sired the founder of modern dance so easily, however. Unveiled in 1973 as "young girls in tunics danced barefoot on the sidewalk to the music of Schubert," a plaque marks her birthplace and an adjoining alley was renamed Isadora Duncan Lane. In 1985 came the first award of the annual "Izzies", the Isadora Duncan Dance Awards to mark the achievements of Bay Area dance artists.

The Barbary Coast

If the precious yellow metal hadn't been discovered in the auriferous sands of the Sacramento Valley, the development of San Francisco's underworld in all likelihood would have proceeded according to the traditional pattern and would have been indistinguishable from that of any other large American city. Instead, owing almost entirely to the influx of gold-seekers and the horde of gamblers, thieves, harlots, politicians and other felonious parasites who battened upon them, there arose a unique criminal district that for almost seventy years was the scene of more vicious-ness and depravity, but which at the same time possessed more glamour, than any other area of vice and iniquity on the American continent.

Herbert Asbury, *The Barbary Coast.*

San Francisco may have been forging a reputation as the cultural center of the American West, but there remained one district where thoughts of Italian singers and Shakespearean drama were far from most people's minds: it was known as the Barbary Coast.

The forerunner of today's Pacific Avenue, Pacific Street in the early days of San Francisco was the main route between the docks and Portsmouth Square. Steadily it and its adjacent streets "abandoned all pretence of respectability" and by the 1860s were lined by melodeons, dance halls, and the rundown bars popularly known as "deadfalls". The few other businesses that existed in the area were clothing outlets which "catered principally to sailors and fleeced them unmercifully with shoddy and worthless merchandise" and auction halls "where goods of all sorts were disposed... at prices far above their actual worth."

The area between the waterfront and Broadway, of which Pacific Street formed a central part, was dubbed the Barbary Coast from a name previously applied by sailors to a barbarous, pirate-infested stretch of the North African coast. Home to San Francisco's main places of entertainment, the chief purpose of most Barbary Coast businesses was to divest customers, or indeed any passers-by, of their money as quickly as possible. Asbury recounts: "From late afternoon until dawn all of the dives were thronged with a motley crew of murderers, thieves, burglars, gamblers, pimps, and degenerates of every description, practically all of whom were busily gunning for the sailors, miners, countrymen, and others who visited the district through curiosity or in search of women and liquor."

Asbury's book, published in 1933 and researched in the 1920s, drew on the recollections of those who lived through the Barbary Coast's heyday, echoing contemporaneous accounts such as that of Colonel Albert S. Evans who, like many "respectable" folk, only dared tour the district in the company of a policeman. Of his visit around 1871, Evans recalled:

> *Women dressed in flaunting colors stand at the doors of many of these 'deadfalls,' and you frequently notice some of them saluting an acquaintance, perhaps of an hour's standing, and urging him to 'come back and take just one more drink.' Ten to one the already half-drunken fool complies, and finds himself in the calaboose next morning, with a broken head, utterly empty pockets, and a dim recollection of having been taken somewhere by some woman whom he cannot identify, and finding himself unexpectedly in the clutches of men he never saw before, who go through him like a policeman, taking from him watch, chain, and every other valuable, and pitch him headlong down a stairway; after which all is a blank in his memory.*

When they were not accompanying visitors from the higher social strata, police patrolled the Barbary Coast "in pairs or in even greater numbers" and were "specially chosen for strength, bravery, and huskiness." The police officer would be "equipped with the regulation night-stick and pistol and also carried, in a large outside breast-pocket within easy reach of his hand, a huge knife a foot or more in length."

In *Lights and Shades of San Francisco*, published in 1876, Benjamin Estelle Lloyd likened the neighborhood to hell itself:

Dance-halls and concert-saloons, where blear-eyed men and faded women drink vile liquor, smoke offensive tobacco, engage in vulgar conduct, sing obscene songs and say and do everything to heap upon themselves more degradation, are numerous. Low gambling houses, thronged with riot-loving rowdies, in all stages of intoxication, are there. Opium dens, where heathen Chinese and God-forsaken men and women are sprawled in miscellaneous confusion, disgustingly drowsy or completely overcome, are there. Licentiousness, debauchery, pollution, loathsome disease, insanity from dissipation, misery, poverty, wealth, profanity, blasphemy, and death, are there. And Hell, yawning to receive the putrid mass, is there also.

While the excesses of the Barbary Coast, parts of which averaged a murder a week, provided colorful copy for newspapers and authors, the area also contributed greatly to the economy of San Francisco. By 1890, it contained the bulk of the 3,117 establishments licensed to sell intoxicating beverages (giving San Francisco a tavern for every 96 people) even without taking into account the approximately 2,000 unlicensed "blind tigers" or "blind pigs" where alcohol was sold illegally. The legitimate takings alone were worth over $9 million per year.

Barbary Coast residents found innovative ways to make money. After her son survived an attempt to shoot him from point blank range, shopkeeper Dora Herz cashed in on his reputation for supernatural powers by locking him in a room and allowing peeps through a hole in the door for ten cents a time. For a modest payment, another local, "Dirty Tom" McAlear, would eat or drink anything, however foul, placed in front of him until he was finally arrested on charge of "making a beast of himself". In custody, he claimed to have been drunk for seven years and was unable to remember the last time he had washed.

The Barbary Coast spawned its share of San Francisco legends. The owner of one dance hall, the Opera Comique, was Happy Jack Harrington. He was "considered the Beau Brummel of the Coast and was invariably attired in the height of fashion. His favorite costume consisted of a high-crowned plug hat, beneath which his hair was puffed out in curls; a frock coat, a white shirt with a ruffled bosom, a fancy waistcoat, and cream- or lavender-colored trousers so tight that he looked as though he had been melted and poured into them. His principal adornment and greatest pride, however, was his silky brown mustache, which was so long that he could tie its ends under his chin." But like many on the Barbary Coast, Happy Jack's celebrity was brief and his downfall hard: convicted of manslaughter after a brawl, he was imprisoned in San Quentin.

A long-time survivor was Abe Warner who opened the Cobweb Palace in 1856 and only left it when he retired in 1897, aged 80. Warner not only refused to remove spiders and or their webs from the bar, causing the whole place to be covered in silvery threads, but also kept "rows of cages containing monkeys, parrots, and other small animals and birds... purchased from sea captains and sailors. One parrot, which had the freedom of the saloon and frequently imbibed too much liquor, called Warner Grandfather and cursed in four languages."

During the 1880s, an area enclosed by Kearny and Montgomery Streets, near today's Transamerica Pyramid, was popularly known as the Devil's Acre with one particularly violent section known as Battle Row. One bar here, the Slaughterhouse, staged an impromptu name-changing ceremony: "the proprietor served free drinks to all comers and at the conclusion of the festivities smashed a bottle of beer against an inebriated customer's head and announced that thenceforth his place would be called the Morgue."

Pretty Waiter Girls

Dance halls and deadfalls were staffed by serving girls, who earned commission on drinks sold to customers and were available for sexual services (usually for 75 cents, payable to the bartender) provided in tiny rooms on an upper floor. Of the women, Asbury notes:

Some were as young as twelve or fourteen years, while others were tooth-less old hags whose lives had been almost continuous saturnalias of vice and dissipation. At least ninety-nine per cent of them were harlots, even the children. Regardless of their youth or decrepitude, they were called pretty waiter girls. They wore gaudy costumes calculated to display or accentuate their charms, if any, and in some of the lower dance-halls and concert saloons a free-spending visitor who was dissatisfied with the degree of revealment was permitted, on payment of a small fee, which rarely exceeded fifty cents, to strip any girl he desired and view her unadorned.

With such lascivious goings-on becoming the norm, it was bizarre that the prominent writer Charles Warren Stoddard should have campaigned against the dancing of the cancan, which he described in the *San Francisco Call*, as "immodest and indecent", appearing particularly upset over its display of female ankles. In a show of propriety, police arrested an offending dancer who was found guilty of indecent exposure and fined $200. Capitalizing on the publicity, many dance hall owners introduced new cancan routines, which were, as Asbury euphemistically puts it, "embellished with new gestures". Another bar pioneered topless waitresses until police ended the practice: the bar responded by dressing its staff in no-less-revealing unbuttoned blouses and promising free drinks to any customers who spotted a serving girl with underwear.

While some dance halls and bars were reasonably fair with their clientele, less salubrious establishments employed devious means to separate a man from his money. If a wealthy customer was seen to be less than generous, he might be given a drugged drink to render him unconscious, at which point he would be robbed and tossed into an alley. Alternatively, if he seemed uninterested in the girls, he might unknowingly be given a dose of Spanish fly (an aphrodisiac) after which it was hoped he would regard money as no object in fulfilling his raging sexual desires. Once a customer had selected a girl for sex, it was common for bartenders to serve the girl, at the customers expense, an aphrodisiac drink, usually, as Asbury states, nothing more than "cold tea at whiskey prices".

Performers at the less prestigious dance halls and melodeons were prized more for their attractiveness than their singing or dancing talent (most would also be sexually available to customers). Sometimes, however, the obvious lack of stagecraft would be developed into an attraction. At one establishment, two sisters nicknamed the Galloping Cow and the Dancing Heifer became a popular act: "two enormous women who had forsaken the wash-tub for a fling at high life... they performed a classical dance, lumbering about the stage like a brace of elephants." The Galloping Cow eventually saved enough money to open her own saloon on Pacific Street, warning that any man who tried to take advantage of her would pay the consequences. When one did, the Galloping Cow first broke a bottle against his head and then broke his back by tossing him over the balcony.

If only to keep a clear head while fleecing customers, serving girls generally kept very sober. One of the largest dance halls, however, the three-story Bull Run at the corner of Pacific Street and Sullivan Alley, specialized in inebriated waitresses, described by Asbury as "the most brazen, hopeless, and abandoned women on the Barbary Coast." Any one of them rendered completely unconscious was liable to be taken upstairs and offered to customers "for 25 cents to a dollar, depending on the age and beauty of the girl."

A Voyage to Shanghai
The chief victims of the Barbary Coast were not in-the-know San Franciscans but out-of-town sailors or "greenhorns", those drawn from rural areas or the eastern US by the excitement of the gold rush. As well being robbed or murdered, a stranger in the Barbary Coast faced the prospect of being "shanghaied", a term derived from a phrase used to suggest any long and arduous sea journey and shortened from "gone to Shanghai". It described the fate of any unsuspecting arrival whose pursuit of booze and carnal pleasures resulted in his waking up aboard ship as an unwitting member of the crew.

San Francisco swiftly became the US's major Pacific port, and its third most important sea trade center after New York and Boston. Some of those on incoming boats deserted for the gold fields, leaving captains in need of fresh crews and ready to pay for them. Any ship arriving in San Francisco would soon be swarming with runners, men who put out from land in skiffs to reach the vessel and earn money by luring sailors ashore with the promise of drink and sex. According to

Asbury, the tools of a runner's trade were "a revolver, a knife, a blackjack or a sling shot, a pair of brass knuckles, a flask of liquid soap, obscene pictures, and as many bottles of rum and whisky, all liberally dosed with Spanish fly, as could be crowded into their pockets."

Runners received a commission from the owners of boarding houses for every sailor they arrived with, though most were accommodated only long enough to be drugged, relieved of their possessions (including their clothes, if these were of any value), and tricked into signing for another voyage, after which they would be robbed of their advance pay—two months advance wages were usually forwarded to crew members, whether they were conscious or not—and taken by skiff to a waiting ship where the captain would pay the runner a fee per head. Since most sailors brought aboard could barely stand, some runners supplemented their income by disguising straw stuffed into clothing as a man, or in some instances by bringing aboard dead bodies.

Along with docked sailors, any able-bodied fellow who wandered into the wrong Barbary Coast bar was liable to be shanghaied by being rendered senseless with a drugged drink and dropped through a trapdoor. Simple assault was used only rarely as any obvious physical injuries would reduce the man's value. Certain bar keepers had their own knock-out concoctions, such as the Miss Piggott Special, named for the tavern owner who perfected a cocktail of whisky, brandy, and gin laced with laudanum or opium. Another weapon that left no marks was the shanghai cigar, custom-made by a Chinatown cigar manufacturer and laced with opium.

Three Hundred Pounds of Passion: 50 cents

In early 1849 a group of "Chilean harlots" were already operating from tents on the south side of Telegraph Hill. As the gold rush took hold, San Francisco could offer the services of working girls from all corners of the globe. By the first half of 1850, Asbury records that two thousand women, "most of whom were harlots", had arrived and that by the end of 1852 "there was no country in the world that was not represented in San Francisco by at least one prostitute." A popular rhyme of the time ran:

The miners came in forty-nine,
The whores in fifty-one;
And when they got together
They produced the native son.

Other than brief liaisons on the upper floors of dance halls and deadfalls, commercial sex at its cheapest and least refined was offered in the purpose-built "cowyards", usually a U-shaped building comprising several floors with "cribs", tiny rooms equipped with a rough mattress, chair and wash basin, arranged along corridors. A crib would be rented by a woman for $2–5 a day, after which she kept her income, although most women were controlled by a pimp or "mack" (a shortened form of the French word *maquereau*) liable to take most or all of her earnings. Some cowyards specialized in girls of a particular nationality, others housed many nationalities and divided them by floor in an informal system of grading. Mexicans were generally cheapest (typically 25 cents) and occupied the lower levels, while most prized were the French girls (the best able to charge 75 cents or more) working from the top floor. The French girls were valued for their apparent refinement and exoticism, even though most had recently been streetwalkers in Paris or Marseilles.

Some girls provided their own business cards to customers. One promised: "Big Matilda: Three Hundred Pounds of Black Passion, 50c." Some venues staged erotic exhibitions known as circuses, offering audiences the chance to watch (and sometimes join in) various combinations of men, women and animals, including on one famed occasion, a Shetland pony.

Such were the profits to be made that the cowyards grew ever bigger. In 1899, one called the Nymphia (a shortening of its original intended name of Hotel Nymphomania) opened with 150 cribs on each of its three floors. Another enormous cowyard at 620 Jackson Street became informally known as the Municipal Crib for the widespread belief (later proved true) that city officials, including the mayor, were receiving a large slice of the profits. Aware of its political links, local tavern owners would seek to curry favor with the city administration by directing their customers to the Jackson Street cowyard, as too did policemen when asked for directions to a crib, while a conductor was known to shout "all out for the whore house" when his street car stopped close by.

Due to the "great variety and extraordinary depravity of the women", one of the most notorious and popular gathering of cribs was adjacent to Union Square on Morton Street, now the classy shopping strip of Maiden Lane. Asbury describes it:

> Every night, and especially every Saturday night, this dismal bedlam of obscenity, lighted only by the red lamps above the doors of the cribs, was thronged by a tumultuous mob of half-drunken men, who stumbled from crib to crib, greedily inspecting the women as if they had been so many wild animals in cages. From the casement-windows leaned the harlots, naked to the waist, adding their shrill cries of invitation to the uproar, while their pimps haggled with passing men and tried to drag them inside the dens. If business was dull, the pimps sold the privilege of touching the breasts of the prostitutes at the standard rate of ten cents each or two for fifteen cents. But on Saturday nights some of the more popular women, who had built up a more or less regular clientele, remained in their 'workshops' from dusk to dawn, while the pimps kept the men standing in line outside, their hats in one hand and money in the other. It was not uncommon for a Morton Street prostitute to entertain as many as eighty to a hundred men in one night.

Superior in quality and higher in price than the cowyards were the parlor houses, well-appointed brothels usually owned and run by women (the madams) and staffed by a group of live-in girls. For many years, the shortage of "respectable" women led to better-connected madams partnering men of noted social standing at balls and masquerade parties. For the madams, such events not only offered a chance to strengthen their social connections but also provided a opportunity to present their newest recruits to the gentleman of the city.

Socially and geographically distanced from the drunken licentiousness of the Barbary Coast, most parlor houses were, by the 1890s, concentrated in the Upper Tenderloin, an area north of Market Street which included parts of Eddy, Ellis, O'Farrell, Mason, Powell and Turk streets. Prices were as high as $5–30, although for the top rate a client would expect to spend the night with the lady of his choice (girls were usually presented for selection when a customer arrived) followed, in some houses, by a full breakfast at no extra charge. While their business was commercial sex, parlor houses in every other respect were bastions of proper behavior; one even exhibited the notice: "No Vulgarity Allowed In This Establishment".

One curiosity of the period was the short-lived parlor house which offered men (chosen from photographs and available for $10 a time) to women customers and made available a silk face mask to customers wishing to preserve anonymity. The only known customers, however, were a few female prostitutes intrigued by the novelty.

The better parlor houses stayed in business for years, despite being infrequently raided by police after intermittent newspaper campaigns or the efforts of vote-seeking politicians as elections drew near. By and large, a blind eye was turned, not least because many prominent San Francisco men were among the regular customers. While madams might be prized for their discretion, theirs was a knowledge that could be, and often was, used to their advantage. Some accordingly became wealthy, owning property and making the most of their social connections. For the majority of working girls, however, the story was quite different. Those living in the relative comfort of a parlor house could do so only as long as their looks lasted. Afterwards, they were liable to fall steadily down the underworld pecking order until finishing up at the worst dives of the Barbary Coast.

Meanwhile, book and newspaper accounts frequently offered titillation disguised as investigative reporting. In 1878, the *New Overland Tourist* carried an article that might today be seen as a manual for sex tourists, offering detailed directions to the scenes of greatest depravity while warning: "We give the precise locality so our readers may *keep away*. Give it a *wide berth* as you value your life!"

While the earthquake and fire of 1906 put pay to the cribs of Morton Street (which would be renamed Maiden Lane in an effort to bury its salacious reputation), damage to the Barbary Coast was swiftly repaired and the cowyards rebuilt. Even as the fire that followed the earthquake raged, demand for sexual services was undiminished. All San Francisco brothels were closed, as they were across the bay in Oakland until the local police chief, faced with "incessant demand", was forced to allow them to open, observing, according to Asbury: "All day long and at night men were lined up for blocks waiting in front of the houses, like at a box office at a theater on a popular night."

The cowyards and parlor houses continued into the 1910s, but their demise was signaled by the election in 1911 of James Rolph Jr. as mayor and a Board of Supervisors intent on cleaning up the city. By now recovering from the disaster of 1906, San Francisco was, its business leaders insisted, no longer a wild mining town but a respectable place of commerce. Joining the fight were church leaders and William Randolph Hearst, publisher of the *San Francisco Examiner*. Simultaneously, new immigration laws stemmed the influx of foreign prostitutes and, for the first time, rendered madams liable to prosecution for employing foreign girls in a "house of ill fame". California's Red Light Abatement Act became law in 1914, in time for the city to close its most notorious haunts before the following year's Panama-Pacific Exposition. Shanghaiing, too, was steadily outlawed, largely due to the campaigning of the Seamen's Union leading to the 1915 Seaman's Act.

The writing had been on the wall for the Barbary Coast from 1913, however, when the *San Francisco Call* described it as "harmless as a serpent bereft of its fangs." Yet strangely enough, despite its degradation, squalor, and hopelessness, the Barbary Coast lingers in San Francisco's collective memory as a cherished piece of the gold rush past, as if its very debauchery somehow compensates the city for a lack of greater historical lineage. Even during its existence, the area was something many San Franciscans took pride in. Recounting his 1870s visit, Colonel Evans noted:

> *Every city on earth has its special sink of vice, crime and degradation, its running ulcer or moral cancer, which it would fain hide from the gaze of mankind... San Franciscans will not yield the palm of superiority to anything to be found elsewhere in the world. Speak of the deeper depth, the lower hell, the maelstrom of vice and iniquity—from whence those who once fairly enter escape no more forever—and they will point triumphantly to the Barbary Coast, strewn from end to end with the wrecks of humanity, and challenge you to match it anywhere outside of the lake of fire and brimstone.*

Others insist that the district wasn't that bad after all. In *Baghdad by the Bay*, Herb Caen quotes Barbary Coast regular Clarence E. Edwords, who claims he found "nothing shocking to our moral sense to equal what I have seen in New York... there was light and laughter that drew the crowds nightly." And upper-crust socialite Amelia Ransome Neville fondly reminisced: "even the streets of dives and dance-halls along the Barbary Coast were irrepressibly gay; never dark and devious like the slums of London or New York. A 'wide-open' town in miners' parlance meant just that, and anything wide open cannot at the same time be dark and devious... It was all mild enough as slums go in seaport cities."

The Breasts of Carol Doda

Selective memories of the Barbary Coast are matched by the affectionate nostalgia now commonly accorded to the "topless craze" that swept through North Beach in the 1960s, though many at the time thought San Francisco was again seeking to outdo Sodom and Gomorrah. Clubs along a neon-lit section of Broadway that during the 1950s hosted jazz, poetry readings, and cutting-edge comedians, were offering (clothed) go-go dancers and imposing minimum drink charges to audiences no longer comprised of impecunious Beats but of a suburban shirt-and-tie crowd.

During 1964, topless bathing suits appeared on the world's fashion catwalks, a fact noted by Davey Rosenberg, publicist for a North Beach club called the Condor. Rosenberg purchased the first topless outfit available in San Francisco and gave it to a Condor dancer, Carol Doda. In June, Doda danced topless on a white piano and brought the club national publicity, not least because the display coincided with San Francisco's hosting of the Republican convention and the city was full of journalists. As Doda's bared breasts had tourists flocking to the Condor, rival clubs were quick to have their performers shed their tops. Among these clubs was the El Cid, which billed dancer Gaye Spiegelman as the "Topless Mother of Eight". Short-lived gimmicks such as a topless shoeshine parlor and topless ice-cream stand encouraged a *San Francisco Chronicle* editorial to conclude with the sarcastic promise of: "Next week: The First Topless Nun!"

No less sensational was Doda spending $2,000 on a twenty-week course of silicon implants adding ten inches to her bust measurements.

By the end of 1965, Doda was appearing in a Las Vegas nightclub with her new breasts insured for $1.5 million. In *The Put-Together Girl*, Tom Wolfe wrote: "Carol Doda's Breasts are up there the way one imagines Electra's should have been, two incredible mammiform protrusions, no mere pliable mass of feminine tissues and fats there but living arterial sculpture—viscera spigot—great blown-up aureate morning glories."

Police raids on Broadway clubs saw frequent arrests of topless performers who would inevitably be acquitted of whatever they were charged with. A related craze for topless waitresses spread to New York where it was banned in 1969, the same year that North Beach saw its first nude entertainment. As tourists packed its sidewalks, Broadway clubs raised their drink prices and employed barkers on their doors to lure customers inside with the promise of female flesh. Legal debates on the issue, largely centering on nudity as a form of self-expression, eventually reached the Supreme Court which concluded that the right to freedom of expression would not be undermined by limitations on "Bacchanalian revelries" in San Francisco clubs. In 1973 the city's Board of Supervisors banned nude acts and placed restrictions on topless performers, insisting that they must be six feet from the nearest patron and the stage at least 18 inches high.

Topless shows steadily faded from fashion. Nowadays, aside from making infrequent appearances with her rock group, the Lucky Stiffs, Doda runs a lingerie shop on Union Street. The Condor (on whose wall a bronze plaque remembers Doda and the topless era) remains in business as a run-of-the-mill sports bar although it enjoyed a brief return to the headlines in 1983 when a doorman making love to a stripper on the club piano, after the club had closed for the night, was crushed to death after accidentally activating the hydraulic system which raised the instrument to the roof. Beneath him, the trapped lady endured a wait of several uncomfortable hours until being freed by a janitor.

The end of the Barbary Coast and the decline of Broadway skin shows did not, of course, mean the end of commercial sex in San Francisco. In 1971 a proposal for the toleration of off-street prostitution to allow police officers more time to tackle "serious" crime seemed likely to be implemented. It was halted, however, by a Grand Jury finding that observed: "We witnessed the unhappy spectacle of considerable influx into San Francisco of 'ladies of the night and midday afternoon'... when news of the department's disinclination to arrest for prostitution became known."

With none of the romance and glamour posthumously accorded to the *fin-de-siècle* parlor houses and their madams, a few blocks of the Tenderloin became synonymous with street prostitution during the 1980s and 1990s, a time when short-lived massage parlors were also dotted thinly about the city. By contrast, the booming upscale end of the sex industry was represented by several look-don't-touch lap dancing and gentleman's clubs, while one long-running North Beach venue, the Lusty Lady, had the distinction of becoming the US's first unionized erotic dancing club in 1998.

A Golden Era: Literary Life in the West

In December 1852 the monotony of life in California's gold mining camps was alleviated by the appearance of a San Francisco-based literary journal, the *Golden Era*. The four-page weekly carried poems, short stories and cuttings from eastern US newspapers, but while it was avidly read, the quality of the contributions, often sentimental poems and short stories, was generally poor—with the exception of work from the likes of Bret Harte, Mark Twain, Joaquin Miller, and the future California poet laureate, Ina Donna Coolbrith.

The *Golden Era* lasted into the 1860s when it was replaced by the *Overland Monthly*, founded by bookseller Anton Ramon seeking a literary title that would rival the east's *Atlantic*. In 1868, Ramon appointed Bret Harte as editor, under whom the *Overland Monthly* published poetry, fiction, and essays that revealed the growing maturity of its contributors (often termed "Western writers" despite the fact that they had originated elsewhere and simply used the US's frontier region as their subject).

Bret Harte's (1836-1902) rise and fall epitomized the fate of writers who gained prominence in San Francisco but failed to win favor with the literary establishment. He arrived in California from New York in 1854 and worked as a miner, teacher and messenger before becoming secretary of the San Francisco's US Branch Mint while editing the *Overland Monthly* and developing his own writing. With the story *The Luck of Roaring Camp* and the poem "The Plain Language From Truthful James", Harte found an audience in the east where publishers besieged him with offers of future work. Leaving San Francisco, Harte joined the eastern lecture circuit where it was noted: "audiences were hostile to him because he looked like a gentleman and not like their idea of a miner." Interest in his work gradually declined until, penniless, Harte took up an offer to become US Consul to Germany and died in England in 1902, never returning to San Francisco despite having penned what for time was the unofficial poem of the city, "San Francisco", which begins:

SERENE, indifferent of Fate,
Thou sittest at the Western Gate;
Upon thy height, so lately won,
Still slant the banners of the sun;
Thou seest the white seas strike their tents,
O Warder of two continents!
And, scornful of the peace that flies
Thy angry winds and sullen skies,
Thou drawest all things, small or great,
To thee, beside the Western Gate.

The *Overland Monthly* also brought the talents of Mark Twain to a wide audience. Trained as a printer before traveling west and briefly working in a silver mine, Twain (1835-1910) gained his first journalistic job in Virginia City, Nevada, and in 1864 reached San Francisco, where he began reporting for the *San Francisco Call*. Twain covered everything from July 4 celebrations to court cases: "Yesterday, in the Police Court, George Lambertson and Ralph Doyle, one a full-grown man and the other a boy of fourteen, pleaded guilty to the charge of exhibiting obscene pictures." It was a time Twain would later described as "sheer, soulless drudgery".

Developed from a story he had heard at a mining camp, *The Celebrated Jumping Frog of Calaveras County*, published in the *Overland Monthly*, brought Twain to national prominence. Like Harte, Twain soon left San Francisco and would never return but, unlike Harte, his writing skills, sharp observations, and cleverly employed wit enabled him to tackle subjects well beyond "Californiana" and become one of the nation's most celebrated writers. In his 1872 *Roughing It*, Twain reflected on the immediate affection he felt for San Francisco: "I fell in love with the most cordial and sociable city in the Union. After the sage-brush and alkali deserts of Washoe, San Francisco was Paradise to me. I lived at the best hotel, exhibited my clothes in the most conspicuous places, infested the opera, and learned to seem enraptured with music which oftener afflicted my ignorant ear than enchanted it, if I had had the vulgar honesty to confess it..."

A Literary Fog

Ironically, since there is doubt as to whether he actually made the comment at all, what might be Twain's most repeated San Francisco quote concerns the city's climate: "the coldest winter I ever spent was a summer in San Francisco." Whatever its origins, however, the comment is apt. Particularly during the summer, temperature-lowering fogs are a common feature, and as such soon became an almost obligatory inclusion in any writer's account of the city.

For some, fogs were a benevolent and almost lyrical aspect of San Francisco. Almira Bailey's *Vignettes of San Francisco* claimed "the San Francisco fog is the hand of a kind nurse on a tired head... like great billows of a bride's veil." In *Rezanov*, Gertrude Atherton described "The soft white fog... rolling over the hills between the Battery and the Presidio, wreathing about the rocky heights and slopes. It broke into domes and cupolas, spires and minarets. Great waves rolled over the sand dunes and beat upon the cliffs with the phantoms clinging to its sides. Then the sun struggled with a thousand colors. The sun conquered, the mist shimmered into sunlight, and once more the hills were gray and bare."

By contrast, fog provided a malevolent backdrop for Dashiell Hammett's San Francisco-set stories, and an appropriately strange and ethereal one for Austin Hall and Homer Eon Flint's *The Blind Spot*, in which a San Francisco house becomes a portal to other dimensions. First published in magazine form in 1921, *The Blind Spot* begins: "On a certain foggy morning in September, 1905, a tall man wearing a black overcoat and bearing in one hand a small satchel of dark-reddish leather descended from a Geary Street tram at the foot of Market Street, San Francisco. It was a damp morning; a mist was brooding over the city blurring all distinctness." And later, as the narration builds towards a climax, *The Blind Spot* finds: "... heavy fog clung like depression; life was gone out—a foreboding of gloom and disaster. It was cold, dank, miserable; one shuddered instinctively and battered against the wall with steaming columns of breath."

Bohemia in Russian Hill

Writers, artists, architects and all kinds of creative characters have shown a fondness for Russian Hill, named for a group of Russian fur-trappers believed to have drowned and been buried on its southeast crest in the early 1800s. Amid a smattering of apartment blocks and modern homes, the neighborhood still retains, despite rampant gentrification, many nineteenth-century cottages and an almost pastoral sense of calm, aided by the steep gradients that limit passing traffic in spite of its central location.

As "Barbary Lane", Russian Hill's Macondray Lane was the home of Mrs. Madrigal in Armistead Maupin's *Tales of the City* novels that began as a *San Francisco Chronicle* column in the 1970s. Nearly thirty years earlier, Jack Kerouac worked on drafts of *On The Road* in Neal and Carolyn Cassady's attic at 29 Russell Place, which, according to Gerald Nicosia, had been fitted out with "a bed on the floor, a three-by-four foot sheet of plywood for a desk, a huge dictionary, a typewriter, paper, Dexedrine, marijuana, bongo drums, a radio and—most alluringly—a tape recorder, which Jack sought to use for 'experiments in new narrative techniques'."

Perhaps surprisingly, the North Beach-based San Francisco Poetry Renaissance of the 1950s that Kerouac and others helped inspire (as, simultaneously and inadvertently, they did the Beat Generation, see

Part Six) was the first nationally acknowledged literary movement to emerge from the city since the 1890s when Russian Hill spawned a thriving bohemia, largely nurtured by Ina Donna Coolbrith. A friend of Harte and Twain and sometimes a coeditor of the *Overland Monthly*, Coolbrith (1841-1928) reached California as a ten-year-old with her mother who was escaping her polygamous Mormon husband (her uncle, Joseph Smith, was the religion's founder). Settling in Los Angeles, Coolbrith wrote her first published verses aged 17 and at the same age entered into a disastrous marriage, her flight from which brought her to San Francisco in 1862. Coolbrith, Harte, and another writer, Charles Warren Stoddard, became known in the city's literary circles as "the Golden Gate Trinity".

At the expense of her own development as a writer (offering what Carol Dunlap in *California People* described as "ritual martyrdom"), Coolbrith became a formative influence on several generations of San Francisco writers, as well as caring for her sister's two orphaned daughters and the daughter of Joaquin Miller. The flamboyant Miller (1837-1914) was a close friend of Coolbrith and at her suggestion had giving up using his real name, Cincinnatus Hiner Miller, to become Joaquin in recognition of Joaquin Murieta, a Mexican bandit at large in California during the 1850s. Miller had also composed a thirty-page poem in honor of this romantic figure (it seems unlikely that Murieta as such ever existed, even though he became the subject of a 1936 Hollywood biopic, *The Robin Hood of El Dorado*). Miller cemented the change by growing his hair to shoulder length, wearing buckskins, a wide-brimmed hat and, according to Gertrude Atherton, boots that "almost reached to his waist". Miller's extrovert nature and desire to be, at Coolbrith's suggestion, "the Byron of the Rockies" earned him a reputation as "a poseur and a bit of a humbug", a theme developed in M. M. Marberry's 1953 biography of Miller titled *Splendid Poseur*.

Coolbrith's commitments to her three surrogate daughters, and for some years to her mother, never allowed her to be financially secure. In 1874, she became an $80-a-month employee at Oakland's first public library where she took great pleasure in developing the reading habits of children, among them the future dancer Isadora Duncan and a bedraggled twelve-year-old called Jack London, later to become one of California's most celebrated literary sons. Coolbrith subsequently became librarian at the Bohemian Club, an all-male institution, which, in recognition of her efforts in organizing its bookshelves and for her selfless impact on the city's literary development, accorded her the rare distinction of honorary membership.

The 1906 fire engulfed Coolbrith's apartment, destroying her letters (she corresponded with literary notables the world over, among them Tennyson, Longfellow, and Rosetti) and the notes for what was to be her autobiography and perhaps the definitive account of San Francisco's first sixty years of literary development. At the 1915 Panama-Pacific Exposition, for which she organized a World Congress of Writers, Coolbrith was declared California's first poet laureate. A rose was named after her by botanist Luther Burbank, as was an 8,000-foot-high mountain close to the pass where she first entered California aboard a covered wagon. In Russian Hill, she is remembered by the steeply terraced Ina Coolbrith Park, close to the junction of Vallejo and Taylor streets.

Another Russian Hill resident was Ambrose Bierce (1842-1914?), whose short stories had appeared in the *Overland Monthly* but who became better known for savagely witty columns under the heading *The Prattler* in the *San Francisco Examiner*. In 1906 Bierce gathered some of his popular epigrams and aphorisms into *The Devil's Dictionary*, offering definitions such as:

> "*BEAUTY: n. The power by which a woman charms a lover and terrifies a husband.*"
> "*HAPPINESS n. An agreeable sensation arising from contemplating the misery of another.*"

Ohio-born Bierce had settled in San Francisco after fighting in the Civil War, but in 1896, like others who gained literary success, he left for the east. The latter period of Bierce's life remains a mystery: it is widely thought he died in Mexico where he went in 1913 to find "the good, kind darkness". More colorful accounts suggest that he committed suicide by jumping into the Grand Canyon or was taken captive by Indians in Brazil.

The 1906 calamity also destroyed a one-time Russian Hill home of Gelett Burgess (1866-1951), whose shiny top hat and diminutive height prompted Russian Hill neighbors to call him the Little Peanut. Despite several novels, Burgess remained best known for "The Purple Cow":

I never Saw a Purple Cow;
I never Hope to See one;
But I can Tell you, Anyhow,
I'd rather See one than be one.

The poem appeared in the Burgess-founded journal *The Lark*, which was printed on bamboo paper and carried a few serious pieces alongside much nonsense verse. To Burgess' lasting chagrin, the success of "The Purple Cow" overshadowed his other work. Furthermore, Burgess and the pranks of the informal *Le Jeune* group of which he was the most prominent member, were made to look increasingly inconsequential as San Francisco's literary style jumped from whimsy to realism.

A Story of San Francisco: Norris and Hammett

The completion in 1869 of the transcontinental railroad gave San Francisco its first fixed link with the eastern US, ending the need for long sea voyages or perilous overland journeys to reach the cultural hubs of New York and Boston, and sharply reducing the city's sense of geographical and artistic isolation. San Francisco was no longer the gold rush frontier town of a few decades before but, thanks to its port, one of the most commercially important cities in the US city with a population that would exceed 300,000 during the 1890s.

With a growing sense of maturity and recognition of its own worth, San Francisco writing became associated with the realism of Jack London (although he wrote little about the city), born on Third Street and who worked for a time in Oakland's dockyards, and Frank Norris (1881-1945), who had arrived as a child with his parents from

Chicago, studied at Berkeley, and became part of the Russian Hill bohemia and a prominent contributor to its literary journals. In 1899 Norris published what would come to be regarded as the city's first real novel: *McTeague: A Story of San Francisco*. Describing the decline of an unlicensed Polk Street dentist whose prospering business and Sundays spent drinking steam beer, playing the concertina, smoking his pipe and admiring his yellow canary are undermined by a former friend's duplicity and a beast-like temper that leads him to kill his wife (leaving her body to be found by schoolchildren) and to suffer his own lingering death in the California desert, *McTeague* presented an unsettlingly realistic portrayal of violence and a ground level view of the emerging urban culture. The novel inspired much publicity, despite mixed reviews, and the 1924 Von Stroheim film *Greed*.

By the 1920s, San Francisco's dark (and, in his hands, almost constantly fog-bound) corners were being explored by Dashiell Hammett. Having worked as a private investigator for the Pinkerton Agency (where his caseload included the Fatty Arbuckle affair), Hammett (1894-1961) began writing advertising copy for a Market Street jewelry shop and selling stories to pulp magazines. While living at 891 Post Street (and subsequently at 1155 Leavonworth Street), Hammett wrote his landmark books, *The Maltese Falcon*, *The Glass Key*, *Red Harvest*, and *The Dain Curse*, realistically describing the low-life milieu and methods of the private detective.

With *The Maltese Falcon*, Hammett also created the iconic American private eye, Sam Spade, who "looked rather pleasantly like a blond Satan," worked from an office on Post Street, and was given to dining on chops, potatoes and sliced tomatoes at John's Grill, an actual restaurant at 63 Ellis Street that now does much to play up its Hammett links. Spade was personified by the distinctly non-blond actor Humphrey Bogart in the most successful screen version of the tale. Hammett departed San Francisco in 1930 for New York, leaving behind his family and "a trail of unpaid bills", and also what would evolve into a mini-Maltese Falcon industry, with at least one walking tour of sites and a plot-revealing plaque on Burritt Street, off Bush Street, which records a key event in the story: "On approximately this spot, Miles Archer, partner of Sam Spade, was done in by Bridgit O'Shaughnessy."

Four decades later, Hammett returned to San Francisco, fictionally at least, in Joe Gores' *Hammett*. Also a private-investigator-turned-writer, Gores took his predecessor back onto the corruption-tainted streets of 1920s San Francisco to solve one last case while simultaneously wrestling with his new-found literary problems, not least the plot of *The Maltese Falcon*.

Atherton, Sterling, and Demarest

Without bequeathing a singularly noted work (and in one case without bequeathing any work at all), three other figures made a noteworthy impact on San Francisco's literary development. Described by Carol Dunlap as "California's first liberated woman", Gertrude Atherton (1857-1948) eloped with and married her divorced mother's suitor at 18, had a son at 19, and revealed talent for scandal soon after with her first novel, *The Randolphs of the Redwoods*, which dealt with alcoholism in a prominent San Francisco family. Already disenchanted with marriage and motherhood, Atherton found herself widowed when her husband's body (he died at sea) arrived on her doorstep in a barrel of rum. Atherton's huge body of work also included *Rezanov*, a fictionalized account of the early nineteenth-century love affair between a Russian officer and the daughter of the Presidio's *comandante*, and *California: An Intimate History*, written for the 1915 Panama-Pacific Exposition. Traveling widely, writing ceaselessly, and advocating female independence, Atherton is remembered by a memorial in Pacific Heights' Lafayette Park.

Poet George Sterling (1869-1926) became a protégé of Ambrose Bierce, who called him a future "poet of the skies, prophet of the suns", and a drinking partner of Jack London, inspiring the character of Russ Brissenden ("flashing insight and perception, the flaming uncontrol of genius") in London's autobiographical novel *Martin Eden*. Sterling left San Francisco in 1905 to become co-founder of the noted bohemian colony at Carmel. He returned to San Francisco to reside at the Bohemian Club while keeping a studio at the Montgomery Block. Though lauded at the time, much of Sterling's work (eighteen volumes were published during his life) has aged poorly. Sterling committed suicide aged 57 in 1926 and is honored in Russian Hill by George

Sterling Glade, off Larkin Street between Lombard and Greenwich streets, where a plaque carries his words on San Francisco:

Tho the dark be cold and blind,
Yet her sea-fog's touch is kind,
And her mightier caress,
Is joy and pain thereof:
And great is thy tenderness,
O cool, gray city of love!

In a city where oddballs and eccentrics are sometimes accorded the status of monarchs, it seems proper to record the literary influence of another Russian Hill resident, Pop Demarest. Although never known to write (or indeed read) anything, Demarest owned a group of simple cottages, originally built for those rendered homeless by the 1906 fire, which he rented to writers at a modest price. Demarest himself preferred a close-to-nature life, for years partly inhabiting a cistern pipe under one of the cottages along with his eighteen cats. He would spend most evenings drinking and dancing (often naked) outdoors to gramophone records. The site of the cottages, between 1078 and 1080 Broadway, is now filled by a condominium complex. Ambrose Bierce, Gelett Burgess, Ina Donna Coolbrith and Frank Norris, photographer Dorothea Lange and her husband the painter Maynard Dixon are among those who owed much to Demarest—who died aged 87 in 1939—including his habitual forgetfulness in collecting their rent.

Shootings, Stabbings, and Feuds: Newspapers and Their Owners

Theatrical impresario Tom Maguire may have been illiterate but he was in a distinct minority in a city where actual and would-be publishers, typesetters, and journalists were available in sufficient numbers for a proliferation of newspapers to serve the print-hungry city. Sam Brannan's *California Star* was founded in Monterey in 1846 but moved the following year to San Francisco where it was soon absorbed by the *Alta California*, which became the state's first daily news organ in January 1850. The ethnic diversity of the region was reflected by French-, German-, Spanish-, and Chinese-language newspapers appearing during the 1850s, followed by others in tongues as diverse as Swiss-Italian, Norwegian, and Japanese.

Founded in 1855 and staying in business until 1929, the *San Francisco Bulletin* was a notable exception to the generally short lives of most city newspapers. Established as a reliable source of news, the *Bulletin* also set what would become an unfortunate precedent for the city's press, when its editor was shot dead for exposing the criminal past of a city supervisor.

In January 1865, San Francisco gained yet another newspaper with the free *Daily Dramatic Chronicle*, founded by the De Young brothers, 19-year-old Charles (1845-80) and 17-year-old Michael (1847-1925), with a $20 gold piece borrowed from their landlord. Stage reviews, jokes and anecdotes, and a few snippets of news appeared in the space between the *Chronicle*'s advertisements. What made the *Chronicle*'s reputation as a dependable news source was scooping other San Francisco papers to the story of Abraham Lincoln's assassination. By 1868, the theatrical news-sheet had become the *San Francisco Morning Chronicle*, which Charles promised would be "a bright, bold, fearless and truly independent paper, independent in all things, neutral in nothing."

Several libel suits and allegations of blackmail between the paper's owners and Tom Maguire were just a taste of what would come. In 1879, the *Chronicle* exposed the checkered past of mayoral candidate Isaac Kalloch, the leading Baptist preacher of the day who had raised the gigantic Metropolitan Temple at the corner of Fifth and Jessie streets and lived very comfortably in a twenty-room mansion. Kalloch had arrived in the city from Kansas which he had left in haste not, he claimed, because of any impending scandal, but because "there are more wicked people of both sexes in San Francisco and he felt compelled of God to go and convert them." Responding to the *Chronicle*'s stories, Kalloch took to the pulpit to suggest that the De Youngs' mother ran a whorehouse and that the other brother, Gustave, was in a lunatic asylum (in fact, he was map publisher). In August 1879, Charles De Young retaliated by firing two shots at Kalloch from a horse-drawn cab outside the temple, leaving Kalloch close to death and himself surrounded by an angry mob of the preacher's followers. Kalloch survived and, aided by a sympathy vote, was narrowly elected mayor in December that year. Charles De Young was imprisoned for nine days (as was Michael, "for his own safety") before being charged with assault and released on bail. Following the shooting, fears of a riot saw barricades erected around Kalloch's temple and neighboring streets patrolled by "an irregular militia... with fixed bayonets."

Once out of jail, De Young left San Francisco for four months before returning to continue the feud by writing a scathing biography of Kalloch. Frustrated by the inaction of the legal system and given a pre-publication copy of the biography, Kalloch's son entered the *Chronicle* offices and shot Charles De Young dead: a crime for which he subsequently acquitted on grounds of self-defense thanks to a witness testimony later found to be false.

Jerome Hart, editor of the *Argonaut*, heard the news of De Young's murder while attending a party on a ship anchored in the bay, where most passengers were not from San Francisco and knew nothing of the event's significance. Hart recalled: "They were surprised that we should break up our party and leave them for so trivial a matter as a murder, when they seemed to think was an every-day matter in San Francisco."

Editorship of the *Chronicle* passed to Michael who became active in Republican politics and one of the city's greatest boosters. In 1880 he commissioned Chicago-based architects Burnham and Root to construct a new home for the paper at the junction of Market and Kearny streets. The city's first steel-framed structure, the *Chronicle*'s new home rose an imposing ten stores high and symbolized the prominence of the newspaper. Three years later, as San Francisco endured an economic downturn, De Young conceived the idea of a winter fair in Golden Gate Park to highlight San Francisco's mild climate and its future prospects. The result was the highly successful

1894 California Midwinter Exposition, attended by 1.3 million people and making a profit of almost $127,000.

One of the Expo's popular features was an art collection displayed in the Egyptian-themed Fine Arts Building. The building was intended to be temporary but remained in place (and lasted into the 1920s before being replaced by the structure that evolved into the present day museum) to became the first home of the Memorial Museum, so-named in memory of the Expo.

De Young took responsibility for acquiring the museum's exhibits on his regular overseas trips. In 1916 he described in *California Living* how "the desire to create a museum took possession of me" and how "during the past twenty years I have taken up different fads on each trip, and worked and worked gathering to complete the particular speciality. I made a collection of knives and forks that took me years to gather, and one of powder horns, picked up at different places all over the globe. The fans filling a number of cases in the present museum were assembled in the same way, as were also the guns and pistols, which were picked up one by one. I used to carry them with me on trams in my hand bag until I got to a place where I could ship them back to the museum."

Under Michael, the *Chronicle* continued to campaign against corruption, most notably against the political machine of Abe "Boss" Ruef, who with the mayor and the Board of Supervisors on his unofficial payroll, effectively ran one of the most dishonest administrations in San Francisco's history. Ruef would eventually serve fourteen years in San Quentin prison but not before a victory parade to mark the re-election of his acolyte, Eugene Schmitz, as mayor in 1905 led to the *Chronicle* building being set ablaze.

Unlike his brother, Michael De Young did not shoot anyone, but in 1884 someone did shoot him. The would-be assassin was Adolph Spreckels, a scion of the Spreckels dynasty originating from Adolph's father, Claus, whose fortunes grew from a monopoly on the California sugar supply. The Spreckels' money had been invested in, among others things, a newspaper, the *San Francisco Call*, that for a time rivaled the *Chronicle*. The source of Adolph Spreckel's anger, however, was De Young's suggestion that the Spreckels family were involved in a share-dealing fraud.

Michael survived the attack and would live until 1925, but the rivalry between the Spreckels and De Young families endured. David Siefkin's history of the St. Francis Hotel, *Meet Me At The St. Francis*, describes the seating arrangements devised by head waiter Ernest Gloor in the status-defining Mural Room to ensure that representatives of the two families would never sit closer than was proper. Alma, Adolph's wife, is quoted as saying of Michael De Young's daughters: "they're nice girls, but we've never been too close since my husband shot their father."

The hostility between the two families was further expressed in rival art museums. The De Young Memorial Museum was forced to share the cultural limelight with the California Palace of the Legion of Honor, bankrolled by Adolph Spreckels and inspired by the art-loving Alma, who had been loudly critical of the De Youngs' hotchpotch collection. The Legion of Honor, whose exhibits include a major collection of Rodin pieces acquired through Alma's friendship with the sculptor, was formally opened in 1921, the same year the Memorial Museum adopted De Young's name. Although both museums were deeded to the city, they remained under separate boards of directors until formally merging in 1972, four years after the after the death of Alma Spreckels.

William Randolph Hearst's *Examiner*

After the ailing Spreckels-backed *Call* closed in 1913 (its publisher, John D. Spreckels successfully devoted his energies to southern California's still extant *San Diego Union*), the biggest and longest-running newspaper battle in San Francisco was fought between the *Chronicle* and the *Examiner*. Yet if the De Youngs were a legend in San Francisco, the *Examiner*'s owner became a legend around the world.

Mining millionaire George Hearst acquired the financially troubled *Examiner,* founded the same year as the *Chronicle,* as settlement for a gambling debt. Not knowing what to do with a newspaper, George was persuaded by his son to pass its control to him, and so in 1887 the 23-year-old William Randolph Hearst (1863-1951) took the first step towards changing the face of American journalism and becoming one of the world's richest men. In a way it was love at first sight. Of the *Examiner*, Hearst claimed he felt "a tenderness like unto that which a mother feels for a puny or deformed offspring."

With the *Examiner* Hearst pioneered the sensationalist style of reporting that would be termed "yellow journalism" (derived from a R. F. Outcault cartoon strip, *The Yellow Kid*). An early indication of the Hearst approach was a hotel fire in Monterey which other city papers would have covered with a single reporter. Hearst, though, chartered a train and transported sufficient writers and sketch artists to the scene to produce a 14-page supplement with the following day's edition. Hearst's flattery of his journalists and ability to pay them high wages encouraged many of the city's top names to work for the *Examiner*, among them Jack London, who covered the Russo-Japanese War, and Ambrose Bierce, who contributed avidly-read columns.

With Hearst's goal of making the *Examiner* the "largest, brightest and best newspaper on the Pacific Coast" achieved, he repeated the success with the *New York Journal*, bought with a loan of $8 million from his mother—whose fortunes also financed the University of California. Hoping that hostilities between the US and Spain in Cuba would escalate, he famously (though some think apocryphally) told his on-the-spot artist Frederic Remington: "you provide the pictures, I'll provide the war." Soon outpacing the *Chronicle*, the *Examiner* became the biggest-selling newspaper in California. The paper carried lurid accounts of the 1921 Fatty Arbuckle affair; in 1947 it ran a campaign against author Henry Miller and his colony of "sex anarchists" at Big Sur; and in 1950 it rubbed salt into the *Chronicle's* wounds by stealing its star columnist, Herb Caen.

Hearst died in 1951 and while the paper remained part of the Hearst media empire, sales of the *Chronicle* (by now aping some of the its rival's tactics) increased and by the late 1950s overtook those of the *Examiner*. The *Chronicle* celebrated the fact with the return of Herb Caen in 1958. In 1965 the battle came to a sort of end with the papers agreeing to share production and advertising facilities while producing editorially independent newspapers, the *Chronicle* publishing each morning and the *Examiner* appearing in six afternoon editions.

In 1999 came a long-anticipated announcement that the Hearst Corporation had bought the *Chronicle*. The acquisition cost $660 million and only took place following the departure from the

Chronicle's board of directors of Nan Tucker McEvoy, a grand-daughter of Michael De Young and the paper's last link with its founding family. Simultaneously it was announced that the *Examiner*, now selling a paltry 109,000 copies, was for sale. In a move which many saw as an ironic twist given the *Examiner's* infamous anti-Chinese stance in the 1870s (see p.152), the Hearst paper was bought by 24-year-old Chinese-American Ted Fang, publisher of the free, thrice-weekly *San Francisco Independent*. In February 2003 the *Examiner*—presumed to be running short of the subsidy that had underpinned its purchase—fired half its staff and declared itself a free weekday paper.

Herb Caen: Nostalgia Ain't What it Used to Be

The full impact of Herb Caen's eight-year defection from the *Chronicle* to the *Examiner* should not be underestimated. Generation after generation of San Franciscans had their take on the city and its people shaped by Caen's deftly-written columns that, for nearly sixty years until his death aged 80 in 1997, mixed snappy news items with humorous anecdotes, always dividing the paragraph-length stories with three dots...

The biggest character in Caen's pieces was always San Francisco itself, a fact that delighted San Francisco-born readers, encouraged those who had arrived from elsewhere, and undermined those who, as Caen wrote, might seek to be one-up by remarking: "when my father first came to this town, even the ferryboats were horsedrawn." Caen himself arrived from elsewhere, born in Sacramento and gaining his first journalistic job there as a sports reporter. He would later lay claim to impeccable San Franciscan credentials, however, insisting that he was conceived during the 1915 Panama-Pacific Exposition when his parents were wintering in the city. In 1938 Caen moved to San Francisco to write a radio column for the *Chronicle*. His success was not instant and it was only after the radio column was nixed that Caen, hoping to keep a toehold on the paper, suggested that he write a column on city life. Becoming as much a feature of San Francisco as the Golden Gate Park or the Ferry Building and a friend to anyone who was anyone, Caen also managed to be an engagingly self-deprecating inside-outsider to anyone who wasn't. The Caen column continued appearing daily (except during the Second World War, when Caen served in the air force) until 1991, after which it slowed to a mere five appearances each week.

Caen's first book, published in 1948, met with little success, but the following year's publication of *Baghdad by the Bay*, a gathering of vignettes and observations of San Francisco life, was reprinted decade after decade and brought Caen a Chamber of Commerce award for "literary contributions to the prestige of our community". It also became a fixture on the bookshelves of the city's better bed-and-breakfast inns, providing guests with bedtime insights into the quirks and foibles of the city. More books followed, as in 1996 did a Pulitzer Prize honoring Caen's "extraordinary and continuing contribution as a voice and conscience of his city". The same year, San Francisco's Board of Supervisors named a section of the Embarcadero "Herb Caen Way...", carefully including three dots.

It was Caen who in the 1950s responded to the invasion of sandal- and beret-wearing followers of the original Beats by dubbing them "beatniks" after the Soviet Sputnik satellite launched the same year. It was he, too, who a decade later described the hippie-infested Haight-Ashbury as "Hashbury" and who in 1984 labeled rock singer Cyndi Lauper "a chipmunk on speed". And it was one of Caen's ex-wives who, when filing for divorce, joked she would name San Francisco as co-respondent. Following his death, the *Examiner* reported "several thousand of Herb Caen's closest friends" joining a candle-lit vigil marking his passing.

So enamored was San Francisco of Caen that it seemed blasphemous to speak ill of him. But a few who dared had a serious point to make. Fellow *Chronicle* columnist Charles McCabe accused Caen of writing about San Francisco in the 1960s as it was twenty years earlier. And three years after Caen's death, the theme was taken up in *SF Weekly* by Matt Smith, who wrote: "As the official voice of San Francisco for 60 years, his Reagan-esque idea that redemption is to be found in some earlier, imaginary era has contaminated the consciousness of all who live here. His columns... suggested that if only San Francisco lived up to an idealized 1940s Old World of upper-crust life—Wilkes Bashford blazers, operas, expensive restaurants, and vacations to Marrakech—it could somehow be saved."

Caen himself seemed to realize that his eulogizing of a bygone San

Francisco was contributing to the city's reluctance to change. In 1993 he wrote: "living here is a constant battle against nostalgia, the San Francisco disease that clouds all vision and judgment." But he soothed agitated readers by adding in the same piece, "no matter how bad we get, we are still better than any place else."

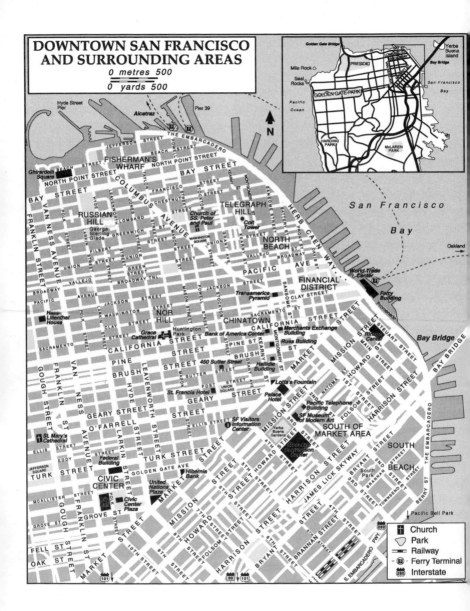

DOWNTOWN SAN FRANCISCO AND SURROUNDING AREAS

0 metres 500
0 yards 500

Inset map labels:
Golden Gate Bridge
Yerba Buena Island
Mile Rock
PRESIDIO
Bay Bridge
Seal Rocks
San Francisco Bay
Pacific Ocean
GOLDEN GATE PARK
HARDING PARK
McLAREN PARK

Main map labels:
Hyde Street Pier
Alcatraz
Pier 39
N
THE EMBARCADERO
JEFFERSON STREET
FISHERMAN'S WHARF
NORTH POINT STREET
Ghirardelli Square
BEACH STREET
NORTH POINT STREET
BAY STREET
San Francisco Bay
BAY STREET
COLUMBUS AVENUE
FRANCISCO STREET
CHESTNUT STREET
TELEGRAPH HILL
RUSSIAN HILL
George Sterling Glade
Church of SS. Peter and Paul
Coit Tower
LOMBARD STREET
GREENWICH STREET
FILBERT STREET
UNION STREET
WASHINGTON SQUARE
UNION STREET
NORTH BEACH
Oakland
GREEN STREET
BROADWAY TNL.
VALLEJO
BROADWAY
PACIFIC AVE
FRANKLIN STREET
VAN NESS AVENUE
POLK STREET
LARKIN STREET
HYDE STREET
LEAVENWORTH STREET
JONES STREET
TAYLOR STREET
MASON STREET
POWELL STREET
STOCKTON STREET
PACIFIC AVENUE
World Trade Center
Ferry Building
BROADWAY
PACIFIC AVENUE
JACKSON STREET
JACKSON STREET
FINANCIAL DISTRICT
Haas-Lilienthal House
WASHINGTON STREET
CLAY STREET
Transamerica Pyramid
CLAY STREET
NOB HILL
SACRAMENTO
SACRAMENTO ST.
CHINATOWN
Merchants Exchange Building
Russ Building
Grace Cathedral
Huntington Park
Bank of America Center
CALIFORNIA STREET
PINE STREET
CALIFORNIA STREET
Bay Bridge
GOUGH STREET
FRANKLIN ST
VAN NESS AVENUE
LARKIN STREET
LEAVENWORTH STREET
HYDE STREET
PINE STREET
BRUSH ST
450 Sutter Street
SUTTER STREET
BUSH STREET
Hallidie Building
BRUSH STREET
POST STREET
UNION SQUARE
St. Francis Hotel
GEARY STREET
Lotta's Fountain
Palace Hotel
MISSION STREET
MARKET STREET
GEARY STREET
O'FARRELL STREET
St. Mary's Cathedral
ELLIS STREET
SF Visitors Information Center
Yerba Buena Gardens
Pacific Telephone Building
SF Museum of Modern Art
SOUTH OF MARKET AREA
SOUTH BEACH
JEFFERSON SQUARE
ELLIS STREET
EDDY STREET
TURK STREET
Federal Building
Moscone Convention Center
HARRISON STREET
FOLSOM STREET
HOWARD STREET
TURK
GOLDEN GATE AVE
Hibernia Bank
James Lick Skyway
BRYANT STREET
BRANNAN STREET
South Park
THE EMBARCADERO
CIVIC CENTER
United Nations Plaza
Civic Center Plaza
MISSION STREET
HOWARD STREET
FOLSOM STREET
HARRISON STREET
BRYANT STREET
BERRY ST
Pacific Bell Park
McALLISTER STREET
GROVE ST
GROVE STREET
MARKET STREET
HARRISON STREET
TOWNSEND STREET
FELL ST
OAK ST
FRANKLIN ST
GOUGH ST
10TH STREET
9TH STREET
8TH STREET
7TH STREET
6TH STREET
5TH STREET
4TH STREET
3RD STREET
2ND STREET
1ST STREET
MAIN ST
BEALE ST
HOWARD ST
SPEAR ST
STEUART STREET
FREMONT ST
Rincon Center
San Francisco Bay
HERB CAEN WAY
DAVIS ST
DRUMM ST
FRONT ST
BATTERY STREET
SANSOME STREET
MONTGOMERY ST
KEARNY STREET
GRANT AVE
MAIDEN LANE
STOCKTON STREET
POWELL STREET
MASON STREET
TAYLOR STREET
Promenade
S. EMBARCADERO FWY.
MARKET STREET

Legend
✛ Church
▽ Park
▭ Railway
- Ⓜ Ferry Terminal
▲ Interstate

PART FOUR

Landmarks, Ruins and Memories

New York has the Empire State Building, Paris has the Eiffel Tower, but San Francisco's most fondly regarded landmarks include an almost featureless tower of reinforced concrete financed by a woman who loved fires, an artful rendition of a Roman ruin, and a famously inaccurate clock tower all but hidden in the high-rise forest of the Financial District. More dramatic and more familiar to the world at large are the Golden Gate Bridge—an engineering marvel that almost never got built—and the tapering profile of the Transamerica Pyramid, which like the equally renowned former prison island of Alcatraz, conceals secrets that few outsiders are privy to.

To San Franciscans of a certain age and nostalgics of any age, some facets of the city have a resonance that belies their modern appearance: Treasure Island is not a flat, man-made island recovering from many years of military occupation but a fantasia of light and a glimpse of the future; the St. Francis is not a pricey tourist hotel but a legend-filled symbol of high society; and a few crumbling concrete blocks lashed by ocean spray on the city's western edge are really reminders of a gigantic saltwater bathhouse that once delighted San Franciscans in their thousands.

Alcatraz Island, 1775, 1934, 1969

As a prison, the reputation of Alcatraz spread around the world, but only in San Francisco does the nearness of the former island penitentiary to the city become apparent. Just a mile and a half from the northern waterfront, the island is plainly visible from many high points and its features, and sometimes even its visitors, are easy to make out. For inmates, such proximity to the city was but one of many unpleasant features of life on "the rock" and became most painfully apparent on New Year's Eve when celebrations at the San Francisco Yacht Club could be heard inside the cells.

Sailing through San Francisco Bay in 1775, Spanish navigator Juan Manuel de Ayala observed the many pelicans on and around a sandstone island that he named *Isla de los Alcatraces* or Isle of Pelicans. It is likely, however, that Ayala was referring to another island, what became Yerba Buena Island, and the name Alcatraz was applied to the wrong chunk of land by the British explorer Captain F.W. Beechey in his 1826 map of the bay.

The advent of US rule in California saw Alcatraz occupied by the army who built steep walls around it, leaving only a dock on the sheltered east side for access, and encircled the island with cannon placements. By 1859, the island could hold a two-hundred-strong force with sufficient supplies to withstand a four-month siege. Two years later, with the US embroiled in civil war, the island became a military prison. Among the first to be confined were three Confederate plotters and Private Matthew Hayland: "an insane man delivered for confinement and safekeeping". In January 1895 the *San Francisco Call* described the arrival on the island of "murderous-looking Apache Indians"—in fact, nineteen Hopi leaders from Arizona who had resisted US government attempts to force their children to attend (anti-Indian) boarding schools.

By the time the army deemed the island prison too expensive to run, not least due to the need to ferry supplies from the mainland, its inmates were under a minimum security regime that emphasized training and rehabilitation. In contrast, when Alcatraz became part of the federal prison system in 1934, the ethos was "maximum security, minimum privilege" and the prison was redesigned to hold the "incorrigibles" of the penal system, those deemed too anti-social or dangerous to be contained elsewhere. The tough regime was inspired by what appeared to be a national crime wave, aided by Prohibition, which had enabled organized crime to flourish.

Inmates were denied radios and newspapers, and almost any contact with the outside world: only twenty percent of the 1,500 (due to the numbering system, the actual roll call is uncertain) prisoners held at Alcatraz ever received a visitor. The right to alleviate boredom with work and exercise had to be earned through good behavior. Only 36 ever attempted to escape; all were recaptured within an hour, save for two who drowned, six who were shot, and seven who escaped in June 1962 (the subject of the 1979 film, *Escape From Alcatraz*), of whom two were quickly recaptured and the remaining five were presumed drowned. Eight Alcatraz prisoners were murdered by other inmates, five committed suicide, and 15 died through illness.

From its earliest days as a federal prison, Alcatraz was the dumping ground for America's least desirable characters. Crime boss Al Capone arrived on the first shipment; the next included bank-robber-turned-kidnapper George "Machine Gun" Kelly. In 1942, in leg-irons and handcuffs and accompanied by three guards, Robert Stroud arrived. Though remembered as the "Birdman of Alcatraz", Stroud's sobriquet was misleading (it stemmed from a 1955 biography of that name and a 1962 film) and had been inspired by his incarceration for murder at Leavenworth prison, Kansas. Held at Leavenworth in solitary confinement, a condition of his life sentence that followed his stabbing to death of a prison guard while seven years into his original sentence, Stroud became fascinated by the habits of sparrows and was later permitted to keep canaries in his cell. Stroud observed the birds' habits, their mating rituals and their illnesses, and wrote a book, *Stroud's Digest of the Diseases of Birds*, which was published to high regard.

Stroud was surprised to find that even at Alcatraz, where he would spend 17 years, he was kept segregated from other prisoners and was refused permission to keep birds. Instead, he studied law and compiled papers for an appeal, ultimately unsuccessful, against the severity of his sentence. Stroud also used his specialist knowledge (he was behind bars from 1909 to his death in 1963) to compile a history of the American penal system. Reasoning that the authorities would seek to prevent the two-volume book becoming known outside the prison, Stroud included an outline of the work as part of his appeal, ensuring that this, at least, would reach an audience. A chapter devoted to the governor of Leavenworth was described as: "A study of how a well-meaning egotist took over the best-fed, best-disciplined and best-behaved prison in the country and in nine months, simply by trying to please everybody, reduced it to chaos and bloodshed."

In a prison so tough that even Al Capone was stabbed with a pair of scissors, tensions inevitably rose. In the most violent and protracted of several uprisings, three prisoners instigated what became known as the Battle of Alcatraz. Lasting two days in May 1946, the battle saw hundreds of heavily armed prison guards joined by eighty marines and 28 sharpshooters from other prisons, while the Coast Guard sent five ships and the US Navy two destroyer escorts ready to open fire on the island. The result was two guards and three prisoners killed, seventeen injured, and two of the ringleaders later executed.

Facing rising maintenance costs—the weakening of the walls by saltwater corrosion was a factor in the 1962 escape—and criticism as petty criminals were incarcerated, the island prison closed on March 1963. The remaining 27 prisoners were transferred and the comment of one of them, Frank Wathernam, seemed to encapsulate the general feeling towards what years earlier had been the great hope of the country's penal system: "Alcatraz was never no good for nobody."

The following year, five Bay Area members of the Lakota nation occupied Alcatraz for four hours as a prelude to a legal claim to ownership of the island under the Great Sioux Treaty of 1868 and the Indian Allotment Act of 1887, which appeared to give the Lakota rights to purchase (at maximum price of 47 cents an acre) unused government land. Never pursued in court, the claim was largely forgotten by the general public until November 1969, when another occupation of the island, this one lasting 19 months, claimed the island for "Indians of all nations".

The second Alcatraz occupation was conceived on the University of San Francisco campus. During 1968 a Third World Liberation Front strike, joined by students and some faculty members, had encouraged Native American students, among them Richard Oakes and Al Miller, to organize. Inspired by the rise of the American Indian Movement (and by the creation on campus of the US's first Department of Native American Studies), Oakes and Miller led fourteen people in an overnight occupation of Alcatraz on November 9. Eleven days later, they were among 89 men, women and children who landed on the island, steadily establishing a school and medical facilities, running laundry and cooking facilities, and electing a decision-making council. While failing to gain legal ownership of Alcatraz, the occupation succeeded in its broader aim of focusing attention on Native American issues, forcing a change in the US government's attitude to native peoples and becoming a catalyst to other Native American actions across the country during the 1970s.

The initial idealism was tainted, however, as rival factions developed and non-Indian groups moved to the island. The accidental death of Richard Oakes' 13-year-old stepdaughter caused the occupation's charismatic leader to leave. By the time federal officials stormed Alcatraz in June 1971, just eleven adults and four children remained. Luis S. Kemnitzer, anthropology professor at San Francisco State University who taught the first Native American Studies class in 1969, remembered: "at the time, I thought that the action was quixotic and a lot of energy expended for ephemeral and will-of-the-wisp goals. I didn't have any idea that it would have the historical importance that it did... Alcatraz was a very complex experience, and it touched and transformed many people."

Alcatraz became part of the Golden Gate National Recreation Area in 1972 and was opened to visitors during the following year. The miserable cells, the mess hall with its tear-gas cylinders fixed to the ceiling, and the prison hospital can all be seen to the accompaniment of the tense oral histories of former prisoners and guards recorded on audio tape.

The Sutro Baths, 1896

Two stone lions and a statue of Diana greet arrivals to Sutro Heights Park, one of San Francisco's most scenic but least visited green spaces, and one that suggests little of the contribution made to the city by its creator, Adolph Sutro (1830-98), the most benevolent of the city's early millionaires. The statuary, the flower-beds, and the ocean views are almost all that remain from the 1,000-acre estate that Sutro raised on this hilltop site, opened to the public for free in April 1885.

A 21-year-old Sutro had arrived in San Francisco and prospered as a tobacco merchant. By 1863 when discoveries of silver in Nevada's Comstock Lode promised riches akin to the gold rush, Sutro had devised a successful method of improved ore-processing and was developing a new tunnel system that would link, drain and ventilate the lode's many mines. Drilling horizontally into the silver-bearing mountain, the tunnel would allow more ore to be extracted while improving working conditions in mines where high temperatures, rising water, and poisonous gases claimed many lives.

For 15 years Sutro sought finance for the tunnel, hindered by devious silver barons eager to protect their profits and monopolies, and by the press which labeled the scheme "Sutro's Folly". Having raised $6.5 million, he gained federal approval and a three-mile tunnel with two miles of lateral branches was completed in 1878, just when the Comstock Lode reached its peak, and began making profits of $10,000 a month. Sutro sold his interests in the tunnel the following year, fortuitously doing so just before the silver boom turned to bust.

Spending the tunnel profits on San Francisco property, Sutro soon owned a twelfth of the entire city, mostly the undeveloped swathes of sand dune that became the Sunset and Richmond districts. By the standards of the time, he lived modestly and gave a side of one of the seven hills he owned (Mt. Parnassus, now Mt. Sutro) to the University of California. Amelia Newsome Ransome noted that Sutro "preferred his library to Nob Hill diversions," perhaps because his library was among the finest private libraries in the US, and his disdain for the uncaring capitalism embraced by most Nob Hill mansion dwellers was well known.

In 1881 Sutro bought the Cliff House, a landmark roadhouse beside the ocean, and spent $50,000 replacing it with a new Cliff

House, an eight-story imitation French chateau precariously perched on a rocky bluff. With restaurants, bars, an art gallery, a mineral museum, and a 200-foot-high observation tower, Sutro's Cliff House became a popular haunt of the well-to-do. Ransom recalled:

> *From its balcony high above the breakers one gazed through binoculars at the seals or sighted ships beyond the Farallones. On clear days these distant islands were silhouetted against the horizon. There was an excellent cuisine at the Cliff House, specializing in fried Eastern oysters, and a bar famous for its mixed drinks. Mixed spirits, however, were never served to ladies. On cold afternoons we sipped port or sherry on the balcony while men drank high-balls, cocktails, or Tom-and-Jerry at the brass rail indoors.*

Four hundred yards offshore from the Cliff House, Seal Rocks housed a colony of (despite the name) California sea lions that provided additional appeal to Cliff House patrons. One sea lion, known as Old Bill Butler, became a well-known San Francisco character and perhaps the only amphibian to be mentioned by columnist Herb Caen, who reminisced how the creature "used to sit in front of the Cliff House and patiently shake flippers with thousands of local yokels each Sunday."

For Sutro Heights Park, which occupied the high ground behind the Cliff House, across today's Great Highway, the philanthropist millionaire commissioned replica life-sized Greek and Roman statuary to line formal gardens, hoping to initiate visitors into the delights of European art. Sutro also sought to undercut by half the fares of the Big Four, the railroad barons who monopolized public transport in San Francisco, by creating his own transit system, the Park & Ocean Railroad, to carry passengers from the city, enabling them to enjoy the park, the Cliff House, and the adjacent beaches, for just five cents. As a result, Sutro's reputation rose among ordinary San Franciscans, and his park was enormously popular, despite the dismissive description of it in Frank Norris' novel, *The Octopus*, which portrayed a honeymooning couple who made "the inevitable bridal trip to the Cliff House and spent an afternoon in the grewsome and made-to-order beauties of Sutro's Gardens..."

Opened in April 1896 with a forty-piece orchestra playing from a floating platform, the Sutro Baths, across Point Lobos Avenue from Sutro Heights Park, brought the joys of saltwater bathing to the masses. Sutro spent $600,000 constructing the baths across a three-acre site with six separate pools filled and drained through an ingenious system of pipes that carried 1.7 million gallons of water from the ocean. One pool (the "ice tank") was kept at sea temperature while the other pools were heated to different levels to suit the mood of bathers, the hottest becoming known as the "soup tank".

Surrounded by palm trees and tropical plants (thriving beneath ceilings composed of 100,000 panes of glass), the pools were large enough to accommodate 25,000 people who could change in one of 500 private dressing rooms, rent one of 20,000 woolen bathing suits and dry themselves on one of 40,000 "Sutro Baths" embossed towels. Several thousand more could occupy tiered seating around the pools while watching high diving or entertainments that might include circus acts and underwater walking races. The bath's three restaurants, meanwhile, could feed a thousand diners at a sitting.

As with the park statuary, Sutro hoped the baths would educate as well as entertain and used them to display some of the items acquired on his European travels. In 1912, *PG&E Magazine* described what visitors to the baths would find after passing through the replica Grecian temple that marked its entrance:

>*…mummies and innumerable other curios from ancient Egypt, a goodly number of specimens of Aztec pottery and art, Damascus plate, beautiful fans from various countries, Chinese and Japanese swords, wooden ware used by the North American Indians and totems from Alaska; while in the gallery proper is found a superb collection of birds and animals, scenes from Japanese life, portfolios of photographs, valuable State papers and hundreds of other works of art and curios.*

And all this for a mere 25 cents admission (ten cents if not swimming).

His five-cent rail fare had been but one feature of Sutro's battles with San Francisco's less altruistic capitalists. Drawing on his high standing among the pubic, Sutro stood as mayor on behalf of the Populist Party (agreeing to do so in the belief that he would not win) and was voted into City Hall's hot seat in 1894. The message of his campaign was simple: opposition to the monopoly of the Big Four, encapsulated in the slogan "The Octopus Must Be Destroyed", using the popular term for the organization whose tentacles reached into every aspect of life. Self-belief and single-mindedness underpinned Sutro's business success but were of limited use to a politician in need of allies. His intended and popular anti-corruption initiatives were stymied through his inability to delegate. He later admitted "I could not manage politicians" and described the end of his two-year term as a "perfect blessing".

Sutro died in 1898, his reputation tarnished by his unhappy mayoral reign. His ashes were buried in a secret spot in Sutro Heights Park, and his son took over the management of the baths. These thrived through the 1920s but the Depression bit into the family fortunes and saw the large pool converted into an ice rink. Swimming ended altogether in 1957 and a continuing slump saw the baths close in February 1966. Hopes that that they would re-open under new ownership were dashed in November of that year when a fire destroyed the buildings. Today, the site of the baths is clearly visible, their scattered remains marking one end of the coastal trail, a challenging footpath route that forges a windswept course high above the Golden Gate.

Sutro's daughter, Emma, lived at the family mansion at Sutro Heights Park until her death in 1938. She raised a new Cliff House after her father's creation was destroyed by fire in 1907. By the 1950s, ownership of the Cliff House was lost and the current incarnation survives as a pale imitation of its forbears while providing a functional visitor center for the Golden Gate National Recreation Area. Offshore, a new generation of sea lions occupies Seal Rocks.

Of Sutro the Merchants Association Review wrote in 1902: "We now eulogize and admire the prophetic inspiration of that far-seeing pioneer, Adolph Sutro, who pronounced many years ago the then somewhat isolated Cliff House Point, one of the most wonderful, remarkable, and picturesque *maritime* locations of the world... [and] showed his admiration of nature's greatest gifts in the creation of Sutro Heights, a beautiful park elevation, overlooking the Cliff House point, affording an unbounded view of the vast expanse of the great Pacific Ocean."

In January 1999 the city's collective amnesia regarding Sutro was the subject of a *San Francisco Chronicle* article by Annalee Newitz asking: "Why did San Francisco forget Adolph Sutro and let his tremendous public projects fall into vandalized ruins?" And, comparing Sutro's battles against the Big Four with contemporary actions against Microsoft's computer software monopoly, she mooted: "Perhaps this is why every several decades we have to learn again that the Octopus must be destroyed. In the remains of Sutro's Baths, and in the populist spirit they embodied, we can find what was forgotten 100 years ago."

The Ferry Building, 1898

Almost apologetically tiny amid the post-modern glass-and-steel high rises that line the lower section of Market Street, a gray sandstone clock tower modeled on the Moorish Giralda tower of Seville Cathedral, Spain, has been telling the time since 1903. The tower, and the Ferry Building of which it forms the most photogenic part, also tell a story of symbolism and survival that runs deep in San Francisco lore.

Reaching 235 feet, the tower rises from a 660-foot-long arcaded structure that holds office and retail space, and for many years was by far the tallest feature on the San Francisco skyline. Rising from the commerce of the Embarcadero, with its piers and ships, and forming a transit terminal for ferry traffic across the bay, the tower became a landmark visible not only all across San Francisco but also on the east side of the bay. In Oakland, city-bound passengers would see the tower from the docks and be able to smell the aroma of coffee carried on the wind from the Hills Brothers Coffee factory on Spear Street.

Through the 1920s and early 1930s, 170 ferries sailed daily across the bay, moving (for ten cents a time) commuters, day-trippers, and passengers on the transcontinental railroad which terminated in Oakland. With fifty million people passing through it annually, the Ferry Building became the busiest transport portal in the US. Under architect Arthur Page Brown, the Ferry Building's construction began in 1896 and was continued following Brown's death by Edward R. Swain. While building work continued for a further five years, the formal opening took place on July 13, 1898, marking San Francisco's recovery from the early 1890s economic depression and its rise to commercial prominence through Pacific trade. With city offices filling one section, the Ferry Building embodied civic pride and optimism for the future.

Yet at 5:16am on April 18, 1906, the hands on the tower clock stopped, their mechanism disturbed by the vibration of the earthquake, which, with the subsequent fire, would leave much of San Francisco a ruin. In the first example of what appears a supernatural ability to survive disaster, the tower—thanks to its steel frame, pioneering use of reinforced concrete foundations, and a thorough dousing with water by a fireboat crew—stayed upright and remained reassuringly visible across the sea of rubble to which much of San Francisco had been reduced.

But while it stayed upright, the tower had lost much of its sandstone facade and the weakening of its internal structure made it far from safe. Fearing its collapse in an aftershock, army engineers made plans for its demolition. Mindful of the building's symbolic importance, the city authorities engaged the Pacific Construction Company to assess the tower's condition. F. A. Koetitzm, the company's chief engineer, reported: "Five of the girders had the connecting bolts at the columns sheared off and had moved laterally away from the column as much as 2". At such ends these girds were resting just one inch on a 3" angle bracket and one felt walking lightly on the floors for fear that they might give way and drop floors, girders, walls and men to destruction."

The building survived the earthquake but could not withstand the decline of ferry traffic that followed the opening of the Bay Bridge in 1937 and the rise of car, bus and rail traffic. By the 1950s, ferry traffic stopped entirely. Despite losing its role as the city's transport hub (prompting Herb Caen to write "every day is Sunday now for this sad old pile of gray—dead and useless except for the clock that goes ticking on when all else is gone") the Ferry Building kept a grip on maritime commerce by housing offices of the World Trade Center in its North Wing and gained more office space with a 1950s remodeling. In his 1961 *San Francisco: An Informal Guide*, Ben Adams writes of the Ferry Building's new interior:

> *...refurbished with chrome, aluminum and marble... more reminiscent of Brussels International Fair than the Cathedral of Seville...*

displays of Alfa Romeo autos, Japanese bicycles, Rhine canned delicacies, Oriental art objects and furnishings, Swedish tools, Indonesian wood carvings. Wander into the Asia House which is a museum as much as merchandise mart. Note the figure of the eight Taoist immortals—especially the charming one of Ho Hsien-Ku, a seventh century daughter of a shopkeeper who, having eaten of the sacred peach, became a fairy and lived on powdered mother-of-pearl and moonbeams. She wanders about picking sacred fungi and is revered as a Protector of the House Holder and Recluses. Of course, most of the emphasis at the World Trade Center is on business opportunities rather than sacred fungi.

Meanwhile, the South Wing still held offices of city and state and, according to Margot Patterson Doss, could also boast "the excellent geological library, laboratories, and a mineralogy museum whose treasures would excite envy in King Solomon."

Although the interior could still thrill, the Ferry Building's place as a highly visible anchor to Market Street was eroded by the steadily rising Financial District and the affront to sensibilities that was the elevated Embarcadero Freeway. Scything between the waterfront and the rest of the city in the hope of easing traffic congestion, the freeway restricted views of the tower and the entire Embarcadero area. Decades of argument regarding the freeway's future were settled in a very San Franciscan manner: by earthquake. The 1989 Loma Preita quake shook the tower but also damaged the freeway so severely that it was demolished in 1992, bringing waterfront views to a new generation of San Franciscans. The same earthquake caused the temporary closure of the Bay Bridge and the restoration of ferry traffic across the bay, which continued in modest measure after the bridge's re-opening.

The unplanned re-emergence of the Ferry Building as a feature on the city skyline brougt renewed impetus to long-running and very varied plans to give the building a role befitting its place in San Francisco history. One such came to fruition in April 2003, when part of the building opened as a gourmet food emporium, hosting a four-times weekly Farmer's Market, offering fresh breads, gourmet olive oils and organic vegetables. Whatever form other developments take, the promise is a full return to public use of what the ever-effusive Margot Patterson Doss called "our twinkling clock tower, water gate, and romantic way station."

City Hall, 1899, 1915, 1999

For two decades, San Francisco's center of civic affairs had been shunted from pillar to post throughout the fast-growing community, but in 1872 a cornerstone for a purpose-built City Hall was laid in a former cemetery at the foot of Larkin Street. In what might be one of the city's worst ever decisions, the building was financed on a year-by-year basis until completion. This presented money-making opportunities to unscrupulous builders and corruptible city officials and also resulted in the structure being obsolete before completion, unable to incorporate the many advances in building technology being pioneered in other expanding US cities.

Twenty-seven years in construction and costing $6 million, City Hall finally opened to great fanfare: seven years later it fell down. True, the collapse was triggered by the earthquake and fire of 1906, which left the building's magnificent dome perched indecently atop a charred steel frame, a sight described in the *San Francisco Examiner* as "like a huge birdcage against the morning dawn." But the destruction did nothing to dispel the rumors of shoddy construction and cheap materials. The president of the Chamber of Commerce commented that the wreck was the result of "mixing bad politics with cement."

Perhaps defending his corner, City Architect Newton J. Tharp noted in his report on the damage: "contrary to popular belief, the bricks and mortar used throughout the entire structure are of the finest and the workmanship of the best. So far, the most rigid inspection of the standing and fallen walls, and of the walls of portions under removal have failed to disclose any large voids or enclosed boxes, barrels or wheel-barrows that have been told in many an old tale as evidence of lax supervision and contractor's deceits." Nonetheless, the vote was overwhelmingly for an entirely new building to be constructed within a fixed budget.

San Francisco would gain not just a new City Hall, but also a Civic Center complex, a mix of city, federal and cultural buildings facing a broad plaza and all derived from the 1905 plan of Daniel Burnham. Pre-eminent in the classically-inspired City Beautiful movement, Burnham envisaged cities of grand boulevards and expansive parks, visionary architectural schemes that excited planners but for reasons of budget, cowardice and sheer impracticality, never became reality. But in San Francisco they almost did.

The $25,000 design competition for a new City Hall was won by the relatively untried firm of Arthur Brown Jr. (1874-1957) and John Bakewell (1872-1963). With a budget half that of the old City Hall, they created the French baroque-derived masterpiece that instills a sense of majesty, even in the heart of present-day San Francisco. The dome can be seen across the city, and the 400-foot-long, finely proportioned Sierra granite exterior is suitably impressive when viewed from UN Plaza. Inside, a marble staircase accesses broad landings where neoclassical sculptures reach from the walls.

The spired copper dome, modeled on that of the Church of St. Louis des Invalides in Paris (where Brown had graduated from the Ecole des Beaux-Arts) is vividly illuminated at night and, as with the California State Capitol in Sacramento, the chance was not missed to make the 307-foot-high dome taller than that of the Capitol in Washington DC. The former asserted California's economic power and independence, the latter provided a reminder of San Francisco's place as America's premier Pacific coast city at a time when this position was being threatened by a rising Los Angeles.

Through the 1990s, City Hall underwent a $293-million seismic restructuring and general remodeling that strengthened its resistance to earthquakes, added contemporary features such as fiber-optic cabling, and restored elements of the original design including the Light Courts which now provide a space for public exhibitions. The dome lost the pale green hue of its deteriorated copper and was restored using gold leaf on a lead-substitute paint, resulting in a gorgeous blue glint that radiates across the city.

The St. Francis Hotel, 1904/The Palace Hotel, 1875

Some of the passengers passing through the Ferry Building in the early 1900s would have been on their way to the St. Francis Hotel, nowadays forming a formidable four-wing sandstone backdrop to the Dewey Monument on the west side of Union Square. Just as the Ferry Building's flower stand became a popular and subsequently mythologized meeting place in the halcyon days of water traffic, the 1856 carved rosewood grandfather clock that has stood in the lobby of the St. Francis Hotel since 1907 became another celebrated meeting place, inspiring the phrase "meet me under the clock", much used by visitors hoping to impress locals.

An unrelated St. Francis Hotel, opened in 1849, had the distinction of introducing bed sheets to a San Francisco where unfussy gold miners were accustomed to sleeping on floorboards or sharing a bare mattress. Funded with $2.5 million from the fortune of deceased railroad baron Charles Crocker, the new St. Francis was completed in 1904. The hotel not only boasted sheets but also an interior liberally festooned with marble pillars, opulent fireplaces, wood-paneled walls and hand-crafted furniture, all discreetly illuminated by sparkling chandeliers. There were tea rooms, lounges and restaurants, where the new electric grills could cook steaks in five minutes, and Turkish baths powered by saltwater piped from the ocean.

Structurally strong enough to withstand the earthquake of 1906, the hotel offered a free breakfast, to actor John Barrymore and opera singer Enrico Caruso among others, before being engulfed by the fire that raged across the wrecked city. In the rebuilt San Francisco, the St. Francis gained a third wing in 1908 and a fourth in 1913, the last providing the oddly asymmetrical face the hotel presents to Union Square today.

While promoting San Francisco as a tourist destination, the hotel did its best to keep its high-spending guests indoors. The property had its own orchestra and theatrical director: a professional actor who would oversee amateur dramatics performed by guests. In the dining room, chef Victor Hirtzler provided entertainment as well as food. With a pointed beard, curling mustache and a red Fez perched on his head at a crazy angle, Hirtzler played up to his guests' image of a European chef by exaggerating his French accent while producing dishes as exotic as any San Francisco had seen. Along with roast leg of reindeer, cactus salad and celery Victor (the vegetable poached in chicken broth, a dish he named after himself), Hirtzler knew 203 ways to prepare eggs, including eggs Sarah Bernhardt (hard-boiled eggs mixed with chicken, truffles and Madeira wine).

Where Victor encouraged humor and a full stomach among guests, Ernest Gloor filled them with terror. As head waiter of the Mural Room (opened in 1935 and the city's pre-eminent ballroom) for 27 years, the Swiss-born Gloor devised seating plans that helped define the city's social pecking order. David Siefkin's *Meet Me at the St. Francis* recalls that Gloor "changed the Monday lunch from a simple meal into an awesome ritual." Guests who hoped to be placed at a center table would dread being banished to the room's margins, signifying banishment to the city's social margins. Under Gloor, the Mural Room was, Siefkin continues, "the one place in San Francisco where your position did not depend on how much money you had, or how much power or how you were dressed, or who your parents were, or what your last name was, or when you arrived, or on any rational reason at all; it depended entirely on what Ernest thought of you." Even those not part of the social elite would hope the hotel's prestige might rub off on them. Herb Caen remarked on "the anxious-to-impress women who sneak into the St. Francis through the Geary and Post entrances and then sweep out grandly under the Powell marquee—so they can join the crowd waiting for the doorman and cab starter to whistle them up a taxi."

Ever seeking to pamper to its guests, the St. Francis introduced the cleaning of money to prevent dirty coins soiling the white gloves of society ladies. Although the practice began with silver dollars it soon extended to all coins (the hotel still keeps a separate stash of crisp notes to issue to guests as change). The coins were washed and polished with a burnishing machine before being dried under 250-watt bulbs and put back into circulation. For 31 years, the process was overseen by Arnold Batliner whose retirement in 1993, aged 88, was marked not only by a party but by Mayor Frank Jordan declaring the day, April 26, Arnold Batliner Day.

Already attracting heads of state, city socialites and leading writers and artists, through the 1920s, the hotel became a magnet for Hollywood movie stars. One arrival was knockabout comedian Fatty Arbuckle, the highest-paid performer of the time who came to celebrate the sale of his next twenty-two films. Given the best suite in the property, Arbuckle ordered records and a gramophone, acquired some bootleg gin, and was joined in his suite by other Hollywood notables and assorted hangers-on for a party. Among the guests was a young actress, Virginia Rappe who, feeling unwell, went to bed in an adjoining room as the not-particularly-raucous party continued.

Arbuckle checked out the next day, unaware that anything was amiss until confronted by reporters. Rappe had been found dead and another partygoer named Arbuckle as being responsible. Lack of evidence against the actor and the suspicious motives of his accuser did nothing to discourage the muck-raking "yellow press" from lurid accusations and innuendo that milked middle America's distaste for what it saw as the godless film community of Hollywood. Arbuckle was tried and acquitted but his career was ruined. Publishing mogul William Randolph Hearst, whose newspapers had mounted the most venomous attacks, observed that the Arbuckle affair "sold more newspapers than any event since the sinking of the Lusitania." Then a six-dollar-a-day employee of the Pinkerton National Detective Agency, Dashiell Hammett recalled catching Arbuckle's gaze on the day of his trial: "His eyes were the eyes of a man who expected to be regarded a monster but was not yet inured to it. I made my gaze as contemptuous as I could. It was amusing. I was working for his attorneys at the time, gathering information for his defence."

As reductions in business travel and increased budget accommodation signaled the end of the era of grand hotels, the St. Francis struggled to stay solvent without sacrificing its lofty ideals. Private ownership ended in 1954 when the hotel became part of the Westin chain, and in 1972 the St. Francis Tower was added. The sleek high-rise tower almost doubled the hotel's capacity but lessened its charm, looming with a sense of menace behind the original wings when viewed from Union Square.

For a certain kind of San Franciscan, however, the St. Francis retains its regal status. The function rooms frequently host major events in the social calendar, while the orchid-decorated Compass Rose lounge provides succor for those oblivious to the rise and fall of Beats, hippies and dotcom entrepreneurs, and whose idea of heaven is lapsang souchong and the creations of the hotel's pastry chefs.

The St. Francis' official history explains that San Francisco, growing in size, affluence and importance at the turn of the twentieth century, badly needed a hotel of grandeur to match the famed hostelries of Boston and New York if the rich and powerful were to be encouraged westwards. What it does not point out is that, from 1875, well before the St. Francis was built, San Francisco had such a hotel. It was called The Palace and was the forerunner of the Sheraton Palace, which occupies the original hotel's location at the junction of Market and New Montgomery streets.

While the St. Francis opened with $2.5 million worth of finery, the Palace was financed to the tune of more than $5 million by banker William Ralston and, with 800 rooms spread across 2.5 acres, was the largest city hotel in the US. Innovations included hydraulic elevators, electric call buttons in each room linked by 125 miles of wiring, 755 noiseless water closets, and so much carpeting from the prestigious New York firm of WJ Sloane that the company opened a San Francisco branch to cater to the hotel's needs. A marble-floored courtyard, overlooked by iron-balconied rooms, formed the center of the seven-story hotel and provided a horse-and-carriage turning circle. Gutted by fire during the calamity of 1906 (unfortunately, an elaborate system of water pipes failed to work), the Palace re-opened in 1909.

Today, the Palace's former courtyard is the enclosed and sky-lit Palm Court, an interior of such beauty that guests have to force themselves out of it to visit the adjacent Pied Piper bar to admire the priceless Maxfield Parrish mural of the same name. Yet for all its grandeur and long list of famous guests, the Palace never quite matched the social élan of the St. Francis. And, in another judiciously phrased version of history, the St. Francis' official story reminisces of the breakfast being served to Enrico Caruso on the day of the 1906 earthquake while neglecting to mention that the great opera singer was actually a guest of the Palace.

The Palace of Fine Arts, 1915

Beside a swan-filled lagoon on the edge of the Marina District, the Palace of Fine Arts—the restored remains of what was a far larger structure—provides a beguiling backdrop for strolling lovers, dog walkers, and anyone in need of an infusion of mystery and enchantment.

The open-sided domed rotunda and its columns, decorated by sculptured staircases that rise to nowhere and tearful maidens (Expo guards were instructed to explain that the ladies were "crying over the sadness of art"), was the centerpiece of architect Bernard Maybeck's contribution to 1915 Panama-Pacific International Exposition. Maybeck (1862-1957) intended the work to instill "sadness, modified by the feeling that beauty has a soothing influence" as visitors passed through it on their way to view the classical art exhibition within the Expo's Great Hall, a route that took them through an arc-shaped, fragmented colonnade decorated by funeral urns and topped by over-sized planter boxes. Even the lagoon, developed from a small natural pond where children would catch frogs was assimilated into the design, its surface dreamily reflecting the sculptured ruins. In *The City of Domes*, journalist John D. Barry quotes one of the Expo's designers describing the Maybeck work:

It's the vision of a painter who is also a poet, worked out in terms of architecture. Maybeck planned it all, even to the details. He wanted to suggest a splendid ruin, suddenly come upon by travelers, after a long journey in a desert. He has invested the whole place with an atmosphere of tragedy. It's Roman in feeling and Greek in the refinement of its ornamentation. That rotunda reminds one of the Pantheon in Rome. Those Corinthian columns, with the melancholy drooping of the acanthus and the fretwork and the frieze, by Zimm, are suggestive of Greece.

Like the Expo's hundred other structures, the Palace of Fine Arts was intended to stand only for the event's duration. Instant and lasting popularity saved it from demolition, however, and, despite being made of chicken wire and plaster, it endured into the 1960s when it was again saved from becoming a genuine ruin with a $7.5-million facelift of reinforced concrete and steel. In 1969 the Exploratorium, an educational science museum, opened immediately west of the Palace in what was the Expo's Great Hall and consumed much of the original colonnade. An intriguing glimpse of the Palace as it looked in the late 1950s is provided by Alfred Hitchcock's San Francisco-set film, *Vertigo*, during a brief sequence in which Spencer Tracey and Kim Novak walk with the structure looming like a real Roman ruin in the background.

The opening of the Panama Canal and the 400th anniversary of the European discovery of California provided good excuses, but a

more pressing reason for the staging of the Expo in San Francisco (other cities had bid for the honor) was to highlight the city's recovery from the earthquake and fire of 1906. Using sand dredged from the bay, land was created from an expanse of mudflats between the Presidio and Fort Mason. The Expo arose across this 635-acre site, enlivened by 1,500 sculptures and murals, and landscaped by Golden Gate Park's John McLaren. Importing rhododendrons from Holland, azaleas from Japan, cinerariae from Brazil, and agapanthus from Africa, McLaren also planted 30,000 trees, including the palms that decorated the main pathways.

Lasting from February to December, the Expo was visited by almost twenty million people; the opening day so excited San Francisco's Mayor Rolph that he ran part of the way to the site. The delights included pavilions from 25 nations (the onset of the First World War had briefly threatened the Expo's opening) and exhibits from many US states, notably that of Oregon which offered a replica Parthenon with trunks of Oregonian redwoods in place of marble pillars. Also displayed was the original Liberty Bell, borrowed from Philadelphia and, among many crowd-pleasing curiosities, a fourteen-ton typewriter.

At the Expo's heart was the 433-foot-high Tower of Jewels, a loosely Aztec-style structure designed by Thomas Hastings (of the noted New York architectural firm Carrere & Hastings). Inscriptions at the tower's base recorded the historical process that led to the Panama Canal's construction while the body was encased by 100,000 cut-glass beads fashioned into imitation jewels and suspended on wires to shimmer in the breeze. Visitors jaded after a full day at the Expo would be revived—and the whole city thrilled—by spectacular nighttime illumination. From positions on the bayside, 48 spotlights threw their colored beams skywards where their glow met the steam pumped from a locomotive at the foot of a pier. Of the light, John D. Barry recalled: "The rotunda and the colonnade began to take on a deeper mystery. Across the surface of the water ran a faint ripple. In the background, over the Golden Gate, the sky was turning to flame. Delicate, gray cobwebs seemed to float in the air like veils, dusk and fog intermingled." And in an apparent fit of rapture, Edwin Markham, author of the popular poem, "The Man With The Hoe", and at the

Expo to promote his book, *California The Wonderful*, observed the evening panorama and exclaimed: "I have tonight seen the greatest revelation of beauty that was ever seen on the earth... beauty that will give the world new standards of art and a joy in loveliness never before reached."

That Maybeck came to create one of San Francisco's most enigmatic and enduring landmarks was due to Willis Polk, the architect overseeing the Expo who gave him the job. Unlike Polk, Maybeck had an academic architectural background, having studied in Paris at the Ecole des Beaux-Arts. But like Polk, Maybeck frequently sought to align diverse architectural styles into a single theme and did so in sympathy with their setting. Settling in Berkeley in 1889, Maybeck taught at the university and fashioned some of the region's most idiosyncratic buildings, among them Berkeley's First Church of Christ, Scientist, and numerous private homes, a fact which prompted one writer to note that "having 'a Maybeck' is like owning a Monet."

Coit Tower, 1933

A 210-foot fluted cylindrical column of reinforced concrete rising from the brow of Telegraph Hill, Coit Tower has few architecturally redeeming features. But this structure nonetheless embodies the mix of personal eccentricity and political controversy that underpins many of San Francisco's celebrated landmarks. Originally, it should be said, Coit Tower was anything but celebrated. It was opposed in its planning, hated by many on its completion, and had its opening delayed for fear of sparking a revolution.

The tower occupies what was once Semaphore Hill, site of a signal station erected by John Montgomery (who, as captain of the *Portsmouth*, first claimed what was then Yerba Buena for the US), who also fortified the summit with a stolen Mexican cannon. In 1850 the station became the Marine Telegraph, comprising two tall wooden masts from which the arrival of ships was signaled with semaphore flags. Such was San Francisco's isolation in the 1850s that ships, mail ships in particular, were eagerly awaited and their approach drew expectant crowds to the dockside.

San Francisco at this time was largely composed of side-by-side wooden structures with canvas coverings. This ramshackle architecture, combined with the lack of full-time fire-fighters and a reliable water supply (an anti-fire regulation called for each household to maintain six full buckets of water), when added to the potential for strong winds to fan flames, made the nascent city highly combustible. Between 1849 and 1851, major fires caused over $23-million-worth of damage and destroyed 3,000 buildings.

Repeated devastation actually aided the development of the city. With the boundless energy that marked its early days, damage was quickly repaired, and comparatively fire-resistant brick- or stone-built structures fronted with iron shutters arose to line broad streets, swiftly giving San Francisco the look and character of a fully-fledged American metropolis. A mark of the city's maturity came in 1866 with the creation of a professional fire brigade. Previously blazes had been tackled by disparate volunteer fire companies, often glorified social clubs, who would race each other to a blaze. Watching the brave but often hapless fire-fighters, sometimes fighting each other as much as the flames, became a regular pastime.

Among those who followed the fire-fighters' trucks was the young Lillie Hitchcock (1843-1929), who arrived in San Francisco as an eight-year-old in 1851. On a celebrated occasion in 1859, Lillie was on her way home from school when, on hearing the city's fire alarm, she dropped her school books and raced to the scene of a fire where she found the truck of Knickerbocker Engine Company No. 5 being pulled by ropes up the side of Telegraph Hill. Seeing the truck about to be overtaken by a rival company, Lillie grabbed a rope, exhorting: "Come on, you men. Pull harder and we'll beat 'em!" A legend was born. A 1900 history of the city's fire service remembers Lillie "romping in short frocks" and being "curiously fascinated by the red shirt and war-like helmet of the firemen, and glorying in the excitement of a big blaze."

Nicknamed "Firebelle", Lillie became a figure at every major fire and sat on top of the Knickerbocker No.5 truck at parades, much to the chagrin of her army doctor father, a graduate of West Point, and his high society associates. While such unconventional behavior might be excused in a young girl, Lillie's obsession with fires and the men (entirely non-sexually) who put them out continued into adulthood. In *California People*, Carol Dunlap recounts: "Typically she would leave cotillions or even weddings to arrive by barouche, with coachmen and dancing partner in attendance, at the latest fire."

Ordinary San Franciscans relished Lillie's rebellious spirit. But even in this unconventional city it was not the done thing for a well-bred lady to gamble, drink, and dress up as a man to get into rough-and-ready nightspots. Lillie did all of these things and further flouted convention by breaking engagements to several would-be suitors until finally marrying a stock exchange caller, Howard Coit. Having already caused a stir in Paris by attending a prestigious masked ball attired as a fireman, Lillie traveled more widely with her husband, being received by Indian maharajas among others of high rank. The marriage over, and depressed by the fatal shooting of a friend in her rooms at the Palace Hotel, Lillie left spent most of her later years in Paris but eventually returned to San Francisco where she died in 1926.

Lillie left $118,000, a third of her fortune, to be spent "in an appropriate manner for the purpose of adding to the beauty of the city which I have always loved," and a smaller sum for a monument to the city's volunteer fire-fighters. The latter, an orthodox statue depicting firemen rescuing a woman, now stands in Washington Square. The other part of Lillie's bequest, however, became the much more dramatic and controversial Coit Tower.

After much deliberation by the city's Arts Committee, two members of whom opposed the plan on the grounds that Lillie herself

hated towers, Park Commissioner John McLaren (the stubborn genius who created Golden Gate Park) was among those who forced the idea through. The city duly hired the architectural firm of Arthur Brown Jr., creator of City Hall, with the project headed by Henry Howard. Although the city boosted funding to $125,000, the architect's plan to sculpt Pioneer Park (a five-acre plot on which the tower was raised) into terraces linked by walkways and winding stairways was never implemented. Reinforced concrete was chosen as the building material for its low cost and, as the effects of the Depression began to bite, the city even sold the tower's scaffolding to keep costs down.

A federally-funded initiative to create work for unemployed artists and a dry run for the wider-ranging projects of the subsequent WPA, a Public Works of Art Project paid twenty-five artists $94 a month each to create a series of murals inside the tower collectively titled *Aspects of Life in California*. Major San Francisco-based artists such as Lucien Labaudt, Clifford Wight, and Ralph Stackpole were among the contributors to the project, which was directed by another, Victor Arnautoff. All had close links with the great Mexican muralist Diego Rivera, whose own murals can be found at the city's stock exchange and the San Francisco Art Institute.

In keeping with the muralist tradition, the artists often cast themselves in the murals, mixed humor, satire, and pathos, and reflected the political mood of the times. Among the depictions of farmers, fruit packers, and scenes of railroads and shipping, a man reaches for Marx's *Das Kapital* in Bernard B. Zakheim's *Library*; a street vendor sells the socialist *Daily Worker* in Victor Arnautoff's *City Life*; while Clifford Wight's *Steelworker* shows a piece of cable twisted into a hammer-and-sickle image.

If the San Francisco Lillie Hitchcock knew as a girl was combustible, a barely less incendiary atmosphere gripped the city when Coit Tower (completed in 1933) and its murals were due to be formally opened to the public in May 1934. That month, a strike by San Francisco's longshoremen had escalated into a four-day city-wide general strike. On July 5, the date remembered as "Bloody Thursday", street battles between pickets and police left three dead and 31 injured as strike-breakers attempted to re-open the docks. A further general strike was supported by the biggest withdrawal of labor ever seen in the US; brought to a standstill, the city was placed under martial law. Unveiling the worker-sympathetic images of the Coit Tower murals in the prevailing mood of insurrection proved too much for the Arts

Committee, who postponed the event. It took another picket, this time led by the Artists' Union, and the removal of the hammer-and-sickle image, before the murals finally went on public view in October 1934.

Lillie's eccentric ways and the bitter struggles of the 1930s now seem very distant memories, as does the fact that 464 people signed a petition against the tower's construction and Gertrude Atherton, a friend of Lillie's, called the finished article "an incinerator".

Though threatened by years of nothing but the barest maintenance, the tower and its murals were successfully restored through the late 1980s. Even the previously overlooked Pioneer Park is gaining a new lease of life from a neighborhood project to plant its gardens, create habitats for birds and butterflies, and bring about the landscaped pathways originally envisaged as an aesthetically pleasing approach to the tower. The only lasting controversy seems to be the trivial one, much mused over by guide books and visiting tourists (with stunning views over the city and beyond, the tower is a justly popular attraction) as to whether its upper portions resemble a firehose nozzle. If they do, it was not something intended by the designers.

Illuminated by night, the tower is a visible and quite unmistakable feature of the city of which it seems very much a part; and, in differing ways, it has exercised the imaginations of poets. Gregory Corso's "Ode to Coit Tower" began "O anti-verdurous phallic were't not for your pouring height looming in tears like a sick tree or your ever-gaudy-comfort jabbing your city's much wrinkled sky you'd seem an absurd Babel squatting before mortal millions..."

And accepting the post of the city's first poet laureate in 1998, Lawrence Ferlinghetti made a speech speculating on ways to improve San Francisco, one being to add a tilt to Coit Tower: "think what it did for Pisa!"

Golden Gate Bridge, 1937
Rapturously described as "a symphony in steel", "an Aeolian harp", and "an eternal rainbow", the Golden Gate Bridge enjoys a fame far beyond its function of allowing 42 million vehicles to travel annually between San Francisco and the rugged green hills of Marin County. One of the world's largest suspension bridges and certainly the most photogenic, the Golden Gate Bridge adorns posters, dishes, T-shirts and postcards,

and is as much an emblem of the city as cable cars, Alcatraz and the Transamerica Pyramid.

Yet such a structure in a such a space was long thought impossible. A fixed crossing over the Golden Gate, a deep channel of cold, fast-moving water linking San Francisco Bay and the ocean, was mooted in 1872 by railroad baron Charles Crocker and more effectively by newspaper editor James Wilkins who, from 1915, orchestrated a campaign to bring the scheme into life. Many engineers thought the challenge overwhelming, the sea too deep, the currents too strong, and the mile-wide span too big. Others opposed the plan, believing it would ruin the natural spectacle. Author Katherine Gerould pleaded: "in the interest of your own uniqueness, dear San Franciscans, do not bridge the Golden Gate."

One who disagreed was the Ohio-born, Chicago-based engineer Joseph B. Strauss (1870-1938). Not only could it be done, affirmed Strauss (who had worked on several hundred suspension bridges), but it could be done relatively cheaply. Where others had suggested a cost of $100 million, Strauss' plan came to $27 million, which would be recouped over forty years through tolls.

The need for a fixed crossing was becoming desperate. Fifty million ferry journeys a year were being made to points north and east across the bay, causing congestion at terminals even with a ferry leaving every three minutes during rush hours. Mindful that a bridge would be a boon to their economies, five northern counties joined with San Francisco to form the Golden Gate Bridge District, a device to tackle the immense legal and political technicalities that the project presented. After much wrangling—and opposition from ferry companies—the go-ahead came in 1929 from the War Department, which owned the required land on both sides of the span. In the depths of the Depression, funding the project with a $35-million bond issue was highly controversial, but it went ahead, construction beginning on January 5, 1933.

Along with many technical innovations, Strauss introduced safety measures that included the first use of head protection (the forerunner of the modern hard hat), glare-free goggles, and a specially-developed face and hand cream to protect workers' skin from strong, salty winds. A safety net placed under the full length of the bridge saved the lives of

19 men (dubbed the Halfway to Hell Club) and only one fatality occurred during most of the construction—a record tarnished by ten deaths three months before completion when a section of scaffolding collapsed and pierced the safety net. With the country struggling to emerge from the Depression, bridge workers enjoyed the luxury of regular employment and high wages, their dollar-an-hour pay financing weekends of carousing in the city. A popular joke had it that while it normally took workers thirty minutes to climb from the ground to the bridge deck, Monday hangovers lengthened the ascent to forty.

Two hundred thousand people crossed the bridge when it opened for pedestrians on May 27, 1937; the next day it carried 25,000 cars. Fifty years later, 300,000 walked onto the bridge to mark its

anniversary. By 1971, the bridge had paid for itself, earning $146 million to cover construction, interest payments, and additional maintenance and construction work. Yet the original intention that tolls would steadily be phased out was never implemented. Tolls were continued to subsidize a loss-making public transport system that included, ironically, ferries. The initial thirty cents toll for private cars (fifty cents for taxis and hearses) had risen to $3 by 1992.

Besides offering endless scope for photographers, the bridge provides the spectacular statistics much loved by travel writers in search of page-filling copy. Consuming 100,000 tons of steel, stretching for seven miles and reaching 220 feet above water level at low tide, the bridge also has 80,000 miles of cabling which could girdle the globe three times over. The towers, each with 600,000 rivets, are as high as a 48-story building while the 4,200-foot-long central span remained the longest in the world until 1964. The only closures have been due to the visits of presidents Roosevelt and De Gaulle, the finding of a Japanese torpedo on a local beach, and three instances of extreme weather. A much-repeated story that the bridge is continually being painted is unfortunately untrue, although a full-time staff of painters carry out on-going touch-up work. While hard to imagine in any color except its rust-like shade of red (actually International Orange), the bridge might have been painted with yellow and black strips, a scheme proposed by the US Navy, or royal blue with yellow polka dots, suggested by two students in the 1930s who also offered to carry out the work.

Officially at least, what few people expected from the bridge was that it would became a popular suicide spot, the first taking place just three months after the bridge's opening. Since they are likely to hit the water at 80mph and the strong currents make swimming almost impossible, jumpers have little chance of survival. Over a thousand people are believed to have ended their lives in this way, including John Doyle, who jumped to his death in 1954 leaving a note saying: "absolutely no reason, except I have a toothache." A record annual figure of 45 suicides in 1995 prompted the introduction of a dawn-to-dusk scooter patrol to spot and talk down potential suicides.

Although the wind singing in its cables (inspiring the Aeolian harp comparison) is usually rendered inaudible by the rumble of traffic across it, the bridge is a rare example of art, engineering and nature brought together in apparent harmony. Even Strauss, who died a year after the bridge's completion, was driven to compose a verse in its honor and to offer a snub to those who said it could never be completed:

At last the mighty task is done
Resplendent in the western sun

Launched amidst a thousand hopes and fears
Damned by a thousand jeers.

Treasure Island, 1939

Just as the outbreak of the First World War had threatened to undermine the 1915 Expo, so the outbreak of the Second World War cast a shadow over the 1939 Golden Gate International Exposition (GGIE), San Francisco's next major public showpiece. Marking the completion of the Golden Gate and Bay bridges, the GGIE also allowed San Francisco to snatch some of the national attention being accorded to New York as that city hosted the 1939 World's Fair. Another parallel with the 1915 Expo was the creation of a new piece of San Francisco on which to stage it. Over three years, 287,000 tons of quarried rock and twenty million cubic yards of seabed were dredged and pumped to create the 400-acre Treasure Island, adjacent to Yerba Buena Island and linked to the Bay Bridge via a 900-foot-long paved causeway.

The GGIE carried the futuristic themes customary for such fairs but also sought to pioneer a new style of transpacific fusion architecture, a synthesis of Pacific Rim design that brought Asian religious symbols together with Mayan pyramids and American streamline moderne. The theme of Pacific fellowship was strongest at the Court of Pacifica pavilion, for which Ralph Stackpole contributed a gaze-stealing eighty-foot statue depicting Goddess Pacifica.

The Expo radiated out from Arthur Brown Jr.'s 400-foot Tower of the Sun and included a forty-acre "amusement zone" offering "Mark Twain's house", a model maternity unit displaying live babies in incubators, and various roller-coasters, Ferris wheels and flea circuses. Most attention, however, was focused on Sally Rand's Nude Ranch, the most up-market of several bared-flesh venues and one that featured dancing girls exploring a wild western theme: they wore bandannas, cowboy boots, hats and gun belts, but very little else. Sally Rand herself was a noted exotic dancer who scandalized Chicago's 1933 World Fair by dancing "nude" (actually in a body stocking) with the aid of two seven-foot-long pink ostrich fans, an act which she later brought to a San Francisco nightclub, the Music Box, with some success. The Expo's less contentious displays included fine art exhibitions, a model of San

Francisco as it might be in 1999, and other foretastes of future life such as "electronic music, atom smashing and chemical agriculture."

The lighting was only slightly less spectacular than that of 1915. General illumination was provided by giant lanterns, some 86 feet high, and 10,000 colored light bulbs secreted in bushes and trees. Special events were marked by the colored beams from 24 giant searchlights converging on a point just above the Tower of the Sun with a glow that could be seen, according to the official guide book, a hundred miles away.

Closure in October rather than the planned December encouraged the belief that the Expo was a financial flop, although its boosters cited the fact that it attracted ten million visitors and had injected $100 million into the Bay Area economy. The Expo enjoyed a four-month revival in 1940 with additions that included "bathing girls in blocks of ice" and a new color scheme: "... the San Francisco-State group stands out in a delicate primrose yellow, while the once-colorless Pacific House is completely coated in coral red."

Built with three large hangars and a landing strip, Treasure Island was viewed as a future San Francisco airport and already provided a base for Pan American's China Clipper, the sea-plane that operated the first scheduled routes between the US and destinations across the Pacific. As it turned out, the US Navy claimed the island as a base in 1942 (and remained in possession until 1993), Japan's attack on Pearl Harbor dampening the Expo's theme of harmony between Pacific nations.

Nonetheless, for a generation of San Franciscans, the GGIE became a memory of innocent fun that stayed with them through the war and beyond. Columnist Herb Caen (who insists that he was conceived during his parents stay in San Francisco to visit the Expo) in a series of tips on "How to Be a San Franciscan", offered the following advice:

> *Never look at Treasure Island without saying dreamily 'Ah, seems like only yesterday that yon drab place was veritable fairyland of lights, gaiety, laughter, hahahaha. And yet, friend, we have lived a lifetime since then. Now we are old—our dreams as dead as the make-believe palaces that once glittered out there on that man-made magic isle.'*

The Transamerica Pyramid, 1972/The Montgomery Block, 1853

The feared "Manhattanization" of the city skyline and the fact that its architectural firm, William L. Pereira & Associates, were based in Los Angeles, led to a considerable amount of opposition to the creation of the Transamerica Pyramid when construction began in December 1969. The protest reduced the intended 55-story, 1,000-foot building into one of 48 floors and 813 feet but failed to prevent the tapering structure becoming a distinctive and ultimately enjoyable addition to the city skyline and its image a staple of souvenir merchandise.

The Transamerica company had its origins with the Bank of Italy, opened in San Francisco by Amadeo Peter Giannini in 1904. Giannini

(1870-1949), born in San Jose to Italian parents, made his name by extending loans to immigrants who were generally regarded as uncreditworthy by established financial institutions. During the 1906 fire, Giannini pushed a handcart laden with his bank's $2 million of gold, hidden beneath fruit and vegetables, to safety. As branches spread across California, Giannini also invested in the nascent film-making industry of Los Angeles, then ignored by other banks, and for a time employed the film-director Cecil B. De Mille as the company's Hollywood loans officer.

In 1928 the Transamerica Corporation came into being as a holding company for Giannini's various companies, including what by now was the Bank of America, soon to be among the world's largest financial institutions. Facing anti-trust suits in the 1950s, Transamerica shed its holdings in the Bank of America and the two became separate organizations. With a certain irony, the Transamerica Pyramid reaches 65 feet higher than the Bank of America World Headquarters (now Bank of America Center), the other dominant feature on the Financial District skyline, completed a year earlier.

The tallest building in San Francisco, the Transamerica Pyramid occupies the site of what, from the 1850s, was the most prestigious. Known as the Montgomery Block, the building was the creation of Henry W. Halleck (1816-72), a graduate of West Point military academy who arrived in San Francisco with the army in 1847. Nicknamed "Old Brains" for his priggish character, Halleck was an ingenious engineer and a signatory to California's 1849 constitution: although his recommendation that the state extend as far east as the Rockies was never implemented.

Brick-built and sitting on on a raft of redwood logs, bolted together and sunk into the mud of what was then the waterfront, the Montgomery Block was regarded as earthquake proof (surviving the 1906 earthquake showed it was, while Halleck's fire-proofing ideas of iron shutters and thick walls also enabled the building to survive the subsequent blaze), but for a time it was known as "Halleck's Folly" largely by its size, four stories spread across an entire city block. Even so, the rapid growth of law and financial companies in the city saw the Montgomery Block quickly filled by occupants paying some of the city's highest rents. The second Vigilante Committee operated here, as did Sun Yat-sen, running the *Young China* newspaper and drafting what would become the first post-Manchu Chinese constitution, while Mark Twain shared the basement steam baths with one Tom Sawyer, the inspiration for Twain's eponymous fictional character.

Relocation of the Financial District changed the Montgomery Block's character. By the 1890s, the building was predominantly occupied by artists and writers enjoying what by then were low rents and spacious accommodation. Nicknamed the "Monkey Block", it became the base for San Francisco's turn-of-the-century bohemia. Residents and regular visitors included Ambrose Bierce, George Sterling, Joaquin Miller, and many others. On the ground floor, Poppa Coppa's Italian restaurant became a celebrated dining spot, while the Pisco Punch (a brandy-based concoction so potent only two were permitted to each customer), sold from the neighboring Bank Exchange bar, similarly became the stuff of legend. One who tried the drink for the first time in 1872 reported: "We had some hot, with a bit of lemon and a dash of nutmeg in it" and, after consuming two glasses, "I felt that I could face small-pox, all the fevers known to the faculty, and the Asiatic cholera, combined, if need be."

Despite enjoying great affection and growing from "Halleck's Folly" into "The Ark of Empire" (the title of a book devoted to its history and its role as "the social vortex of the city, of all of California" by Idwal Jones), the building was ignominiously demolished in 1959 to make way for a car park.

The Transamerica Pyramid has much about its design of which Halleck may have approved. The tapering form provided a practical solution to the problem of maximizing interior space while allowing sufficient light to reach the streets to comply with building regulations. The structure stands atop a concrete and steel foundation buried 52 feet beneath ground with the memory of Halleck's redwood logs kept alive by the Redwood Park on the building's east side, planted with eighty redwoods from the Santa Cruz mountains and landscaped into a popular venue for lunch-time concerts. Where Halleck relied on thick brick walls to lessen fire risk, the Pyramid's safety measures include the emergency staircase and smoke tower concealed in one of its wings and a life support control center located in an underground command post. To withstand earthquakes, the building uses a truss system to carry horizontal as well as vertical loads, while the strengthened white pre-cast-quartz aggregate exterior also allows for lateral movement. Its most serious test came in 1989 with the Loma Prieta earthquake, during which the building shook for a minute and the spire swayed 12 inches but no damage or serious injuries resulted.

A 27th-floor observation room once provided a popular public viewing point, but from the late 1990s, views to non-employees have been restricted to those seen on TV screens on the ground level lobby from cameras mounted on the building's roof: a dramatic panorama of the city also available to Internet users. What the views do not show, however, is the spire's distinctive yellow glow in the San Franciscan night.

PART FIVE

United Nations

If the eastern US was settled by Europeans, then the western US was colonized by Europeans who had become Americans and were under the spell of Manifest Destiny (the mid-1800s doctrine of American expansionism): intent on putting down roots in the Great American Desert, as uncharted lands were known, and taming its wild landscapes—as they did its "wild" natives—to create a God-fearing land of plenty for the chosen people.

Concealed by mountain ranges and deserts, San Francisco and California were spared. Beyond easy reach of wagon trains, they promised little to make the treacherous overland journey—or even the slightly less dangerous sea voyage—worthwhile. The discovery of gold changed everything, making San Francisco a magnet not only for determined Americans but for about one-third of the gold rush invaders who came from outside the US. Lust for gold brought Central and South Americans, Asians, Europeans, Australians, and many more from seemingly every corner of the globe.

Even before the gold discovery, Yerba Buena had been a multicultural hotchpotch. The windswept trading post had a black man as its treasurer, a white American appointed as its Mexican *alcalde*, an Englishman overseeing trade tolls and, in the person of William Heath Davis, a Bostonian/Polynesian merchant whose memoirs would reveal much of the period to later generations. Before them, Spanish missionaries had created Mission Dolores and brought the European diseases that helped destroy the region's native population.

After the gold rush, San Francisco was an international port with an international population that prompted lyrical tributes to its apparent multi-ethnic harmony. Of unknown authorship, a poem called "Mission Dolores" was published in 1884:

Wide Thy Golden Gate stands open to all
Nations of the world,
Free beneath its stately portals
All flags are in peace unfurled.
Beauteous Gate, when loitering Sunset
Covers Thee with burnished gold.
Mighty Gate, when surging ocean Thy
Strong cliffs alone withhold.
Treacherous Gate, deceiving many with a
Name most fair-Blessed Gate, where millions
Find the golden boon of liberty.

A few decades later, journalist H. L. Mencken remarked on visiting San Francisco: "What fetched me instantly (and thousands of other newcomers with me) was the subtle but unmistakable sense of escape from the United States." Sunset Book's 1969 pictorial guide *San Francisco* offered the following cosmopolitan image:

Your background is Hungarian—or Danish or French or Irish or
German or Russian. You want to keep in touch with your heritage but
don't feel like an evening at a Japanese theater or a Greek taverna or a
Mexican cantina. So you read any of a score of the city's newspapers
about floods in Dublin or credit cards in Zurich or crops in Normandy
or medical centers in Stockholm. In San Francisco you may be a
newcomer but you're never a foreigner.

Appropriately enough in October 1945, San Francisco's War Memorial Opera House hosted the formal founding of the United Nations. The event was not free of fear and suspicion, however. A widely recounted anecdote concerned the Soviet Union's delegation staying at the St. Francis Hotel who, believing their rooms were bugged, pulled apart the suspect wiring and in doing so stopped all the hotel clocks: the wiring being part of the central system running from the lobby's grandfather clock. The UN's relocation to New York prompted Adlai Stevenson, visiting the Bay Area while campaigning for the US presidency in 1952, to remark: "I firmly believe that if the UN had remained here it would work much better. San Francisco has shown the world that people of diverse races and cultures can live together in peace."

Stevenson might have been right in regard to the UN. But while the ethnic diversity of San Francisco has created a city where New Year is a rolling celebration of January 1 and the lunar new years of China, Vietnam and Thailand, and where special events mark Japanese Cherry Blossom, Irish St. Patrick's Day, Mexican Cinco de Mayo and (for many years) French Bastille Day, it does so with a history punctuated by native genocide, anti-Chinese hysteria, Japanese internment, and institutionalized discrimination against Latinos and African-Americans.

A Mission

On June 26, 1776, Spanish missionary Francisco Palou conducted Mass in a rough encampment beside a lake named by the colonists, La Laguna de Nuestra Señora de Los Dolores. Mission Dolores (formally Misión de San Francisco de Asis) was subsequently erected nearby, surviving to became the oldest building in San Francisco and giving a name to the Mission District, occupying the flat lands between what are now Potrero Hill and the Castro. Palou wrote:

No sooner had the expedition gone into camp than many pagan Indians appeared in a friendly manner and with expressions of joy at our coming. Their satisfaction increased when they experienced the kindness with which we treated them and when they received the little trinkets we would give them in order to attract them, such as beads and estables. They would repeat their visits and bring little things in keeping with their poverty, such as shellfish and wild seeds.

The natives here are all well formed. Many of them have beards, others are hairless and rather ugly. They are accustomed to tear out by the roots the hair of the eyebrows, and this renders them ugly. They are poor Indians without much of a house than a hedge of branches to protect them somewhat against the high winds which prevail and which molest them very much. The men go entirely naked, except that they cover the shoulders with a sort of small cape pieced together from otter skins and pelican feathers. The women cover themselves with nothing but tules strung together around the waist.

On October 8, a barbecue celebrated the dedication of the mission and Palou noted: "Only the savages did not enjoy themselves on this happy day." The "savages" had reason to be fearful. Mission Dolores was the sixth of the 21 missions founded by the Spanish in California and all—along with the garrisons, or *presidios*, built with them—were stakes in Spain's claim to the territory as European powers vied for supremacy in North America. A tenet of the mission system was the capture and conversion of natives while using their labor to build and maintain the missions, tend animals, and cultivate the mission land. Such enclosure and the introduction of diseases, such as measles, to which the natives had no immunity, signaled an end to California's native cultures and very nearly the end of the natives themselves.

In *Seventy Five Years in California*, William Heath Davis describes how natives were brought to the missions:

> *The Indians were captured by the military who went into the interior of the country in pursuit of them, detachments of soldiers being frequently sent out from the presidio and other military posts in the department on these expeditions, to bring the wild Indians into the missions to be civilized and converted to Christianity. Sometimes two or three hundred would be brought in at a time—men, women and children—from the foothill region of the Sierra Nevada and the San Joaquin and Sacramento valleys. They were immediately turned over to the padres at the different missions, generally with a guard of a corporal and ten soldiers to assist the priest in keeping them until they had become somewhat tamed. They were kindly treated, and soon became domesticated and ready and eager to adopt the habits of civilized life. They gradually lost their desire to return to their former mode of life.*

At the time of Spanish settlement, California was home to around 300,000 natives divided into slightly more than a hundred nations (some extending no further than their home village) each with a distinct language and culture. Prevalent on the San Francisco peninsula were the Costanoan, derived from the Spanish word Costaños, or "coast people" (in their own dialect, they were Ramaytush). Published in 1925, the authoritative *Handbook of the Indians of California* by Alfred Kroeber (a University of California anthropology professor)

described the native population of Mission Dolores as an "extraordinary jumble". Remarking on the impact of the Spanish arrival on Costanoan culture, Kroeber notes tersely: "Costanoan basketry has perished," while the mission system had "effaced even traditional recollections of the forefathers' habits, except for occasional fragments of knowledge." He concluded that, by the end of the mission era, the Costanoan were "extinct as far as all practical purposes are concerned."

Mission Dolores was never among the most important California missions but nonetheless held "ten thousand head of cattle, many thousand head of horses and mares, and a vast number of sheep" on land that stretched to San Mateo, twenty miles south. Taking advantage of Spain's waning empire, Mexico declared its independence in 1822. Geographically remote and commercially unimportant, California's running was effectively passed to the Californios, mostly Mexican-born California settlers and their families. In theory, mission possessions were to be divided among Californios and the natives; in practice, vast tracts of land and the cattle and horses on them were taken by the Californios. In 1833, Heath Davis found two thousand natives living at Mission Dolores: "Among them were blacksmiths, shipwrights, carpenters, tailors, shoemakers and masons, all of whom had learned these trades at the mission, under the superintendence of the padres. They had also learned the Spanish language, as a general thing had acquired habits of industry, and had become civilized and Christianized. Many of them could read and write."

In the Californio period, some natives stayed close to mission complexes, some spread across the countryside, while others used their farming skills on the ranches of the Californios (whose own skills were in horsemanship and socializing). When California's missions were secularized in 1834, they contained 30,600 natives; eight years later there were just 4,450 recorded on former mission land. Secularization reduced the missions to parish churches; the outbuildings of Mission Dolores were used as a hotel, brewery and gambling parlor.

The near-disappearance of California's Native Americans added to the curiosity that gripped San Francisco on the arrival of Ishi, the last surviving member of northern California's Yahi people. Ishi, who never revealed his real name but was known by the Yahi word for "man", was discovered in 1911 in the foothills of northern California's Lassen Peak, near the town of Oroville. Incarcerated in the local jail, Ishi was exhibited as a "wild man" until placed in the care of Alfred Kroeber who provided him with living quarters at the then San Francisco-based university museum of anthropology. In her biography of the lone Yahi, Kroeber's wife, Theodora, wrote: "Ishi was the last wild Indian in North America, a man of stone age culture subjected for the first time when he was passed middle aged to twentieth century culture." Respiratory complications resulting from his first cold led to Ishi's death from tuberculosis in 1916. And it would not be until 1969 and the occupation of Alcatraz that Native Americans would again feature prominently in San Francisco news.

With a small museum and a contemplative mood evoked by its tiny, dimly-lit chapel, Mission Dolores today provides a subdued reminder of Spanish times. Various religious items were carried by mule and cart from Mexico, while the geometric patterns on the chapel's ceiling, based on native basketry, are thought to be the only lasting examples of Costanoan culture. Kroeber's "extraordinary jumble" are among the 5,000 natives collectively remembered by a sculpted Indian maiden in the mission's well-tended cemetery, although their remains are scattered across a much larger burial plot on which arose the surrounding streets and buildings. The cemetery proper also bears the marks of San Francisco's multicultural history: it holds the remains of luminaries of the Spanish settlement (not least Palou himself), of the Californio period, and early Americans including James P. Taylor and Charles Cora, both hanged by the Vigilance Committee in 1856.

The mission is occasionally used for services and more often for baptisms; it is dwarfed by the vivacious Spanish Revival style and twin towers of the neighboring Basilica of San Francisco, founded in 1926 and serving the large and predominantly Latino Catholic population of the present-day Mission District.

The Mission District

As the new American city of San Francisco grew beside the bay, three miles distant, the mission area remained neglected "with fields of flowers basking in soft sunshine around the old adobe residences of the Spanish families and other buildings, and with vistas of green willows marking the spots where the creek waters ran. Birds trilled their lays on every hand and the pall of gray fog that haunted the sandy wastes westward of the city never reached that region." The absence of "gray fog" became apparent to property speculators and in 1850 a construction company acquired permission to build a plank road carrying Mission Street (now, as then, the longest road in San Francisco, measuring 7.29 miles) from Third to 16th Streets.

By 1860 a street car service was operating on the thoroughfare linking the city with a six-acre pleasure resort called Woodward's Gardens on the west side of Mission Street, complete with zoo, boating lake, aquarium, art gallery, and a museum offering "a large and valuable collection of zoological specimens from all parts of the world." Operating until 1883, the gardens' popularity was immense and prompted one visitor, the San Francisco-born Robert Frost, to later write a poem, "At Woodward's Gardens", based on his tormenting of a resident monkey with a magnifying glass.

The Mission District's growth was hastened by the 1906 fire, which caused widespread destruction to low-income housing in the south of Market Street area and North Beach, and brought an influx of

working-class Irish, Poles, Dutch, Slavs, Scandinavians, Peruvians, Colombians, and Chileans, into the area's relatively spacious family homes (some of which are now among the city's best examples of Italianate and Stick-style architecture). By the 1930s Mission Street was dubbed the "miracle mile" for its shops, nightclubs and movie theaters. A small Mission District Mexican population, established from the 1910s, was joined by a steady stream of Nicaraguan and Salvadoran settlers fleeing turmoil in their homelands, while the need for armament workers during the Second World War brought a further wave of Latino immigration. The neighborhood's Latino population doubled each decade from the 1950s, and Central American strife during the 1970s and 1980s brought many more arrivals, mainly from Guatemala and Nicaragua.

With produce markets, bakeries and *taquerias*, and Latin rhythms spilling onto its main streets, the Mission District has an effervescence that makes the rest of San Francisco seem sleepy. While providing inexpensive sustenance to locals, Mission District eateries have also brought *lomo saltado*, *pupusa* and many other Latino staples to the tastebuds of Bay Area restaurant-goers, while food critics otherwise locked in debate over the latest gourmet dining venue will sometimes devote column inches to the relative merits of Mission District *burritos*. Seeing the district in terms of its food is not a new phenomenon. In a 1923 series for the *San Francisco Examiner* called "San Francisco's

Foreign Colonies", Robert H. Willson described visiting the Mission District where he found a restaurant whose name he refused to reveal lest it be overrun:

> *This little restaurant seats no more than 20 people and therefore it is still possible to pat out the tortillas by hand. The place is so plain and simple in all its appointments that the stranger will be astounded by its cuisine. A bowl of sopa de verduras and a plate of tortillas, fresh from the fire; a salad of lechuga y tomates; chiles verdes, with just a tang of the cebolla; a plate of chiles rellenos con queso, the sweet green peppers stuffed with cheese, fried in batter and served with a pungent sauce; and then what you will—carne con chili, tender bits of beef in a real salsa de chili colorado; or enchiladas, home made; or gallina en pippian; or albondigas; or perhaps, a fine breast of pollo en molle. Always at the end, of course, the frijoles, but here such frijoles as make of the common bean a delicacy fit for the epicure.*

Aside from its food, another highly visible aspect of the Mission District are the murals, which bring banks of color to the sides of shops, banks, schools, and seemingly any flat and upright surface. Now celebrated and formally adopted by the city as part of its cultural heritage, the earliest Mission District murals evolved through the efforts of privately-funded artists' collectives, the most celebrated (their fame largely carried by word of mouth) concentration appearing in Balmy Alley, between 24th and 25th Streets, during the 1970s and 1980s. Reflecting the time, many of these groundbreaking works provided pithy visual comments on US policy in Central America.

Seen throughout the neighborhood, murals can be witty, satirical or politically provocative whether depicting local scenes, Latin American history, commenting on local or international affairs, or aiding community awareness of dangers such as drunk driving. Arrivals at the Mission Street BART station are greeted by an expansive example showing faceless figures apparently supporting a BART train on their backs, an allusion to the controversy surrounding the extending of the transit system to the district.

One of the artists on the BART project, Michael Rios, also created one of the district's biggest and boldest murals, *Aspire To*

Inspire: Tribute to Carlos Santana, spread across three buildings at Van Ness Avenue and 22nd Street. Against a background that fuses Aztec and San Francisco motifs, musicians including John Lee Hooker, Jimi Hendrix, Miles Davis, John Coltrane, and Bob Marley are depicted as heroes and role models, as is Carlos Santana. Born in Mexico, Santana played as an eleven-year-old guitarist in the clubs of Tijuana but put together his first band in San Francisco, where he had moved with his family and learned English while attending Mission High School. Santana's fusing of rock music and Afro-Caribbean rhythms with his eponymously named band made a spectacular impact at the 1969 Woodstock festival and led him to worldwide success, selling millions of albums. Santana's eschewing of the trappings of the rock star lifestyle in favor of a more spiritual path earned many admirers, while his renewed success and scooping of industry awards for his album *Supernatural* in 2000 heightened his local esteem.

Despite the fact that many immigrant arrivals were college-educated, the Mission provided the bedrock of the city's unskilled labor force for decades, while enduring high unemployment and disproportionate concentrations of people living beneath the poverty line. From the late 1970s, low rents and easy connections to the rest of the city encouraged a mini-bohemia to develop around Valencia and 16th Streets, with a proliferation of cafés hosting poetry readings and writers' workshops, a period which also saw the arrival of women-orientated shops and nightclubs.

By the late 1990s, however, the character of the Mission District was being undermined by the growth of the Internet- and technology-based economy. With many people coming to San Francisco and its surrounds to join the expanding ranks of multimedia and dotcom companies based in neighboring SoMa, local landlords saw the potential of converting low-rent family homes into expensive loft-style apartments aimed at the beneficiaries of the technology boom, which forced locals to commute to Mission District jobs from homes much further afield. Meanwhile, in a more traditional spread of gentrification (to the horror of Valencia Street locals, the immediate area was described as "the hippest in America" by *Vanity Fair* magazine), chic cafés and clothing boutiques were appearing and, by the time of the sharp downturn of the e-economy during 2000, the future of one of San Francisco's most distinctive neighborhoods seemed to be hanging by a thread.

Chinatown

The dragon-tailed lampposts, steamy dim sum shops, herbalists and hard-to-find temples of Chinatown still serve the Chinese community, even though most of San Francisco's Chinese live outside the area. Some only return to visit the market stalls of Stockton Street, bringing traffic to standstill on Saturdays, while the abundance of Grant Avenue gift shops offering woks, meat cleavers and souvenir chopsticks attests to the neighborhood's immense tourist appeal.

Chinatown and the Chinese were not always so warmly embraced. Describing the city in 1852, *The Annals of San Francisco*, reported: "The manners and habits of the Chinese are very repugnant to Americans in California. Of different language, blood, religion and character, inferior in most mental and bodily qualities, the Chinaman is looked upon by some as only a little superior to the negro, and by others as somewhat inferior." Herbert Asbury's otherwise engaging and informative *The Barbary Coast*, written in the 1930s, loses its balance writing about the "yellow torrent" and a "deluge of yellow men" from the "Flowery Kingdom" when describing the Chinese influx into California during the gold rush. Or as Asbury outlined it with barely concealed contempt: "The Chinese invasion of San Francisco and California began in the summer of 1848, about five months after the discovery of gold at Sutter's Fort, when three frightened subjects of the Son of Heaven—two men and a woman—disembarked from the brig *Eagle* and vanished in the foothills behind Yerba Buena Cove."

Asbury's "frightened subjects" were a precursor to what by 1852 were 22,000 Chinese in California, growing to 71,000 by 1879. A handful of Chinese merchants, established in San Francisco from its pre-US years, helped spread to China news of the gold discovery and the need for workers. With their home provinces wracked by famine and war, many Chinese viewed *Gum San*, or "Gold Mountain", as California became known, as promising sufficient riches to make the journey worthwhile. In return for a cut of future earnings, the merchants (banded into various fraternal organizations and effectively functioning as a Chinese embassy) guaranteed employment, assistance to sick workers, and return travel to China. Handbills distributed in China promised: "Nice rice, vegetables and wheat all very cheap. Three years there will make poor workman very rich and he can come home at any time. Everything nice to make man happy... Don't heed wife's counsel or the threats of enemies."

On arrival, some stayed in San Francisco to provide much-needed services such as cooking, boot making and laundry. The latter became a staple occupation, aided by a fresh water shortage and high prices that led to some gold miners sending their dirty clothes to Hawaii or Hong Kong to be cleaned. The first Chinese laundry opened in 1851 on the corner of Grant and Washington Streets and was so popular that it was soon working round-the-clock.

Many more Chinese headed inland to the gold-producing areas where by 1852 one in ten of the state's 250,000 miners were of Chinese origin. The discovery of gold brought settlers from all over the world, but the only ethnic group to be subject to the $20-a-month Foreign Miners License Tax—introduced from 1851 and theoretically imposed on all non-US workers—were the Chinese, and paying it greatly reduced their income. This, coupled to gold mining becoming more reliant on machinery than manpower, encouraged the Chinese to leave the gold fields and seek work in San Francisco.

In 1865, however, railroad baron Charles Crocker put an all-Chinese group of laborers to work on the construction of the Central Pacific Railroad. Part of the monumental undertaking that became the first fixed link between the US's east and west coasts, the railroad had to cross some of the country's most remote and mountainous areas. So bad were conditions during the winter of 1866 that two Chinese workers were buried fifty-feet-deep by a snowfall and were reportedly discovered frozen to death but still upright and holding their shovels. Despite the racial hostility directed towards them, ten thousand Chinese toiled on the railroad, earning a reputation as reliable workers that prompted descriptions such as that of Henry K. Norton who, in a volume of Californian history published in 1924, observed:

Probably the most conspicuous characteristic of the Chinese is their passion for work. The Chinaman seemingly must work. If he cannot secure work at a high wage he will take it at a low wage, but he is a good bargainer for his labor and only needs the opportunity to ask for more pay... With proper instruction their industrial adaptability is very great. They learn what they are shown with almost incredible facility, and soon become adept.

Completed to much fanfare in 1869, the railroad was expected to lift California out of its post-gold rush slump. Instead, it enabled eastern companies to undercut their western counterparts, leading to a further downturn and the loss of many jobs. Seeking a scapegoat, labor unions blamed the Chinese who by 1872 held half the factory jobs in San Francisco while Chinatown merchants enjoyed manufacturing monopolies on products such as bricks and cigars.

Most Chinese became members of a "tong", an American term for a Chinese-American secret society. Besides looking after their members' interests, Tongs provided a means for settling disputes in the absence of proper legal representation (Chinese were effectively excluded from the US legal system) and controlled Chinatown's gambling, prostitution, and opium supply. Such vices were decried as immoral by outsiders but Chinese workers, single males who sometimes worked twenty hours a day and were denied any other form of pleasure, viewed them as necessities. The popular press whipped up "yellow peril" stories, stoking anti-Chinese feeling, while pamphlets warned of "The Establishment of a Heathen Despotism in San Francisco: Nations of the Earth Take Warning" and described the Chinese as an "Enslaved and Degraded Race of Paupers, Opium-eaters and Lepers." Opium dens in particular provided great scope for lurid reporting. Charles Warren Stoddard wrote:

We enter by a small door that is open for a moment only, and find ourselves in an apartment about fifteen feet square. We can touch the ceiling on tiptoe, yet there are three tiers of bunks placed with headboards to the wall, and each bunk just broad enough for two occupants. It is like the steerage in an emigrant vessel, eminently shipshape. Every bunk is filled; some of the smokers have had their dream and lie in grotesque attitudes, insensible, ashen-pale, having the look of plague-stricken corpses...

We address them, and are smiled at by delirious eyes; but the ravenous lips are sealed to that magic tube, from which they draw the breath of a life we know not of.

By contrast, a rare and comparatively reasoned Westerner's insight into Chinatown life was provided by Jesse B. Cook, assigned to the Chinatown squad before becoming San Francisco's Chief of Police in 1908:

The opium den was another thing that the Chinese resorted to because they had no other place to go. At that time nearly every store in Chinatown had an opium layout in the rear for their customers. All the Chinaman had to do was bring his opium. In those days the Chinese were allowed to smoke opium, provided they did not do so in the presence of a white man. If a white man was present it meant the arrest of all who were in the room at the time... Opium has a peculiar, sweet smell, not at all distasteful, and many times when coming home from Chinatown after going through dens, people in the cars sitting near me, would be sniffing, smelling the opium in my clothes and wondering what it was. When I got home it would be necessary to undress in an outer room and air my clothes to get the opium fumes out of them.

Of the clashes between rival gangs that became known as the tong wars, Cook wrote:

During my first term in Chinatown in 1889, the Chinese did not use revolvers in their tong wars, believing they made too much noise. A lather's hatchet sharpened to a razor edge was their chief weapon. With this they could chop a man all to pieces and generally, when they did leave him, would drive the hatchet into his skull and leave it there. The men using these weapons were known as Poo Tow Choy, or little hatchet men. One night at the corner of Jackson and Washington Streets, two Chinamen with hatchets chopped another all to pieces. This happened about six feet behind a Chinaman who was selling peanuts on the corner. Although this man was questioned, he insisted that he did not know anything had happened nor that anyone had been killed, in spite of the fact that the back of his clothes was all spattered with blood. The murder-

ers were later captured, sent to the penitentiary for life but about ten years after were deported to China.

In ending—there is nothing in the world that will make a China-man "madder" than for anyone to say to him "Sock Nika Tow," which translated means "Chop your head off."

With the US suffering economic depression, the anger directed at San Francisco's Chinese took legal form in the 1882 Exclusion Act, which outlawed further Chinese immigration to the US for the purposes of finding work, and by the subsequent Scott Act prohibiting the immigration of Chinese women except as wives of merchants, a measure preventing the expansion of the US's existing Chinese population. Between 1852 and 1874, Chinese were also prevented from testifying in court against a Westerner: an inequality of which Mark Twain noted: "Any white man can swear a Chinaman's life away but no Chinaman can testify against a white man."

Nonetheless, Chinatown even then (when it chiefly comprised of flimsy wooden buildings divided by narrow alleyways) was attracting the adventurous. Prominent New York-based journalist Charles Nordhoff, visiting San Francisco in the early 1870s, advised: "Ladies and children may safely and properly walk in the main streets of the Chinese quarter by day. The tourist who wishes to investigate farther should get a policeman stationed among the Chinese to show him around after dark. He will see some strange and unpleasant sights; and ladies and children must be excluded from this tour." Nordhoff's investigations revealed:

…in cellars, they make cigars, in shops they work at sewing machines— the men, I mean; here in an entryway, the Chinese cobbler cobbles a shoe, the boy waiting at his side to put it one when it is done. Here are eating houses where smoked duck, pigs' heads, livers and gizzards of fowl, whole chickens cooked in oil, sodden pork and sausages are sold. Here is their church, or temple, with queer images of wood and tinsel, before which sandalwood is burned or small firecrackers are sparkling.

Nordhoff also attended the Chinese theater and noted the strange music that accompanied the show, as in more colorful manner did *The*

Annals of San Francisco which described the musical entertainment in a Chinatown gambling den:

> *At the innermost end of some of the principal gambling places, there is an orchestra of five or six native musicians, who produce such extraordinary sounds from their curiously shaped instruments as severely torture the white man to listen to. Occasionally a songster adds his howl or shriek to the excruciating harmony. The wailings of a thousand love-lorn cats, the screams, gobblings, brayings, and barkings of as many peacocks, turkeys, donkeys, and dogs,—the "ear-piercing" noises of hundreds of botching cork-cutters, knife-grinders, file-makers, and the like,—would not make a more discordant and agonizing concert than these Chinese musical performers in their gambling-houses.*

One visitor delighted with Chinatown was Oscar Wilde. Recounting his trip in an 1883 lecture he said: "Chinatown, peopled by Chinese labourers, is the most artistic town I have ever come across... In the Chinese restaurant where these navvies meet to have supper in the evening, I found them drinking tea out of china cups as delicate as the petals of a rose-leaf... When the Chinese bill was presented it was made out on rice paper, the account being done in Indian ink as fantastically as if an artist had been etching little birds on a fan."

Attacks on Chinese were frequent, and two orchestrated mob attacks on Chinatown occurred in 1877, spearheaded by Denis Kearney. Rousing San Francisco workers against what he saw as the twin threats of China and capitalism, Kearney and his followers also threatened the wealthy occupants of Nob Hill. The violent nature and lack of education of his followers led to a nickname, "hoodlums", which passed into common usage to describe a lawless youth or petty gangster.

Aiding the perception of Chinatown as a place of great exotic appeal was the fact that its residents were, until the overthrow of dynastic rule in China, compelled to wear traditional clothing with men's hair tied in queues. Such rules were upheld by the emperor's spies who would pass word of any transgressors back to China where their family would face the consequences. Conflicting with this, however was a Board of Supervisors ruling in 1876 that every imprisoned male would have his hair "cut or clipped to an uniform length of one inch from the scalp." The law was repealed only after one Chinaman, Ho Ah Kow, who had lost his queue in jail, sued for $10,000 damages.

A New Chinatown

Asbury called Chinatown living quarters "flimsy shacks and odorous cellars", of which "no attempt was made to cleanse them until the bubonic-plague scare of 1901, when health officers invaded the district and fumigated it with three hundred pounds of sulphur." Charles Nordhoff mused: "if the whole Chinese quarter of San Francisco, as it is now arranged, could be blown up with gunpowder, and decent accommodations provided for the people who inhabit it, civilization and Christianity and free government on the Pacific coast would make a great gain."

It was not gunpowder but the 1906 earthquake and fire that razed the district, easily consuming its wooden shacks. As the city was rebuilt, suggestions that the new Chinatown should be located on the city's fringes at Hunter's Point were rooted partly in anti-Chinese feeling and also in the knowledge that Chinatown had occupied what by now was extremely valuable land. The relocation proposal was met with annoyance at the highest level in China, where the government asserted that the Chinese consulate would, no matter what, be rebuilt on the site of the old Chinatown. Fearing loss of its valuable trade with China, the city authorities decided Chinatown would stay where it was.

The other great change for the Chinese and Chinatown was the overthrow of the Manchu dynasty in 1913 and the founding of the Chinese republic. Sun Yat-sen, a major contributor to the new China, had operated in San Francisco briefly during 1894 and for a longer period from 1904 (he was permitted to enter despite the Exclusion Act). He espoused republican views through the *Young China* newspaper, which he edited from offices in Spofford Street and later at the Montgomery Building. Sun Yat-sen's time in San Francisco was marked in 1938 by the unveiling of Beniamino Bufano's stainless steel and pink granite sculpture in the small and easily overlooked St. Mary's Square, which also holds a Chinese-American war memorial, across California Street from St. Mary's Cathedral.

As it arose in the 1920s, the new Chinatown acquired a unique form of architecture. Sometimes termed "San Francisco Chinese", the style originated with two prominent Chinese merchants commissioning (in the absence of any local Chinese architects) the firm of T. Patterson Ross and A. W. Burgen to adapt traditional Chinese features to American materials and building regulations. The result was a riot of chinosiserie, lantern-style street lights, and spectacular additions such as the 1907 Chinatown Telephone Exchange, 743 Washington Street (now housing a branch of the Bank of Canton), and the Sing Chong Building, 601-615 Grant Avenue, its pagoda towers beckoning tourists through what is now the Chinatown Gateway, a 1970 addition

at the junction of Grant Avenue and Bush Street. Another break from the past was the re-naming of Dupont Street as Grant Avenue, presumably to lose connotations of vice, Dupont Street having been the site of numerous brothels.

Paper Sons, Paper Daughters

The 1906 fire destroyed the city's public records and led authorities to fear an influx of "paper" sons and daughters, Chinese claiming kinship with a US resident having bought false documents in China and learning by rote the details of the family they claimed to be a part of. While it is likely that relatively few Chinese arrivals were attempting to deceive US immigration officials in this way, guilt was assumed and it was up to the would-be immigrant to prove their innocence through a series of interrogations.

The new arrivals were held (as were Japanese and Koreans) at Angel Island. With 740 rocky acres making it the largest island in San Francisco Bay, Angel Island was a former military prison that became an immigration processing center in 1910. Family members were separated and lived in segregated dormitories, sanitary conditions were poor, and the camp was surrounded by barbed wire and watched over by armed guards. Some arrivals passed through successfully and quickly, others were held for weeks, sometimes months, before a decision was made on their future. Some applicants denied entry committed suicide rather than endure loss of face by returning to China.

An interpreter employed at the island recalled: "I used to think it was easier for a camel to enter the eye of a needle than for a Chinaman to pass through the Golden Gate." In the thirty years to 1940, 175,000 passed successfully through Angel Island but not without bitter memories. Some wrote or carved despairing poems onto the walls, later discovered by chance by a park ranger (the island became a state park in 1958). One reads:

America has power, but not justice.
In prison, we were victimised as if we were guilty.
Given no opportunity to explain, it was really brutal.
I bow my head in reflection but there is nothing I can do.

Although the Exclusion Act was not fully repealed until 1965, the entry of China into the Second World War as an enemy of Japan improved relations with the US, and a small annual quota of Chinese immigrants was permitted. This reversed Chinatown's decline in population as, subsequently, did a soaring birthrate.

Celebrated Chinatown

The new-look Chinatown and the new-look Chinese, now able to wear Western clothes and integrate with the rest of the city, encouraged the promotion of Chinatown as a tourist destination. Souvenir shops lined Grant Avenue, while restaurants, teahouses and nightspots aimed squarely at Westerners were tucked into a network of streets and alleys. Crooner Frank Sinatra and actor Ronald Reagan were among the celebrity guests as too, after a concert in the city in 1964, were the Beatles who arrived for a drink at the Rickshaw Bar (long since closed) on Ross Alley. The transformation from mysterious ghetto to tourist-friendly neighbourhood seemed complete when columnist Herb Caen lauded its quirky charms:

Chinatown. Where you instantly label yourself a 'tourist' if you order chop suey—an American invention. Where the clock in the Western Union office tells you what time it is at the moment in China. Where an Italian newsboy named Chester has been peddling newspapers at the corner of Jackson and Grant Avenue for so many years he can now speak Chinese—with an Italian accent. Where a spot called the Shanghai Low casts modesty and even credibility to the winds by advertising: 'A Visit To Our Cafe Is The Equal Of A Visit To China'. Where Lum & Co. operate a grocery that, for no reason at all, is called 'The Italian Grocery'.

Among the restaurants was Sam Woh's, still at 813 Broadway and continuing its tradition of inexpensive, mediocre food and rude service despite the death of its famously grouchy waiter, Edsel Ford. The restaurant is one of the more unlikely footnotes in the story of the Beats, being the spot chosen by Jack Kerouac, Gary Snyder, Kenneth Rexroth, Allen Ginsberg and others to unwind after Ginsberg debuted the epoch-making *Howl* at the Six Gallery. A modern-day restaurant guide concludes: "If you like abuse with your noodles, Sam Woh's is the place."

In literature, too, Chinatown's image was changing. An entire genre of "yellow peril" literature, epitomized by Sax Rohmer's absurdly caricatured villain Doctor Fu Manchu, was replaced by more realistic fare. A start had been made in 1912 with the publication of Sui Sin Far's short story collection, *Mrs Spring Fragrance*, which included a table-turning comment from a Chinese character proposing to write a book on Americans: "Ah, these Americans! These mysterious, inscrutable, incomprehensible Americans!" Published in 1945, Jade Snow Wong's *Fifth Chinese Daughter* continued the theme of women writing about Chinatown realities, as did Amy Tan in the 1980s with the enormously popular mother-daughter novel, *The Joy Luck Club*. Meanwhile, C.Y. Lee's 1956 *Flower Drum Song*, a novel inspired by Grant Avenue ("the colourful thoroughfare stimulates a man's imagination") was adapted into a hit Broadway musical by Rodgers and Hammerstein. Chinese life outside Chinatown provided a background for Gus Lee's 1991 *China Boy*, a semi-autobiographical account of growing up in a 1950s San Francisco "proudly conscious of its untempered and eccentric internationalism"; more precisely in Haight-

Ashbury, where: "I was trying to become an accepted black male youth... This was all the more difficult because I was Chinese."

As the Chinese community spread further across San Francisco, the narrow confines of Chinatown drew newer arrivals from the Philippines (by the 1970s, a tiny "Little Manila" was established on the fringes), Korea, Laos, and Vietnam. Grant Avenue remains the public face, with shops laden with everything from jade statues to decorated chopsticks. Running parallel, Stockton Street's market stalls cater to a more Chinese clientele in a pedestrian crush that deflects attention from remnants of earlier times, such as the 1857 Kong Chow Temple, which, in a fine example of a Chinatown mixed-use building, occupies the top floor of no. 855 while the ground level houses a post office.

The oldest Chinese temple in the US is found amidst the painted balconies of Waverly Place: the Tien Hau, at the top of no.125, which dates from 1852. The temple is devoted to the Goddess of Heaven and Sea, popular in early Chinatown for offering protection to travelers, sailors, and prostitutes among others. While Buddhist and Confucian beliefs remain strong among the Chinese community, many converted to Christianity in the late1800s, attracted, in part, by a promise of free English lessons.

In recent decades, many Chinese have left the confines of Chinatown for larger homes, particularly in the Richmond district, where Chinese businesses predominate along Clement Street. Meanwhile, a new generation of Chinese-American architects have made a mark on Chinatown, none more dramatically than Clement Chen with the 1971 Chinatown Holiday Inn, a concrete tower adorned with Oriental flourishes that looms above Portsmouth Square. The square, unrecognizable as the place where the captain of the *Portsmouth* came ashore in 1846 to proclaim US rule in San Francisco, now forms the top of an underground car park and holds the concrete benches that provide elderly Chinese with an impromptu venue for games of chance.

Japantown

In contrast to Chinatown's usually congested streets, Japantown is a quiet and relatively unvisited pocket of the city, more a reminder of San Francisco's Japanese community than a part of it. Walled by the miserable Geary Expressway and occupying just six blocks, Japantown contains Japanese religious sites, shops and restaurants, but only a few hundred of San Francisco's 12,000 Japanese-Americans live in the neighborhood. The community has, however, enjoyed a significance greater than its numerical size, due in part to the value of the city's trade with Japan.

Although a handful arrived in California through unofficial means, citizens of Japan were prohibited from emigrating until 1868. From then, a trickle (the 1870 census showed 33 of the US's 55 Japanese living in California) arrived to work on California's farms, their skills in growing fruit and vegetables often embarrassing the established farmers. Further resentment towards them stemmed from the Japanese habit of seeking to lease land rather than simply toil on it, which led to the state's 1913 Alien Land Law. Under its terms, anyone not eligible for US citizenship (which the Japanese were not) was banned from owning or leasing land. In return for the US-born children of Japanese emigrants being allowed into "white" schools, Japan prevented further emigration of laborers, and in 1924 the US Exclusion Act halted all immigration from Asia.

In San Francisco, where a Japanese consulate opened in 1870, the Japanese became established on the fringes of Chinatown and in an enclave around South Park, numbering 590 by 1890. After the 1906 fire, many Japanese relocated to the fringes of the Fillmore District in the Western Addition, raising the temples, tea-houses and community centers that soon led to the area becoming known as "Japanese Town". Prominent Japanese included Makota Hagiwara (?-1925), the master gardener who had created the majestic traditional-style Japanese Tea Garden for Golden Gate Park. Besides devising the gracious mix of cherry trees, ponds, a five-tiered pagoda, stone lanterns, and winding paths, Hagiwara developed a Japanese tradition by enclosing a printed fortune-telling message inside a pastry cookie, served to patrons with tea. Thereby, the fortune cookie was introduced to the US and, by the 1920s, the idea had spread to the restaurants of Chinatown, soon to became a staple of Chinese eateries throughout the US.

Entrepreneurial, valuing education and family life, the Japanese exhibited traits perfectly in tune with "American" values. Nonetheless, discrimination was rife and their offspring who had graduated through

the US education system commonly found professional jobs denied them and were typically employed in family businesses. This contributed to the tight-knit nature of the community, which had grown fivefold in thirty years but still numbered only 5,280 (out of San Francisco's 636,000 population) in 1940.

"A Jap's a Jap"

On December 7, 1941, Japan's attack on the US Navy's Pacific Fleet at Pearl Harbor drew the US into the World War and brought anti-Japanese sentiment throughout California to fever pitch. The next day, bank accounts of Japanese and Japanese-Americans throughout the US were frozen and community leaders, whether or not US citizens, were arrested and interned by the FBI. In February 1942, President Eisenhower acceded to the demands of military commanders by signing Executive Order 9066, giving them powers to remove persons deemed a risk to security. Anyone of Japanese descent (assessed as having 1/16th or more Japanese blood), regardless of citizenship, was deemed such a risk (rumor suggested the real reason was to prevent the strengthening of Japanese-American dominance in agriculture as farming was expanded during the war), and San Francisco's Japanese population were among the 110,000 ordered to prepare themselves for relocation to inland regions. Even the Japanese Tea Garden in Golden Gate Park was renamed the "Oriental Tea Garden".

On the contentious issue of treating US citizens as enemies, the Western Defense commander, General DeWitt, addressed a House Naval Affairs committee: "It makes no difference whether the Japanese is theoretically a citizen. He is still a Japanese. Giving him a scrap of paper won't change him. A Jap's a Jap." On May 21, 1942, the *San Francisco Chronicle* reported: "Last night Japanese town was empty. Its stores were vacant, its windows plastered with "To Lease" signs. There were no guests in its hotels, no diners nibbling on sukiyaki or tempura. And last night, too, there were no Japanese with their ever present cameras and sketch books, no Japanese with their newly acquired furtive, frightened looks."

It was thought that the Japanese might settle permanently in the relocation areas. Due to the hostility of locals and the reluctance of the Japanese to attempt to forge new lives in some of the US's most inhospitable landscapes, however, this rarely happened and instead the building of "relocation camps" was ordered. Here, the Japanese were held behind locked gates and barbed wire fences, and guarded by armed troops: internment in all but name.

Photographer Dorothea Lange visited one of the camps, Manzanar, in California's Owens Valley. One of her photographs, showing the internees' huts obscured by a dust storm, encapsulated the harshness of the environment. In Dorothy Swaine Thomas and Richard S. Nishimoto's 1946 book, *The Spoilage*, the mood of the imprisoned Japanese is expressed by a Manzanar inmate, Joseph Yoshisuke Kurihara. Born in Hawaii in 1895, Kurihara had neither visited nor had any direct connection with Japan and he had served in the US Army during the First World War:

> *After living in well furnished homes with every modern convenience, suddenly forced to live the life of a dog is something which one can not so readily forget. Down in our hearts we cried and cursed this govern-ment every time when we were showered with sand. We slept in the dust; we breathed the dust; and we ate the dust. Such abominable existence one could not forget, no matter how much we tried to be patient, under-stand the situation, and take it bravely. Why did not the government permit us to remain where we were? Was it because the government was unable to give us the protection? I have my doubt. The government could*

*have easily declared Martial Law to protect us. It was not the question
of protection. It was because we were Japs! Yes, Japs!*

Immediately after the war, Kurihara renounced his US citizenship and
left for Japan among the first group of voluntary deportees in 1946.
Ironically by war's end, the US had convicted just ten people for spying
on behalf of Japan, none of them Japanese. Meanwhile, the so-called
Nisei regiment, mostly made up of Japanese-American volunteers from
Hawaii (with a few from the relocation camps), fought so heroically in
Europe that they became the most decorated regiment in US Army
history. The anger and resentment that simmered in the Japanese
community for decades was alleviated, to some extent, in 1988 by a
formal apology from the US government and the payment of $20,000
to each surviving detainee.

Unhappy Returns
The end of the war did not mean the end of problems for San
Francisco's Japanese community, some of whom were not released for
months after Japan's surrender. Many had been forced to sell businesses
at less than their market value while their homes, left vacant, were soon
threatened with demolition as the city feared the uninhabited area
would become a health hazard. War industries, particularly ship
building, had drawn a new workforce to San Francisco, including many
African-Americans who swelled the population of the Fillmore District
and Western Addition, steadily pushing back the traditional boundaries
of Japantown.

Rather than start afresh in the old area, many returning Japanese
settled instead in the Richmond and Sunset districts, one unforeseen
result of their incarceration being a fuller integration into city life.
Japantown still held community landmarks such as the Buddhist
Church of San Francisco, opened in 1898 and maintained by non-
Japanese converts to Buddhism during the war years. It, like other
religious centers, provided temporary accommodation for returning,
homeless Japanese.

Through the 1950s and 1960s, the increasingly dilapidated
Victorian dwellings of Japantown were razed to make way for the
widening of Geary Boulevard, facilitating the Expressway and Japan

Center, a three-acre indoor shopping mall stocked predominantly with Japanese goods and containing Japanese restaurants. Owned by the Kintetsu Corporation, a gigantic transport, leisure and tourism company, Japan Center's construction forced the closure of many family-run businesses and, not least with its fortress-like appearance, symbolized Japantown's transition from a community base to a shopping destination and sanitized cultural attraction.

Not before time, the late 1990s brought improvement plans, with a park development enhancing the five-tiered Peace Pagoda, previously rising forlornly beside the Expressway; while 1999 saw the return of the artful fountains of Buchanan Mall, a short retail street landscaped by Japanese-American artist Ruth Asawa.

The Western Addition and the Fillmore District

The Geary Expressway created a split within the Western Addition, separating the commercial section known as the Fillmore District from the poorer, mainly residential area south of the Expressway. Originally, the Western Addition had been exactly that: a result of the Van Ness Ordinance of 1858 that permitted the city's grid-plan street system to be extended west of Van Ness Avenue. With spacious homes set around green squares, the area became part of a middle-class suburbia that eventually, combined with Haight-Ashbury, reached as far west as the new Golden Gate Park.

Triggered by the temporary relocation of department stores from Downtown following the 1906 fire, a commercial strip developed around the junction of Geary and Fillmore Streets, becoming known as the Fillmore District. To absorb displaced San Franciscans, many family homes were converted to apartments and the Western Addition population became ethnically diverse, mixing Jews, Filipinos, Russians, Mexicans and others, as well as the city's major concentration of African-Americans, numbering between 4,000 and 5,000 by the late 1930s.

Leidesdorff and Mary Ellen Pleasant

Much earlier, when San Francisco was still Yerba Buena and part of Mexico, a handful of blacks and "mulattos" (typically the offspring of Spanish or Mexican settlers and Native Americans) were among few hundred residents of the settlement. By far the most prominent and influential of these was William A. Leidesdorff (1810-48). Born in the Virgin Islands to a Dutch father and islander mother ("of Negro blood"), Leidesdorff had built a fortune through maritime trade on the New Orleans-New York route before captaining his 106-ton schooner west, landing at Yerba Buena in 1841.

Acquiring Mexican citizenship and a 35-acre land grant, Leidesdorff founded a school, built the settlement's first hotel (optimistically named the City Hotel) and become community treasurer: his 1847 ledger records San Francisco's municipal assets at $4,476. He also raised a home of sufficient grandeur to host civic functions and receive visiting dignitaries. Sue Bailey Thurman's 1952 *Pioneers of Negro Origin in California* says of Leidesdorff: "He had the urbanity of a seasoned diplomat, politician, and man of affairs. His cuisine offered the finest foods and wines and he could boast the only flower garden in all Yerba Buena." Leidesdorff's death, aged 38 in 1848, saw flags lowered to half mast and his funeral cortege acknowledged with a military salute as it traveled to Mission Dolores where he was buried beneath the chapel floor.

As Yerba Buena became San Francisco and the gold rush began, the city saw its first influx of African-Americans. Some were freed black slaves, some had arrived as slaves and bought their freedom, others had escaped from slave-owning states and traveled west. While California's constitution outlawed slavery, a condition of admission to the union was observation of the Fugitive Slave Law, calling for escaped slaves to be captured and returned to their owners.

Some escapees who reached San Francisco (via the secret network known as the Underground Railroad) were installed in jobs and homes by Mary Ellen Pleasant, a woman who, even by the standards of pioneer-era San Francisco, remains an extraordinary enigma almost a hundred years after her death. Varying biographical accounts suggest that Mary Ellen Pleasant (who used several names during her life) was born around 1814 on a slave plantation in Georgia, the daughter of the Virginia governor's son and a voodoo priestess. From Marie Le Veaux, New Orleans' legendary voodoo practitioner, she received instruction in using spiritual methods to benefit the poor at the expense of the rich. After working for several families and assisting in the movement of escaped slaves to Canada, Pleasant avoided her own arrest by moving to San Francisco in 1852.

On the journey she befriended a Scotsman, Thomas Bell, soon to become a prominent San Francisco banker over whom Pleasant would covertly wield considerable influence. Buying and selling properties, facilitating the meeting of rich San Francisco gentleman and eligible young ladies, and finding jobs for runaway slaves in the homes of the city's rich and powerful, Pleasant amassed a fortune and gained unparalleled inside knowledge of the workings of San Francisco. Much of her fortune, mostly gone by the time of her death in 1904, was spent on charitable works and challenging anti-black laws. Most famously, she was instrumental in winning the 1868 "Trolley case", concerning the treatment of black passengers on streetcars, that set a precedent in the California Supreme Court.

Pleasant gained the derogatory nickname "Mammy" from the popular press, which, particularly towards the end of her life, speculated darkly about the source of her wealth—at least some of which derived from blackmailing leading businessmen—and hinted that she may have had a hand in the unexplained death of Thomas Bell. After her own death in 1904, the *San Francisco News* looked back almost fondly, writing in 1935:

> *What old-timer does not remember the lean, erect, shrewd-eyed Negress with her old black straw bonnet, gold hoop earrings, spotless kerchief fastened with a winking moss-agate brooch, moving among the stalls of the old Sutter Street market? Mammy, who was reputed the wickedest woman in San Francisco, who figured in every important lawsuit for nearly half a century, but who lied so cunningly that the most astute lawyer never tripped her.*

Perhaps only in San Francisco could a suspected voodoo practitioner and blackmailer also be remembered, as Pleasant was, as a "mother of civil rights". Near the junction of Octavia and Bush streets (by the site of her mansion, now occupied by a hospice), a sidewalk plaque remembers Pleasant and lies beside six eucalyptus trees that she planted and which, allegedly, she haunts, making sporadic appearances as a black crow.

The Rise of the Fillmore

In the post-slavery era, many African-Americans reached the Bay Area having been employed on the construction of the transcontinental railroad. Some finished up where the tracks did, in Oakland, while others crossed to San Francisco to became part of the growing black population increasingly centered on the Western Addition. Due to the reluctance of white landlords elsewhere to rent to black tenants and the discriminatory practices of federal housing projects, and with homes vacated by the internment of the Japanese, the Western Addition became the main destination of 40,000 African-Americans who arrived in San Francisco for jobs in war-time industries. But while many blacks had left the overt racism of the southern states, they found San Francisco much less the city of equality than they might have hoped.

Black journalist Thomas Fleming filed unpaid reports on the 1934 waterfront strike for the strike-supporting African-American paper *The Spokesman* (at that time no mainstream San Francisco newspaper would employ a black journalist; none did until 1962) and later recalled of the docks:

> *Blacks could only work on two piers in San Francisco. The rest of them? If you even went near them, you might get beat up by the hoodlums. And there were only two shipping lines that you could ship out to work on. During the strike, there were some vigilantes patrolling the entire Bay Area... Apparently they were displeased with some of the editorials we were writing, because we came to work one morning and all the plate glass windows were smashed out. They had gotten inside and smashed the keys on the keyboard of our Linotype machine, and they pasted up a note: 'You niggers go back to Africa'.*

San Francisco's black population doubled each decade from the 1940s to the 1960s and, with its churches, restaurants, businesses, shops and nightclubs, the Fillmore District became the heart of community life. As the jazz clubs of North Beach began vibrating with the new sounds of bebop through the 1950s, the top musicians would frequently cross the city to the Fillmore District, rounding off their San Francisco night with a jam session at Jimbo's Bop City at 1690 Post Street. In *Around The World In San Francisco* (1950), author Leonard

Austin offered a well-meaning if stereotypical observation of Bay Area black life: "It is a world of deep spiritual emotions and simple faith; at times bitter, at times hysterically joyous; the world of healing services, spirituals and blues, of 'bebop' and 'jive talk', of fish fries and barbecued ribs, of hot chitterlings and sweet potato pie."

In the post-war economic slump, however, it was black workers who lost their jobs fastest. Meanwhile, many of the Western Addition's former white and Jewish occupants who had left for suburbia rented their properties to African-Americans. The prevalence of absentee landlords contributed to homes becoming rundown and helped fuel "slum clearance" initiatives that roused much local hostility.

Black Panthers and St. John Coltrane

By 1960, African-Americans accounted for one in ten of San Francisco's population and, aside from the Western Addition, strongly black areas included West Oakland and Hunter's Point, a hilly area on San Francisco's southwestern fringe. The latter was the subject of *Hunters Point: A Black Ghetto*, by Arthur Hippler, which quoted a white policeman's response to any resident threatening to stray beyond its boundaries: "Get back upon the hill where you belong, nigger. If I see your black ass down here again, I'll shoot it off!" Hippler's book provided an alternative report on a three-day riot following a white policeman's shooting of a 16-year-old black youth in Hunter's Point. Spreading into the Western Addition and West Oakland, the disturbance signaled a loss of patience, particularly among young blacks, with established black rights campaigners such as the National Association for the Advancement of Colored People (NAACP) and the Civil Rights Movement.

As bulldozers were carving their way through the Western Addition, destroying black homes and black businesses in the name of urban renewal, two militant black Oakland-based activists, Huey Newton and Bobby Seale, decided to take a more direct approach and founded the Black Panther Party. Originally called the Black Panther Party for Self-Defense, in response to the brutality of Oakland police, the Black Panthers drew inspiration from revolutions in Cuba and China, from Malcolm X, and from a broader anti-establishment mood engendered by opposition to US involvement in the Vietnam War.

Somewhat bizarrely, Newton had also been influenced by student activists in Berkeley; he had been in a police station cell in 1964 at the time of a mass arrest on the Berkeley campus and had witnessed the students' mocking of police procedures.

As branches formed across the US, the Black Panthers contributed enormously to a raising of African-American consciousness, but, not least by carrying guns on a march to the California state capitol in 1967, they generated considerable fear among middle-class whites in general and the FBI in particular, whose director, J. Edgar Hoover, declared them to be "the greatest threat to the internal security of the country". The FBI's pursuit of leading Black Panther figures resulted in several shoot-outs and theatrical courtroom battles, leading to prominent members being killed, imprisoned, or becoming fugitives.

Those who survived often adopted less confrontational, community-based work such as arranging free food and healthcare for the needy and promoting the inclusion of black history studies in school curricula. The Black Panther Party continues to be active throughout the US, and the writings of its members are still discussed. To some young blacks, however, the Panthers even seem to have adopted what they stood against. In 1997 a new Black Panther Party in Texas, advocating armed struggle, fought and lost a legal battle to use the original Panthers' name and logo.

Others in the Western Addition during the 1960s opted for a more spiritual path. Shortly before his death in 1967, saxophonist John Coltrane appeared at San Francisco's Jazz Workshop. One audience member who found the performance particularly inspiring was Franzo Wayne King. A jazz fan from a family of Pentecostal preachers, King had been operating a "listening clinic", also known as the Yardbird Club (after another sax legend, Charlie "Yardbird" Parker), in his living room to spread the joys of the music he regarded as "African classical".

King recalls Coltrane providing him with a "baptism in sound", and it prompted him to found a temple, named the One Mind Temple Evolutionary Transitional Body of Christ which, by the 1980s, had evolved into the St. John Coltrane African Orthodox Church with King ordained as a bishop. Held for 29 years at a Western Addition storefront at 351 Divisadero Street, the church's four-hour Sunday services would find the robed bishop playing sax, accompanied by a drummer, pianist, a gospel choir, and the congregation playing any instruments they cared to bring, mixing improvisation, exultation, and prayer. The financially unsupported church also provided training to local people in music and computer skills, and made free meals for the hungry several times a week. A new landlord and a massive rent increase, reflecting the area's gentrification, drove the church to a new and probably temporary location at 930 Gough Street.

Neither Black Panthers nor prayer could stop the redevelopment of the Western Addition. The project destroyed the commercial and social heart of the black community, while the four-lane Expressway created an unofficial divide between the north and south sides. The former subsequently gained overspill from affluent Pacific Heights and saw Fillmore Street become a trendy shopping strip with upscale clothing and furnishings stores. The south side (now called the Lower Fillmore) simply remained poor, despite efforts to revitalize the area as a Jazz Preservation District, lining streets with trees and markers to the musicians who once graced its clubs, including a massive mural on the wall of the Boom Boom Room at 1601 Fillmore Street, a live music venue opened by blues legend John Lee Hooker in 1997.

Among the new arrivals to the Western Addition in 1951 was Willie Brown, a 17-year-old former shoeshine boy from Texas who would later spend 31 years representing San Francisco at the California Assembly, fourteen of them as Speaker, and who, in 1995, became the city's first African-American mayor. Reflecting on life in the Fillmore District and the impact of the redevelopment, he told a PBS documentary: "It was a devastating blow to African-Americans in San Francisco, a blow from which we, frankly, have never really recovered. There is no true African-American community comparable to what it was in the Fillmore. This great life, that was comparable to the Harlem Renaissance, was destroyed by the redevelopment process."

The Richmond

Between Golden Gate Park and the hills of the Presidio, stuccoed family homes lining the quiet streets give the Richmond the look and mood of typical American suburbia. But amid the 1960s Americana exemplified by Mel's Drive-In, a favorite for traditional milkshakes and burgers, the population includes representatives from most corners of Asia and a diverse assortment of East European émigrés, some of whom worship beneath the onion domes of a Russian Orthodox cathedral inside which lies the body of a saint.

Arriving via Alaska, the first recorded Russian in San Francisco (then Yerba Buena), was Nikolai Petrovic Rezanov, a Tsarist diplomat appointed head of the Russian-American Fur Trading Company. Settling in 1806, Rezanov became betrothed to the 16-year-old, Donna Concepción, daughter of Yerba Buena's *comandante*. In a much-romanticized tale, Rezanov died while returning to Russian to seek the Tsar's permission to marry. His intended learned of his fate much later and was only able to cope with her grief by becoming a nun and devoting herself to charitable works. The doomed romance inspired a poem from Bret Harte and *Rezanov*, a 1906 novel by Gertrude Atherton ("Theirs was one of the few immortal loves that reveal the rarely sounded deeps of the soul while in its frail tenement on earth.").

San Francisco's first Russian settlement, of around fifty families, established itself in Potrero Hill during the second half of the nineteenth century. Some had fled conscription into the Tsarist army, many were dissenters from the Orthodox Church. As well as Russian Baptists, they included Doukhobors, Subbotniks and members of pietistic sects such as the Molokans. Most observed the peasant lifestyles they had been used to, keeping chickens, goats and sheep, and building makeshift steam baths in their backyards. Such practices lasted into the 1950s, and Sundays in the neighborhood, as described by Ben Adams in *San Francisco: An Informal Guide*, were a scene of "Molokan and Baptist churches... filled with bearded patriarchs and their shawl-draped wives."

The success of the Bolsheviks in 1917 brought educated and aristocratic Russians to San Francisco, largely from the officer ranks of the defeated White Army, who settled around Sutter and Divisadero

Streets. To this area and the neighboring Richmond were drawn Chinese-born Russians following the rise to power of Mao Zedong, among them Shanghai businessmen who carried their money with them and looked to invest it in new Richmond district businesses. From the opposite direction came East Europeans displaced at the end of the Second World War, including Czechs, Slovaks, Poles, and Hungarians. Parts of Geary and Clement became filled with East European cafés, bringing to the culinarily adventurous San Franciscan, already well-acquainted with Asian fare, new experiences such as *sashlik* and *pelmeni*, and giving restaurant reviewers the chance to crow: "you can't beat piroshki to take home at 15 cents each." Describing Richmond eateries, Margot Patterson Doss wrote of: "Hungarian foods as lush as Zsa Zsa Garbor and every bit as tempting."

In the early 1960s one of the most revered figures of the exiled Russian Orthodox Church arrived in the Richmond. Born in Russia in 1896, John Maximovich had risen through church ranks, serving in France and China where he facilitated the transport of several thousand Russians to the US. Already credited with performing miracles and frequently referred to as a saint, Archbishop John (as he then formally was) was given the task of healing rifts within the San Francisco Russian community and solving problems that were delaying completion of the new Holy Virgin Cathedral of the Church-In-Exile on Geary Street. At the latter at least, John was successful. A biography of the archbishop records the cathedral's 1964 opening:

The elevation of the magnificent crosses, the grandeur of which is visible when sailing in the San Francisco Bay, was proceeded by a solemn procession (over a mile) with masses of people participating. The procession was almost cancelled due to heavy rains, but the Saint, without any hesitation, led the procession with hymns into the drenched streets of the City. As the procession began the rain stopped. The crosses were blessed in front of the new cathedral and when the main cross was elevated, the sun broke through and a dove lighted upon the brightly shining symbol of Christ. This visible triumph of the elevating of Orthodox crosses, symbols of Christ's victory, shining on the hills of a contemporary Babylon where Satanism has been openly professed, was the crowning victory of the life of the Saint on earth.

The gold-leaf encrusted domes of the cathedral (also known as The Joy of All Who Sorrow) catch the eye above the rooftops of the Richmond, but resplendent though they are, they do little to suggest the incredible beauty of the interior where the walls are lined by icons, religious paintings, and mosaics, and lit by a voluminous chandelier. The room is unknown to most San Franciscans, closed to all but those who attend Mass, with photography forbidden (as is speaking and the wearing of skirts). The hushed, reverential atmosphere stems partly from the fact that the body of John himself (he died in 1966) has lain here for 25 years in the ornate crypt and now in a coffin on the main floor.

The return of San Francisco's Japanese community following its incarceration during World War II found many opting for the Richmond district rather than returning to the much-changed Japantown. Similarly, as San Franciscan Chinese became able to, they left the usually cramped accommodation of Chinatown for affordable and much more spacious homes in the Richmond. Parts of the neighborhood, particularly, the commercial strip of Clement Street, were dubbed the "New Chinatown" as they gained Chinese shops and restaurants. A walk along the street today reveals a Pan-Asian diversity rich even by San Franciscan standards. Alongside Chinese and Japanese eateries are cafés and restaurants offering Malay, Singaporean, Thai, Cambodian and Vietnamese cuisine, while some employ chefs sufficiently dexterous to combine several—if not all—of these at once.

North Beach

Now compressed by an expanding Chinatown and tourist overspill from Fisherman's Wharf, North Beach was settled in the late 1800s by Italians who made it the base of the city's soon-to-be pre-eminent ethnic group. The old days are remembered chiefly by a dwindling number of enduring family businesses, including some of the cafés for which North Beach became renowned, and a couple of long-serving churches.

Originally North Beach lived up to its name, defining the city's northern waterfront with a sandy beach. Local wharves were worked by a multicultural mixture spanning Portuguese, French, Basque, Spanish, Mexican, Chilean and others, who occupied low-rent apartments in a breezy valley between Telegraph and Russian Hills. Landfill extended the district several blocks north to what became Bay Street and the population steadily dispersed. The creation of Columbus Avenue, named after the Genoa-born explorer and cutting a busy diagonal scythe through the right-angled streets, encouraged the easy northward spread of a small Italian population that had taken root beside Portsmouth Square.

From the 1890s, poverty in their homeland encouraged Italians to settle in the US. In San Francisco, Italians made up 5,000 of the 300,000 population in 1890 but forty years later accounted for nearly one in ten of the city's 634,000 people. North Beach was by now characterized by three- and four-story Edwardian homes erected with more speed than finesse following the 1906 fire (one of the great legends of the disaster records parts of North Beach being saved by Italians covering buildings with wine-soaked blankets). It offered affordable housing, while easy access to the bay brought, for many, the opportunity to resume fishing for a living.

At times served by five Italian-language newspapers, North Beach became the nerve center of the Italian-American community and spawned those who shaped the city's future. Already prominent were financiers such as Amadeo Giannini, whose Bank of Italy (the future Bank of America) provided loans to underpin local businesses. In 1912, Giannini's one-time partner and founder of the Transamerica Corporation, locally-born John Fugazi, acknowledged the neighborhood's importance by donating a community center, Fugazi Hall, its rich terra-cotta facade grabbing the eye on Green Street. Still a social center, the hall also provides office space, mounts a small Italian historical collection, and for years has hosted the zany and seemingly ever-running satirical musical *Beach Blanket Babylon.*

Notable San Francisco Italians also included Domingo Ghirardelli (1817-94), whose skills as a *chocolatier* were discovered by the wealthy James Lick who helped create a market for Ghirardelli chocolate in San Francisco. Ghirardelli consequently gave up his adopted Peru and arrived in the city in 1849, opening a chocolate factory in what is now the Fisherman's Wharf shopping complex of Ghirardelli Square.

Naples-born conductor Gaetano Merola (1881-1953) first visited San Francisco in 1906 and in the 1920s staged a popular, if financially ruinous, open-air opera season at the sports stadium of Stanford

University, apparently inspired by the venue's resemblance to the Roman Baths of Caracalla. Settling in the city, Merola founded the San Francisco Opera Company and remained its director until he collapsed and died in 1953 while conducting an outdoor recital of *Madame Butterfly* at Golden Gate Park's Stern Grove. Never a dull character, Merola was once described as "the master of the shrug" and, having discovered a vocally-talented policeman in Santa Cruz, promptly added him to an opera bill as "the singing cop".

One of San Francisco's most charismatic and effortlessly controversial politicians, Joe Alioto (1916-1998) was the son of an Italian-born fish wholesaler and restaurateur who had settled in San Francisco in 1895. Alioto's two-term reign as city mayor began in 1967 and saw a crack down on student protests, the removal of low-income groups from prime locations to speed up the detested "Manhattanization" of the skyline, the boosting of finance and tourism, and many years of embroilment in libel battles against press allegations of Mafia connections.

A cleaner cut North Beach hero was Joe Di Maggio, born in 1914 as the eighth of nine children of an immigrant fisherman from Sicily. Di Maggio played baseball for the San Francisco Seals before being signed by the New York Yankees during 1936 in return for five players and $25,000. Di Maggio's greatness on the diamond (two of his brothers were also noted players) was matched by a gentlemanly and taciturn manner away from it. Spending his winters in San Francisco, Di Maggio acceded to popular demand by renewing his vows to his second wife, actress and sex symbol Marilyn Monroe, on the steps of North Beach's Church of SS. Peter and Paul. Di Maggio's may have seemed the perfect rags-to-riches story but his marriage to Monroe lasted just nine months, reputedly not aided by his expectation that a wife's place, even if the wife was Marilyn Monroe, was in the home. Many thought that Di Maggio assumed Monroe would eventually return to him; he sent flowers to her grave for twenty years after her death in 1962. Hopeless romantics might dwell on the fact that had Monroe stayed at home, she and Di Maggio may have spent their twilight years strolling arm-in-arm through the Marina District, where Di Maggio spent most of his later years with his sister before moving to Florida where he died in 1999.

Built over two decades and completed in 1942, the Church of SS. Peter and Paul, "a monument which glorifies God and reflects honor upon our city, our colony and our far away Italy," faces the north side of Washington Square and offers Mass in English, Italian, and Cantonese. Surely one of the few Christian places of worship to boast the street number 666, the Romanesque church is also unique in having a role in a Cecil B. De Mille film, *The Ten Commandments*, partly filmed here during its construction. The church's facade and its twin towers are gorgeously illuminated at night, casting a spectral glow over the compact greenery of Washington Square.

Just as North Beach has no beach, Washington Square has no apparent connection with George or any other Washington and, with five sides, is not even square. It does, however, have amateur art shows, provides a space for Tai Chi, holds a monument to the city's firemen (part of the bequest of Lillie Hitchcock Coit), a statue of Benjamin Franklin, and an inscribed bench recalling Juana Briones, a woman of legendary kindness in pre-US San Francisco whose 1836 adobe home, approximately at the corner of today's Powell and Filbert Streets, was then the only house between the Presidio and the bay.

The Italian influx into North Beach helped revive the fortunes of the Church of St. Francis of Assisi, its bright Gothic exterior reflecting the morning sunshine from the corner of Columbus Avenue and

Vallejo Street. The first parish church built in San Francisco after Mission Dolores and the first Catholic church in California since the Spanish missions, St. Francis' was founded by the city's French community in 1860. The exterior survived the 1906 fire and the gutted interior was rebuilt. The French congregation gave way, of course, to Italians. Today, most parishioners are Chinese.

Italians brought a plethora of cafés to North Beach. Among those that remain, Caffe Trieste, at the corner of Vallejo and Grant, has been owned by the Giotta family since its 1956 opening and stages opera performances by members of the family on Saturday afternoons. Opera from a jukebox percolates through the conversation at another survivor, Caffe Puccini, squeezed into a triangular space between Vallejo and Green Streets, also valued for its prestigious vantage point overlooking Columbus Avenue and the sketchbooks on its walls contributed by several decades-worth of visiting artists and non-artists. Trieste, in particular, was a favorite haunt of the Beats, including Lawrence Ferlinghetti whose City Lights bookstore still occupies its original premises on the west side of Columbus and, appropriately, carries the best gathering of books by and about the Beats.

Across the slender Jack Keroauc Alley (so-named as a result of a 1970s campaign to get the city to honor its literary heritage; though gone is a huge mural of Arthur Rimbaud and Charles Baudelaire) from City Lights is Vesuvio. The facade of this café and bar still bears the inscription "we are dying to leave Portland, Oregon" as it did when opened in 1949 by Henri Lenoir, a 1930s arrival from France who not only displayed new works by artists but had a Dada-esque liking for creating and exhibiting pieces of his own. These included a "beatnik kit" of beret, dark glasses, and sandals, and many eccentric pieces that formed a museum-like display at his other bar, Specs, long under different ownership but still surviving, along with some of Lenoir's exotica, on tiny William Saroyan Place.

While many Italians remained in the area through the 1950s and 1960s, there was a general exodus to more spacious and comfortable homes across the city as North Beach became the city's nightlife center. Comedy clubs showcased cutting-edge performers such as Lenny Bruce and Mort Sahl; jazz was played in cellar clubs such as The Place; and at the Condor Club the breasts of dancer Carol Doda caused traffic jams along Broadway as the flesh-crazed rushed to see the sensational "topless" entertainment that began in 1964.

A few sex shops and peepshows still cling to Broadway, but much of North Beach's nightlife is now focused on its restaurants, among which only a few convey a convincing sense of the Italian past: the Gold Spike, with simple Italian staples served in large quantities amid a sea of business cards, is one of them. Other landmark businesses include Molinari's Deli, 373 Columbus Avenue, with an artfully arranged window display of meats and cheeses, and the Victoria Pastry Shop, 1362 Stockton Street, unrivaled for multi-tiered wedding cakes.

PART SIX

Turning America on its Head

Since the 1950s San Francisco has repeatedly incubated social, political, and cultural movements that, against all odds and expectations, became sufficiently powerful to challenge convention and bring about significant change in many aspects of life in the city and far beyond. Barely noticed by most San Franciscans when they took place, a handful of incidents and events became the stuff of myth: the poem read from an upturned fruit case that begat the Beat Generation; the Berkeley student removing his shoes and climbing onto a police car roof heralding nationwide campus revolt; the drag queen attack on a cafeteria that was a precursor to gay pride; the LSD-fueled dances which would inspire new music and new lifestyles, and take psychedelia from Haight-Ashbury to the world.

Yet the nostalgic glow that comes with hindsight obscures the fact that such things began with a small group of people and went, even in famously tolerant San Francisco, hard against the grain. Every achievement was a strike against a city establishment that at first resisted, then grudgingly accepted, and ultimately celebrated the changes—as often as not heralding them as yet another example of San Francisco's innovative thinking and warm-hearted inclusiveness.

A Howl in North Beach, 1955

On October 7, 1955, from a makeshift stage in an art gallery near the junction of Union and Fillmore streets, a 29-year-old, sporadically-published poet named Allen Ginsberg began reading an embryonic work called *Howl*. The reading set in motion a chain of events that would not only create the first San Francisco literary movement since the Russian Hill bohemia of the 1890s, but also led many to believe the very fabric of American society was about to be unraveled.

San Francisco offered writers few material rewards. Those seeking fortune and fame were better served by New York, center of US book publishing, or Los Angeles, where the film industry was a ready market for those who could shape their words into screenplays. But the city by the bay did offer something others did not. Arriving in 1927, Kenneth Rexroth recognized what it was, later noting that San Francisco was unique among US cities in not having been settled overland by the "westward-spreading puritan tradition" but instead shaped by "gamblers, prostitutes, rascals, and fortune seekers who came across the Isthmus and around the Horn. They had their faults, but they were not influenced by [religious leader] Cotton Mather."

Born in Indiana, orphaned, and coming of age during the Chicago renaissance of the 1920s, Rexroth (1905-1982) convinced his guardian that street life, bars, and cafés provided a better education than school. Teaching himself Chinese, Greek, Japanese, and Latin, Rexroth became a man of great erudition (some claim he read each new edition of the *Encyclopaedia Britannica* from cover to cover), a poet and journalist of anarchist ideals, and would play an immeasurably important role in the Bay Area literary scene. Described by Carol Dunlap in *California People* as the "ultimate cultural cosmopolite of post-World War II California," Rexroth lived at the legendary Montgomery Block on Portsmouth Square before moving to a six-room apartment at 250 Scott Street in Haight-Ashbury where he hosted weekly seminars drawing the city's prominent writers. To Rexroth, San Francisco was:

...like an untouched Mediterranean village—like St. Tropez or the Cinque Terre in those days—and yet it was a great city, and in its own way not a provincial one but the capital of its own somewhat dated culture... More important, nobody cared what you did as long as you didn't commit any gross public crimes. They let you alone and however much you might have puzzled them they respected you as an artist. At no time in all the years I have lived in San Francisco have I ever met with anything but respect verging on adulation from neighbors, corner grocers, and landladies. They were proud to be associated with an artist or poet. With Greenwich Village landladies or Left Bank concierges, this is simply not true.

Although he was a generation older, Rexroth was seen by the fledgling Beat writers as a like-minded soul, one with the practical benefit of being a talent scout (of sorts) for publishers. Rexroth, meanwhile, was excited by their readiness to break free from literary and social conventions. One of his admirers was Lawrence Ferlinghetti who attended the weekly salons: "We would listen, and we'd ask him questions... He was a very brilliant man and put many of us on our feet with a stance we could grow with." Poet Philip Whalen recalled: "It was always very interesting, because there were young poets there, and older ones, visiting luminaries from different professions and arts. People said it was boring because Kenneth talked all the time. But Kenneth was a marvelous talker, so I didn't mind if there was anybody else famous there or not."

Armed with a letter of introduction from poet William Carlos Williams, Allen Ginsberg made contact with Rexroth on his arrival in San Francisco in 1954, becoming a regular at the weekly get-togethers, which by then had become what Gerald Nicosia termed "a salon for maverick writers and anarchists." These viewed Rexroth "as a 'hip square' and general sponsor of talent." Attending New York's Columbia University in the late 1940s, Ginsberg (1926-97) had befriended Jack Kerouac (1922-69), a sports scholarship dropout, and William Burroughs (1914-97). With them, Ginsberg was discovering Eastern religions, mood-altering drugs, the wild new sounds of bebop jazz, and the pleasures of multitudinous sexual unions. Although the three, and a growing band of kindred spirits, produced very different writing, they were as one in their quest to find an existence of greater meaning than the conformity, conservatism and consumerism of the post-war US. As Cold War paranoia and anti-Communist witchhunts steadily gripped the country, San Francisco bucked the trend, remaining a place of tolerance and possibility that for a short time would provide a safe haven for the free spirits of what became the Beat Generation.

Bizarre as it now seems, Ginsberg briefly embraced the conventional. In San Francisco, he was working as a market researcher and, although he had enjoyed many homosexual encounters, was ensconced in a steady relationship with a woman with whom he lived in a Nob Hill apartment at 755 Pine Street. Years later, he recalled: "I really wanted to get married, settle down and have a life in advertising."

But when the relationship ended, partly through Ginsberg's on-going sexual relationship with Neal Cassady (a talismanic figure among the Beats, depicted as Dean Moriarty in Kerouac's *On The Road*), Ginsberg moved to North Beach to share a Montgomery Street apartment with a Russian painter, Peter Orlovsky, who became his lover and life-long partner.

In a great day for the future counterculture, Ginsberg was made redundant when his job was taken by a computer. Ginsberg himself had suggested a computer would be more efficient and looked forward to the enforced layoff and six weeks of unemployment insurance that would bring time for writing. In August 1955, from a first-floor room at 1010 Montgomery Street in North Beach sitting at an old office typewriter, Ginsberg began *Howl*, determined to write "what I wanted to without fear, let my imagination go, open secrecy, and scribble lines magic lines from my real mind... write for my own soul's ear and a few other golden ears." And he shaped each line into a length matching the length of his breath: a poem to be spoken rather than read, its sound to burst into the air like notes rising and dipping from a free-blowing saxophone.

North Beach's attractions included low-rent apartments, an abundance of cafés and bars, and the camaraderie of City Lights, which opened in 1953. The first bookstore in the US devoted to quality paperbacks, City Lights encouraged prolonged browsing, declaring itself a library for people who buy books. Its name taken from the Chaplin film, City Lights had earlier been the title of a short-lived popular culture journal founded by Peter Martin, a tutor at San Francisco State College. To help finance the venture, Martin invited Lawrence Ferlinghetti (b.1920), at the time a poetry critic (a grand term for what at first were unpaid reviews) for the *San Francisco Chronicle*, to put up $500 as a half share in a bookstore that would occupy the floor beneath the magazine's office. The magazine's demise saw Martin head to New York after selling his share in the bookstore to Ferlinghetti.

The shop was an immediate success and steadily took over more and more of the building it occupies to this day. Open daily until midnight or 2am, City Lights became a natural focal point, described by Ferlinghetti as "not an uptight place but a center for the intellectual

community." Ferlinghetti was keen to move into publishing and used the City Lights name to launch the Pocket Poets series, small books that gathered verses from the luminaries of the Bay Area beginning with his own *Pictures of the Gone World* in August 1955. Across an alley (then Adler Alley, now Jack Kerouac Street) from City Lights, was another friendly haunt, Vesuvio, a bar and café run since 1948 by Henri Lenoir, who encouraged the patronage of the bohemian set with what he described as "the non-bourgeois atmosphere created by the avant-garde paintings I hung on the walls." Up the hill on Grant Avenue, the Coffee Gallery, no. 1358, touted "orgies of poetry", while the "Blabbermouth Nights" at The Place, no. 1546, invited performing poets to compete for daft prizes and free drinks.

North Beach also had jazz clubs, notably the Jazz Cellar on 576 Green Street, which staged Rexroth-inspired poetry and jazz fusions. Some found the North Beach jazz clubs too mainstream; wilder fare was found in less touristic areas such as the Fillmore District and south of Market along Folsom Street, "the little Harlem on Folsom Street", according to *On The Road*, in which Jack Kerouac described a typically frenzied night: "Out we jumped into the warm, mad night, hearing wild tenorman... the behatted tenorman was blowing at the peak of a wonderfully satisfactory free idea, a rising and falling riff that went from 'EE-Yah!' to a crazier "EE-de-lee yah!'"

A dramatic but much less likely influence on Ginsberg was the Sir Francis Drake Hotel at 450 Powell Street. Seeing its silhouette one foggy night and hearing the clanging of a cable car bell, the word

"Moloch" jumped into Ginsberg's mind. The poet entered the hotel's ground-level cafeteria muttering "Moloch Moloch" and using the word (the name of the Old Testament's Semitic deity to whom parents sacrificed their children) and its associated images to fuel Part II of *Howl*, as the poem steadily evolved. In his journals, Ginsberg would later refer to "the vegetable horror of the Sir Francis Drake Hotel."

A very different hotel, the Wentley, situated at 1214 Polk Street, provided low-cost apartments to many of the new San Francisco bohemia, while its ground-floor Fosters Cafeteria gained an unlikely entry into the footnotes of Beatitude for its affordable food and impromptu salons (the hotel also provided a title, *The Hotel Wentley Poems*, for a collection from one of its occupants, John Weiner). It was at the Wentley that Ginsberg and Orlovsky first met, and of their sitting together in the cafeteria, Ginsberg wrote of "a kind of celestial cold fire that crept over us and blazed up and illuminated the entire cafeteria and made it an eternal place."

Six Poets at the Six Gallery

The Six Gallery at 3119 Fillmore Street was a large, uncluttered art show space in what had formerly been an auto repair shop. The October 7 reading had been organized in fits and starts with some of those on the bill only finding out about their appearance when they read about it on handwritten notes which promised a "...remarkable collection of angels on one stage reading their poetry. No charge, small collection for wine, and postcards. Charming event."

Kenneth Rexroth was appointed master of ceremonies and the evening began with the San Francisco-born surrealistic poet Philip Lamantia—whose work had been published by André Breton in 1943—reading prose poems by his friend, John Hoffman, who had recently died from, it was said, an overdose of peyote. Next onto the tiny stage (actually an upturned fruit crate) was Michael McClure, aged 23 and giving his first reading, followed by Philip Whalen, a large man who, as Warren Coughlin, would be described in Kerouac's *The Dharma Bums* as "a hundred and eighty pounds of poet meat."

According to Barry Miles' biography *Ginsberg*, the audience numbered around 150 and comprised the "whole bohemian poetry intelligentsia of the Bay Area... gathered together in one room for the first time, and there was an atmosphere of great gaiety and excitement." Claiming to be too shy to read onstage himself, Jack Kerouac provided encouragement from the floor and later claimed, in a fictionalized account of the night in *The Dharma Bums*: "I was the one who got things jumping by going around collecting dimes and quarters from the rather stiff audience standing around in the gallery and coming back with three huge gallon jugs of California burgundy." Philip Whalen's reading was followed by a short break after which Ginsberg, having freely imbibed of the wine that was being passed around, stepped onto the stage to begin the public debut of *Howl*.

In *Scratching the Beat Surface*, McClure remembered: "It was like a hot bop scene. Ginsberg was real drunk and he swayed back and forth. You could feel the momentum building up. Some of the people started to shout 'Go!' 'Go!'... Ginsberg read on to the end of the poem, which left us standing in wonder, or cheering and wondering, but knowing at the deepest level a barrier had been broken..." Whalen concurred: "Ginsberg getting excited while doing it was sort of scary. You wondered was he wigging out, or what—and he was, but within certain parameters. It was a breakthrough for everybody. The mixture of terrifically inventive and wild language, with what had hitherto been forbidden subject matter, and just general power, was quite impressive." In *The Dharma Bums* Kerouac wrote:

> scores of people stood around in the darkened gallery straining to hear every word of the amazing poetry reading as I wandered from group to group, facing them and facing away from the stage, urging them to slug from the jug, or wandered back and sat on the right side of the stage giving out little wows and yesses of approval and even whole sentences of comment with nobody's invitation but in the general gaiety nobody's disapproval either. It was a great night.

And McClure captured the feeling of inspiration and excitement that *Howl* had provoked: "In all of our memories no one had been so outspoken in poetry before—we had gone beyond a point of no return. None of us wanted to go back to the gray, chill, militaristic silence, to the intellective void—to the land without poetry—to the spiritual drabness. We wanted to make it new and we wanted to invent it and the process of it as we went into it. We wanted voice and we wanted vision."

Kenneth Rexroth was in tears, his wife later telling Ginsberg that he had been waiting all his life for such a moment. Ginsberg had surprised himself with his own power and the power of *Howl*, only the first part of which was then completed. Much later, he would write of his sympathies for Gary Snyder, the final poet who had the unenviable task of following Ginsberg to the stage.

Although the world did not yet know it, what became the San Francisco Poetry Renaissance had begun and what would later be lauded as the Beat Generation had experienced one of its defining moments. In celebratory mood, the poets and their friends headed for Chinatown and dinner at Sam Woh's, a restaurant famous then as now for its rude staff, then continued to North Beach and The Place before concluding the night, in true Beat style, with an orgy. One who was at the reading but didn't join the party afterwards was Lawrence Ferlinghetti. Due to his ownership of City Lights, Ferlinghetti was regarded by Ginsberg (according to Ferlinghetti himself) as "a square bookshop owner". Nonetheless, Ferlinghetti sent a telegram to Ginsberg aping Ralph Waldo Emerson's enthused words to Walt Whitman a century before on his first reading of *Leaves of Grass*. Ferlinghetti wrote: "I greet you at the beginning of a great career. When do I get the manuscript?"

To shape *Howl* into its final form, Ginsberg left North Beach for a small cottage in Berkeley (the subject of "A Strange New Cottage in Berkeley", a poem later included in the *Reality Sandwiches* collection), described by Kerouac in *The Dharma Bums* as a place boasting "a good three speed Webcor phonograph that played loud enough to blast the roof off". A repeat of the Six Gallery event was staged in Berkeley in May 1956. Ginsberg's reading of the now completed *Howl* included the (partly) Sir Francis Drake Hotel-inspired section. Ginsberg yelled lines that included "Moloch whose mind is pure machinery! Moloch whose blood is running money! Moloch whose fingers are ten armies! Moloch whose breast is a cannibal dynamo! Moloch whose ear is a smoking tomb!" and the crowd joined in, booing and hissing at each repetition of "Moloch". In the audience was a New York poet, Richard Eberhart, who wrote an article for the *New York Times Book Review* describing the literary renaissance taking place in San Francisco. Much of the piece, published in September, was devoted to Ginsberg and *Howl*: "Its positive force and energy come from a redemptive quality of love, although it destructively catalogues evils of our time from physical deprivation to madness."

Naked Before the World

Ferlinghetti had sent a copy of *Howl* to the American Civil Liberties Union (ACLU) hoping for support in what he anticipated would be problems with the work's overt sexual imagery (homosexual at that) and what, in other contexts, might be considered obscene language. For the fourth book in the City Lights Pocket Poets series, Ferlinghetti ordered a thousand copies (with Ginsberg wondering if that number would ever sell) to be printed in England and shipped back to the US. At US Customs, 520 copies were confiscated but when the ACLU made it known it would challenge this action, officialdom relented and the book went on sale.

During May 1957, two police officers bought a copy of *Howl* at City Lights and returned to arrest the person behind the counter for selling obscene material and Ferlinghetti for publishing it. Reporting the arrests, a *San Francisco Chronicle* headline declared "The Cops Don't Allow No Renaissance Here." Its account of the trial, which began in August, described "a packed audience that offered the most fantastic collection of beards, turtle-neck shirts and Italian hair-dos ever to grace the grimy precincts of the Hall of Justice." With the aid of the ACLU, Ferlinghetti won the obscenity case with ease. The immense publicity surrounding the trial brought the San Francisco scene to national attention and helped the book become one of the best selling poetry collections of all time, complete with dedications to Kerouac, Burroughs, and Cassady from Ginsberg. These dedications promised that the other poets' books "will be published in Heaven" and there was an introduction from William Carlos Williams concluding: "Hold back the edges of your gowns, Ladies, we are going through hell."

Ginsberg had lived in San Francisco for only three years and he would soon move on. Yet it was San Francisco, and perhaps only San Francisco, where Ginsberg and others could dream and experiment, and find an encouraging, supportive audience while they created challenging and fearless words. Greatly contributing to the poetic success of *Howl* was Ginsberg's openness and honesty, living up to John Clellon Homes' attempt to define Beat writing as something that "involves a sort of nakedness of mind; and ultimately of soul; a feeling of being reduced to the bedrock of consciousness." Also, as Ferlinghetti later remarked, the poem with its uninhibited sexual language made Ginsberg "a worldwide symbol of sexual depravity."

Ginsberg's friends often noted his lack of self-consciousness. At a reading in Los Angeles, Ginsberg challenged a drunken heckler to show his bravery by removing his clothes. As the heckler backed away, Ginsberg took his own clothes off, declaring: "The poet always stands naked before the world."

Beat Goes Beatnik

Ginsberg and Kerouac greeted the national recognition of the San Francisco Poetry Renaissance by leaving the city and going to New York, where the *Village Voice* proclaimed "Witless Madcaps Come Home to Roost." The publicity surrounding the trial of *Howl* and the publication the following year of Kerouac's breathless and perfectly realized novel, *On The Road*, became the cornerstones of what by now was widely known as the Beat Generation: a term first publicly used in a 1952 *New York Times* article by John Clellon Holmes (author of the seminal, if relatively orthodox, Beat novel, *Go*) who credited its first—and appropriately spontaneous—use to Kerouac.

The other important event of 1957 was the Soviet Union's launch into orbit of the first satellite, Sputnik. San Francisco columnist Herb Caen took this as a cue and dubbed the would-be Beats who were beginning to flood into San Francisco as "beatniks" because they were "as far out" as the space craft. Ginsberg referred to "beatnik" as that "foul word" and raged in a letter to the *New York Times Book Review* after a review had used the term in relation to Kerouac: "... if 'beatniks' and not illuminated Beat poets, overrun this country they will have been created not by Kerouac but by the industries of mass communication which continue to brainwash Man." But North Beach *was* being overrun by turtleneck sweaters, sunglasses, and sandals worn by those who looked to ape the Beats only as a brief excursion from more conventional lives. The neighborhood's cheap rooms and literary hangouts became a thing of the past as rents increased and entertainment moved from poetry and jazz towards the "topless era" of the 1960s. Two landmarks that endured and flourished were City Lights and Vesuvio, where a window now displayed a bearded, sunglasses-wearing dummy advertising a "beatnik kit".

Victims of a changing North Beach included the gloriously named Co-Existence Bagel Shop at 1398 Grant Avenue, which, according to Ben Adams' *San Francisco: An Informal Guide*: "opened as a fourth-rate Jewish delicatessen which actually served bagels, it soon turned into a small, smoke-filled bistro which attracted a motley and disparate crowd... young people seeking they knew not what, artists and pseudo artists, organization men trying to escape the grey flannel suit for the weekend, and leather-jacketed boys on motorcycles looking for noise, excitement and a fist fight." It closed partly because of "the beat bartenders who gave away oceans of beer and tons of potato salad." In its place came the Bugle Shop selling, among other novelties, sandals for dogs.

In *On The Road*, Kerouac described leaving San Francisco: "Mission Street that last day in Frisco was a great riot of construction work, children playing, whopping Negroes coming home from work, dust, excitement, the great buzzing and vibrating hum of what is America's most excited city—and overhead the pure blue sky and the joy of the foggy sea that always rolls in at midnight to make everybody hungry for food and further excitement." Ten years on from the events of the book, real life for Kerouac was very different. The now famous author was continually bothered by police (taking out their frustrations over the *Howl* verdict) and by those jealous of his new status as a counter-cultural icon. Gerald Nicosia in his Kerouac biography, *Memory Babe*, states: "What finally drove him out of California was not the police but the new cliques of lookalike pseudo-hipsters... [from whom] he received more challenges than an aging gunfighter."

Kenneth Rexroth wrote in 1957: "There is no question but that the San Francisco renaissance is radically different from what is going on elsewhere... nowhere else is there a whole younger generation culture pattern characterized by total rejection of the official highbrow culture." Yet Rexroth hated being described as the "father of the Beats" and had not missed an opportunity to snipe at Kerouac since one of

Kerouac's friends had an affair with his wife, driving Rexroth to a nervous breakdown. He hated the commercialization of something that to him had been a dissident movement capable of bringing about social change (by July 1959, even *Playboy* was in on the craze, running a Miss Beatnik photo spread). The poetry and jazz fusions he had encouraged had degenerated into "bums with pawn shop saxophones put together with Scotch tape, and some other guy with something called poetry..." Rexroth left San Francisco to teach, and later retire, in Santa Barbara.

Through the 1960s, as San Francisco evolved into a counterculture citadel, Ginsberg would periodically return, becoming a Karmic presence at events such as the Human Be-In of 1967, which he co-organized, and never lost his core beliefs as he became acknowledged as one of the US's greatest poets. Looking back on *Howl* Ginsberg said "I was curious to leave behind after my generation an emotional time bomb that would continue exploding in US consciousness in case our military-industrial-nationalist complex solidified into a repressive police bureaucracy." While in *Ginsberg*, Barry Miles wrote: "Allen single-handedly *willed* the Beat Generation into being by his unshakable belief that all his friends were geniuses."

Across the Bay: Berkeley and the 1960s

Dominated by the 1,230-acre campus of the University of California, Berkeley lies on the east side of San Francisco Bay and is the only place in the US that regularly makes San Francisco look conservative. With a long history of deviation from the norm, Berkeley elected a socialist mayor in 1911, was among the first US cities to approve votes for women, and by the 1920s was swelling its already ethnically diverse population by attracting ten percent of all the US's foreign students.

Founded by pacifist, poet and journalist Lewis Hill in 1949, Berkeley's KPFA became the country's first community-supported radio station and one that, as the mainstream media played its part during the 1950s in generating anti-Communist hysteria, allowed broadcaster William Mandel to host the US's only talk show providing balanced coverage of the Soviet Union. In May 1960, as part of the House UnAmerican Activities Committee's (HUAC) investigations into political subversion in US society, Mandel, along with a few Berkeley students and a greater number of faculty members, was subpoened to appear before HUAC at San Francisco City Hall. When police turned fire hoses on several hundred demonstrators outside the hearings, an action widely reported as protesters being "washed down the steps of City Hall," it served to raise the political awareness of Bay Area students as well as garner public sympathy for the protesters, as did a hamfisted attempt by HUAC and the FBI to present the incident as "a student riot" in a supposedly factual film, *Operation Abolition.* Four years later, Berkeley students were among those who joined the Civil Rights Movement and traveled during the summer break to segregated southern states to assist in the registration of black voters; locally, some joined a successful campaign to force San Francisco hotels to employ black workers.

The Free Speech Movement

Returning to Berkeley in 1964 for a new academic year, students found that a tradition of allowing campus supporters of political groups to campaign from makeshift tables on a patch of ground between Sather Gate and the campus proper (long regarded as a no-man's land where university rules forbidding political activity were not applied) had ended, as building work had made the whole area part of the campus. Believing that their right to free speech was being impinged, fifty students invaded Sproul Hall, the university administration block, on September 30. The impromptu invasion became a sit-in that lasted until 3am, when the participants, ill-prepared for a longer stay, left and organized a free speech protest on Sproul Hall's steps at noon later that

day. In response to the occupation, the university authorities took the unprecedented step of indefinitely suspending eight students.

The free speech issue and the action against the eight students galvanized the campus and the next day, Jack Weinburg, a Berkeley graduate, was among those who gathered before Sproul Hall and defied campus rules by erecting a table from which to hand out pamphlets. Arrested by campus police, Weinburg adopted the techniques of civil disobedience and fell to the ground, forcing police to carry him to a police car parked on the plaza. Within seconds, students sat on the ground around Weinburg forcing the arresting officers to walk around or over them as they lifted Weinburg and eventually placed him in the back of the police car. Surrounded by students, however, the car was unable to move. In a spontaneous gesture, Mario Savio, one of the students involved in the occupation of Sproul Hall, climbed to the roof of the car (having first removed his shoes and mindful of the police request to "be careful of the antennae") to address the crowd. As more students arrived at the scene, other speakers also removed their shoes and spoke from the car roof, as did at least one who sang while accompanying himself with a guitar. With the police car now effectively impounded by students in a protest with no leaders, the situation reached an impasse. Through the day, the crowd was swelled by more students and assorted spectators, including drunken fraternity house members shouting abuse at those surrounding the police car. Savio recalled: "We had a difficult situation: we'd caught a police car, and we didn't know what to do with it." Eventually, a university chaplain climbed to the roof of the police car to defuse a potentially violent confrontation.

The Berkeley police got their car back but the event marked the birth of what became the Free Speech Movement (FSM). With negotiations between the university authorities and students over the future of the suspended eight and other campus issues reaching stalemate (many problems stemmed from the university's regents acting in *loco parentis* to the students), the FSM planned an occupation of Sproul Hall for December 2 and distributed a leaflet reading: "Come to the noon rally (Joan Baez will be there) bring books, food and sleeping bags." On the appointed day, Mario Savio (1943-96) made what would become the Free Speech Movement's landmark speech:

There is a time when the operation of the machine becomes so odious, makes you so sick at heart, that you can't take part; you can't even passively take part, and you've got to put your bodies upon the gears and upon the wheels, upon the levers, upon all the apparatus, and you've got to make it stop. And you've got to indicate to the people who run it, to the people who own it, that unless you're free, the machine will be prevented from working at all!

Led by Joan Baez singing "We Shall Overcome", around 1,500 students entered the administration building intending to stay. Unlike the earlier action, the occupation was equipped with food and supplies and well-organized, with sentries posted to entrances, monitors appointed to each of the four floors, and areas set aside for sleeping, study, film shows and the informal classes of what was dubbed the Free University of California, its curriculum including "Wild Spanish" and the Baez-hosted "Music and Non-Violence".

As the increasingly agitated university authorities made repeated efforts to persuade the occupiers to leave, state governor Edmund Brown put local police forces on alert. The students, however, had lookouts at local police stations in touch with Sproul Hall by walkie-talkie. By 4am, with the likelihood of police action increasing, the occupiers prepared themselves for a tear gas attack. David Lance Goines' *The Free Speech Movement* quotes activist Ron Anastazi: "I was going up and down the aisles pouring water on handkerchiefs and scarves that people were holding up, some of the girls were sitting there holding up embroidered handkerchiefs and kerchiefs, and these kids were just shaking, and I was shaking, we were all so scared. And yet, they were staying there and doing it. That was the most profound moment. I really felt an incredible oneness with everyone; we are not going to give in."

Shortly after 4am, police arrived and over several hours effected what became the biggest mass arrest in California's history, with 773 students taken to prison. As the occupation and arrests became national news, students and faculty members launched a campus strike that would last until December 8, when the faculty formally agreed their support for the FSM's demands. These forced the governing body to lift the student suspensions, amend rules regarding political activity on campus, and adopt a less autocratic system.

Power to the People Park

As the 1960s progressed, Berkeley became a barometer of the social and political unrest spreading through the US. Biased media coverage of the city's first major anti-Vietnam War protest in August 1965 prompted the founding of a community newspaper, the *Berkeley Barb*. Reflecting local feelings more accurately than the established media, the *Barb* at its 1969 peak sold 90,000 copies a week and carried a bizarre mix of radical politics and the kind of sex ads other publications refused. The *Barb* eventually lost its way following a rebellion against its infamously miserly owner (later found to be stashing the publication's profits in a Swiss bank account) by its staff who departed to start the *Tribe*, a similar publication but without the sex ads, which operated for a time from a Berkeley laundromat.

A prominent local issue was the university's razing of older sections of the city to create space for new student dormitories and garages. The gradual loss of historic shingle- and stucco-fronted homes did little to warm the university to the community, and even less when those evicted from the doomed buildings were students and activists. One such land clearing took place in 1968 near the corner of Telegraph Avenue and Haste Street. Intended as a new athletics field, the plot was left undeveloped and quickly became strewn with rubbish and abandoned vehicles. By April 1969, the state of the site prompted local shopkeepers to discuss making better use of the land. Shortly after, the *Berkeley Barb* took up the theme and encouraged people to assemble at the clearing bearing shovels, top soil and "lots of smiles" to create "a cultural, political, freak out and rap center for the Western world." The call was heeded and, on April 20, several hundred turned out to rake the land, lay soil, plant shrubs and trees. First called Power to the People Park, the plot has since been known more simply as People's Park.

The university responded by issuing a formal reminder of its ownership of the land and warned that the park would be fenced off. The arrival, early on May 14, of police-guarded workmen to construct an eight-foot-high chain link around the park led to several thousand students gathering the following day in Sproul Plaza. Demanding the removal of the fence, the students marched along Telegraph Avenue toward the park, where they stopped before the police lines and chanted. Chaos ensued after a fire hydrant was activated, police launched tear gas at the crowd and later fired first birdshot, then the more injurious buckshot. Protesters divided into small groups, some hurling rocks and other missiles at police, some overturning cars. As a result, 128 protesters were wounded, one permanently blinded, while a bystander watching from a rooftop died of buckshot injuries four days later.

Ronald Reagan, the actor-turned-politician who had been elected state governor in 1966 (despite the fact that his only previous political experience was as president of the Screen Actors Guild) and who had earlier spoken out against the FSM, ordered three battalions of the National Guard into Berkeley. They began a 17-day occupation of the campus while enforcing a citywide curfew and a ban on public assembly. Further protests and sporadic outbreaks of violence (and several spontaneous "parks" appearing elsewhere) climaxed on May 20 with at least 800, some accounts suggest several thousand, students gathered in Sproul Plaza being sprayed with CS gas from an army helicopter. Carried on the wind, the gas caused injuries across the whole of Berkeley. Ultimately, destruction of the park was prevented although the fence remained in place until May 1972 when it was torn down during a demonstration against US action in Vietnam.

Still fiercely protected by locals, who forced the removal of volleyball courts built on the park by the university during the 1990s, the park's future continues to be an issue. With a free clothes and food distribution point, the park currently provides a refuge for the poor and homeless, has a children's quarter and a DIY gardening section, while its creation, the continuing battle for its existence, and its place in community history, are recorded by a Telegraph Avenue mural.

The legacy of the FSM, whose success encouraged other student actions across the US as a precursor to large-scale demonstrations against involvement in Vietnam, is perhaps best illustrated by the innumerable political, environmental, and economic campaigns that continue to be publicized from makeshift tables arranged along Sproul Plaza. In 1998, in an intriguing turning of the tables, the prospect of a more formal reminder of the FSM became apparent when the university chancellor, Robert M. Berdahl, acknowledged a $3.5 million gift from a student-radical-turned-computer-software-mogul for a permanent tribute to the FSM (a café/museum and preservation of the FSM archives) with a speech that began:

> *Thirty-three years ago on this campus a student named Mario Savio removed his shoes and mounted the top of a police car to defend the right of free speech, and life has never been the same ever since on the Berkeley campus or any other major university in the United States.*

A Private Revolution: Haight-Ashbury, 1964-7

In the mid-1860s, the area west of Divisadero Street was beyond the formal boundaries of the city and was known as the Outside Lands. Comprising sand dunes and rugged hills, the area had been occupied by dairy farms and by the wooden shacks of squatters, who claimed rights to the land. Some of the newest "squatters" had been installed by property speculators who hoped for substantial profits once the legal complexities of land ownership were settled. In an 1868 compromise, the squatters were granted most of their claim and the rest of the disputed territory went to the city, which planned new streets and earmarked plots for schools, fire stations, and parks, including the future Golden Gate Park.

Carrying the cable cars that connected Haight-Ashbury (named for its two main streets) to the city, Haight Street attracted bars, restaurants, and hotels. Immediately north, a narrow rectangular strip of greenery, the Panhandle, was laid out and became a popular carriage-ride for wealthy San Franciscan families. Another attraction was an amusement park, the Chutes, which opened on Haight Street in 1895. Aided by the development of Golden Gate Park, Haight-Ashbury's popularity soared and through the 1880s and 1890s scores of elegant and spacious Queen Anne homes (together with a smattering of other in-vogue styles) arose, most serving the middle classes as weekend retreats. The new homes encouraged more businesses to open along Haight Street, and by the end of the nineteenth century Haight-Ashbury was established as a well-to-do resort area.

Untouched by the fire of 1906, Haight-Ashbury's ample homes (still today one of the largest groupings of Victorian and Edwardian

architecture in San Francisco) promised refuge to those made homeless by the calamity, and many were converted into apartments to cope with the intense demand. The city's westward expansion steadily engulfed Haight-Ashbury and, in the economic decline of the 1930s, absentee landlords neglected the upkeep of their properties while renting them to low-income tenants. In 1924, Anita Day Hubbard wrote of the "comfortable maturity about the little city San Francisco knows as Haight-Ashbury." Decades later, Jay Stevens described the area as having "tumbled so far down the socioeconomic ladder that by World War II it was considered suitable for worker housing."

Altered States

From the late 1950s, Haight-Ashbury's low rents were attracting students from San Francisco State College and the city's bohemian fringe, such as Kenneth Rexroth who hosted his influential weekly salons at 250 Scott Street. As the one-time jazz and poetry clubs of North Beach became topless bars, Haight-Ashbury promised affordable and characterful accommodation. For less than the price of a North Beach apartment it was possible, according to Charles Perry's *The Haight-Ashbury*, to "rent two floors of an old mansion and get leather wallpaper, expansive window seats and art nouveau stained glass and scrollwork." In *The Grateful Dead*, author Hank Harrison noted: "North Beach, the beatnik ancestral home had more or less been vacated, left to the Mafia and the junkies and the established mercantile heads... the underground spirit had shifted to the Haight-Ashbury and the San Francisco State College... the college was the real functioning nexus; the Haight was a stomping ground, a sort of paradise for the intellectuals to find cheap rent."

A handful of Haight-Ashbury occupants took to wearing vintage clothes (sold for a few dollars at local thrift stores), appearing as pseudo-Edwardian dandies amid the Haight-Ashbury social mix of African-American, Chinese, Filipino, Portuguese and Spanish. Besides treating their homes to a primitive form of period restoration, such as replacing electric light bulbs with gas lamps, the students and bohemians also introduced a completely new element: a mind-expanding drug called LSD.

Created in a Swiss pharmaceutical laboratory in the 1930s, lysergic acid diethylamide (abbreviated to LSD and later to be known on the street simply as "acid") was a hallucinogenic drug able to induce altered mental states in its users. These might include changed perceptions of time and seemingly mystical insights into the meaning of existence. Substances capable of providing broadly similar effects such as mescaline, peyote and psilocybin had earlier excited the Beats; in the 1950s English author Aldous Huxley had, while living in California, sampled mescaline and influentially described the experiences in *The Doors of Perception* and the subsequent *Heaven and Hell*. Using volunteers, the US military (seeking a new psychological weapon or truth serum) and the psychiatric profession had conducted experiments with LSD without reaching any firm conclusions, although a Harvard psychiatry professor called Timothy Leary became so enthused by its potential that he had lost his job for giving LSD to students off campus and set up a rural retreat to explore the drug's life-enhancing potential in a carefully controlled setting.

Among the nascent hippies of mid-1960s Haight-Ashbury, however, LSD suddenly seemed to find its calling. Harrison recalled: "after LSD everything was color; prior to LSD, everything was black-and-white schmaze."

Can *You* Pass the Acid Test?

Among those enrolling at Stanford University's writing course in 1958 was Ken Kesey (1935-2001), who found he could earn $75 a day by participating in drug experiments at the nearby Menlo Park Veterans Hospital. Kesey was dosed with LSD, psilocybin and mescaline, among other substances, in controlled conditions. Working night shifts at the same hospital, Kesey had access to the drugs cabinet and conducted less controlled experiments on himself. He also found time to write a novel that, in 1962, would be published to wide acclaim as *One Flew Over the Cuckoo's Nest*.

Kesey's interest in LSD deepened and to mark the publication of his next novel, *Sometimes A Great Notion*, he decided to update Keroauc's

On The Road by traveling to New York on a wildly-painted bus equipped with living amenities, a powerful sound system, Beat-totem Neal Cassady at the wheel, a sign at the back warning "Caution: Weird Load", and a destination board at the front proclaiming "Furthur". The journey would eventually be documented by Tom Wolfe as part of *The Electric Kool-Aid Acid Test*, recounting the adventures of Kesey and his loose-knit group dubbed The Merry Pranksters.

Although legal, LSD was only officially available through the New York-based pharmaceutical company, Sandoz. Using his homemade laboratory in Berkeley, however, an occasional student called Augustus Owsley Stanley III manufactured what he claimed to be enough LSD for a million and a half doses. As the potency of Owsley's acid and his personal philosophy became widely known, Timothy Leary offered a commendation: "I've studied with the wisest sages of our time... and I have to say that (Owsley), college flunk out, who never wrote anything better (or worse) than a few rubber checks, has the best up-to-date perspective on the divine design than anyone I've ever listened to."

In September 1965 a costumed Kesey and his Merry Pranksters attended a Beatles concert at San Francisco's Cow Palace, hoping to turn the audience on with LSD (not realizing that the audience would consist of screaming adolescent girls), and later that evening met Owsley at Kesey's woodland-enclosed home. Wolfe wrote: "The world's greatest LSD manufacturer, bar none, standing out in the dark in the middle of nowhere amid the boho-slug multitudes under the shadowy redwoods." Owsley became the Pranksters' chemist, supplying the active ingredient for what became a series of Kesey-organized events called acid tests.

Advertised with a small poster in a Santa Cruz bookstore cryptically asking "Can *You* Pass the Acid Test?", Kesey and his Merry Pranksters hosted the first test, with friends and friends of friends paying a dollar entrance charge, consuming LSD, and hearing music randomly created on guitars and flutes as Kesey announced: "the world is a spaceship and the captain has lost his mind." As word spread, the next acid test attracted 400 people and had live music from a local band, The Warlocks, turning blues-based songs into long improvisations with the aid of electronics and tapes, as displays of colored light were projected onto the walls.

The acid tests quickly evolved into advertised events in public halls. In January 1966, two thousand people attended one at San Francisco's Fillmore Auditorium at 1805 Geary Street. The Warlocks, now called the Grateful Dead, provided music aided by masses of expensive sound equipment donated by Owsley (presumably from LSD manufacturing profits) who also assisted Kesey in wiring the hall with microphones, cameras, loud speakers, and TV screens for instant replays to the crowd. Charles Perry recalled: "They had packed so much electronic equipment the whole hall had a low, dull buzzing sound... The walls were covered with balloons and streamers and there was a baby's bathtub full of LSD-spiked punch in the middle of the floor."

The acid tests culminated later that month with a three-day Trips Festival at the Longshoremen's Hall at 400 North Point in Fisherman's Wharf, publicized by an advertising agency releasing balloons above Union Square and unfurling a banner with a single word: "now". Kesey described the festival as part of "a need to find a new way to look at the world and attempt to locate a better reality." The festival was attended by the jazz critic of the *San Francisco Chronicle*, Ralph J Gleason, who would later author one of the definitive books of the period, *The Jefferson Airplane and the San Francisco Sound.* Of the Trips Festival he wrote for the *Chronicle*:

There were five movie screens on the walls and projectors for the flicks and the light mixes spread around the balcony. A huge platform in the middle of the room housed the engineers who directed the sound and the lights... A huge pair of red and yellow traffic lights blinked constantly. Strobo-scopic lights set at vantage points beamed down into the crowd and lissome maidens danced under them for hours, whirrling jewelry... A platform in front of the stage was for the dancers who free-form twisted all night long... Long-legged girls in leotards leaped around the hall with shrill whistles blowing... The man who jumped from the balcony to the trampoline didn't really make much of an impression, the evening was such a conglomeration of impressions.

Others began organizing acid tests and, following the Trips Festival, rumors spread of a huge Kesey acid test being arranged for

New York's Madison Square Garden. But Kesey was arrested for marijuana possession and, facing a likely jail term, unconvincingly faked his own death before going into hiding in Mexico. Another blow came during October 1966, when after months of controversy over the safety of the drug and its impact on the nation's youth, LSD was classified as a narcotic and made illegal.

Electric Music for the Mind and Body

The unclassifiable bohemia that was growing in Haight-Ashbury from 1964 included young musicians who had previously played acoustic folk or bluegrass. The universities at Berkeley and Stanford had both spawned lively folk/protest scenes but Haight-Ashbury musicians began gravitating toward electric instruments, encouraged by the "British invasion", an assault on the blandness of US Top 40 fare led by the Beatles and the Rolling Stones (inspired in part by black American music that few white Americans had ever heard), and the new electric sounds of former folkie Bob Dylan.

The fact that most musicians already knew each other or, in the confines of Haight-Ashbury, quickly became acquainted, engendered a cooperative spirit and a desire to create music to please themselves and their friends—not least because both bands and audience would often be tripping on LSD. With legal restrictions on live music dating back to the dance band era contributing to a lack of venues, the new Haight-Ashbury musicians mostly played free shows in public places or sporadic benefits for community causes.

Arriving from Berkeley, Marty Balin (b.1942) opened what was described as San Francisco's "first folk nightclub", The Matrix, at 3138 Fillmore Street in the Marina District. With himself as its singer, Balin set about forming a house band for the venue, having chosen the name, The Jefferson Airplane. Balin recruited Skip Spence as drummer despite the fact that Spence was a guitarist (he later joined another seminal band, Moby Grape, in that role) who had never played drums. The band debuted at the Matrix's opening night on August 13 and soon gained a following partly, it was noted, for their weird name.

Two months later, the Jefferson Airplane joined other Haight-Ashbury bands at the Longshoremen's Hall for a "Tribute to Dr.

Strange" (not a formal tribute at all but an appealing name for an event). Also appearing were the Charlatans, noted for their Haight-style Edwardiana, hair that was "longer than the Beatles'", and a piano player whose Haight Street shop sold "antique clothes, knickknacks, a little art and a lot of marijuana stash jars." On the bill, too, were the Great Society whose singer, Grace Slick (b.1939), would shortly join the Jefferson Airplane.

During November and December there were further shows (always described as "dances" partly for legal reasons but also to symbolize the lack of the usual division between "performers" and "audience") as benefits for a guerrilla theater group called the Mime Troupe. Since the late 1950s, the Mime Troupe had been staging free shows in city parks and abandoned churches, its members frequently arrested by police for nudity and use of swearwords. The benefits were organized by the Mime Troupe's business manager, Bill Graham. Ralph Gleason described a December 10 benefit at the Fillmore Auditorium:

> ...a most remarkable assemblage of humanity was leaping, jumping, dancing, frigging, fragging and frugging on the dance floor to the music of the half-dozen rock bands—the Mystery Trend, The Great Society, the Jefferson Airplane, The VIPS, the Gentleman's Band, the Warlocks and others. The costumes were free-form, Goodwill-cum-Sherwood Forest. Slim young ladies with their faces painted à la Harper's Bazaar in cuts-and-dogs lines, granny dresses topped with huge feathers, white levis with decals of mystic design; bell-bottoms with splits up the side! The combinations were seemingly limitless.

Grace Slick remembered the night:

> As you walk onto the dancefloor, you have the feeling you've just entered seven different centuries all thrown together in one room. The interior of the building is a turn-of-the-century rococo, and a man in red briefs and silver body paint is handing out East Indian incense. A girl in full Renaissance drag is spinning around by herself listening to some Baroque music in her head, while several people in jeans and American Indian headbands are sitting in a circle on the floor smoking weed. Close by, a good-looking man in a three-musketeer costume is placing ashtrays on the

cheap fifties Formica tables that circle the edge of the room. Over in the corner, people are stripping off their clothes, and while the acid is taking effect, they're getting body-painted so they'll glow in the dark as the night progresses.

There were also a three-foot-high sign proclaiming "LOVE", a bar that served only soft drinks, and table offering apples for sale: "The only dance I've ever been at (outside of Halloween) where they sold apples. Craaazy!" reported Gleason.

In Haight-Ashbury, 1090 Page Street (what Hank Harrison would call "the underground City Hall") was becoming a meeting place for musicians where "floors were hardwood parquet, set in the most unusual patterns, but the rosewood-and-oak spiral staircase and balustrades were decayed as if a dampness had haunted the place. In the basement stood the gazebo-like bandstand, with the moonstone glass windows around it..." Resident at 1090 was Chet Helms who was organizing regular dances at the Avalon Ballroom, at the junction of Sutter Street and Van Ness Avenue, and encouraging local musicians to jam in 1090's basement, events that became so popular that he began charging 50c admission and once had 300 people trying to get inside. Also living at the house was a magician, "a strange oriental anthropologist named Mr Sito", and, in the attic, bass player Peter Albin who co-founded Big Brother and the Holding Company to became the Avalon's resident band. On June 10, 1966, the band debuted their new singer, Janis Joplin, a woman from Texas who during a previous San Francisco stay had sung acoustic blues in North Beach.

Another band, formed by musicians who had met at the Dr. Strange tribute, was the Quicksilver Messenger Service. They were promised an ounce of marijuana by the Committee Theater, active since the late 1950s with satirical comedy shows and increasingly interested in multi-media events, as payment for recording a version of "Star Spangled Banner". The result was so good it earned the group not one but two ounces of weed.

The Grateful Dead moved north along the peninsula from Palo Alto, eventually taking up residence at 710 Ashbury Street after the existing tenants were unceremoniously forced out. The band's manager,

Rock Scully, described the house as "one of those high-ceilinged, crumbling old Victorian mansions the Haight is full of. Once homes to railroad magnates and robber barons, now crashpads for the hippie *Anschluss*. Big bay windows, billowing like sails into the street, and a stoop worthy of Henry James: gingerbread porch, stained glass in the entry, a front door the Bank of England would be proud of." Frequent basement jam sessions attracted hundreds of onlookers, as did the band's appearances on the back of trucks at the nearby Panhandle or on the edge of Golden Gate Park.

Writing in September 1965 in the *San Francisco Examiner* under a heading "A New Haven For Beatniks", Michael Fallon used for the first time the word "hippie" (derived from Norman Mailer's term "hipsters" in reference to the Beats) to describe the scene growing around a Haight-Ashbury coffee house, the Blue Unicorn on 1927 Hayes Street. The Blue Unicorn had been a meeting place for the legalize marijuana movement and the Sexual Freedom League (advocating precisely what its name suggested), and offered chessboards, sewing kits, a piano, books, art, music and other amenities for patrons' use. The Blue Unicorn quickly attracted Haight-Ashbury's small but steadily expanding off-center population: the "hippies" who themselves would have hated such a categorization. A series of leaflets offering "the Unicorn Philosophy" were written and handed out by owner Bob Stubbs. One proved to be remarkably prescient: "We have a private revolution going on. A revolution of Individuality and diversity that can only be private. Upon becoming a group movement such a revolution ends up being imitators rather than participants..."

Summer in the City

The year 1967 began in stupendous fashion with the biggest and most extraordinary event held to date. It took place in the Polo Field section of Golden Gate Park and was called The Human Be-In (there were two other names, the Pow Wow and the Gathering of Tribes, though the first was the one that stuck). The *Berkeley Barb* promised: "we shall shower the country with waves of ecstasy and purification. Fear will be washed away; ignorance will be exposed to sunlight; profits and empire will lie drying on deserted beaches; violence will be submerged and transmuted in rhythm and dancing."

Before 25,000 people, Allen Ginsberg and Gary Snyder provided poetry and prayers; LSD crusader Timothy Leary orated; Jerry Rubin, the radical political activist who had been released from jail the previous night, passed around a hat to raise bail money; and providing music over a malfunctioning sound system music were the Grateful Dead, Quicksilver Messenger Service, and the Jefferson Airplane. Owsley's latest batch of super-strength LSD, nicknamed White Lightning, was handed out. The day concluded with the blowing of a conch shell and a mass collection of rubbish orchestrated by Ginsberg. Hank Harrison observed: "one could see fans, feathers, plumes and tufts; bells, chimes, incense, pennants, banners, flags and talismans; beaded charms, lettuce-and-tomato sandwiches, balloons, paradise flowers, and animal robes, bamboo, fruits and baskets; folded hands, closed eyes, bright brows and smiles, stoned people; prayer cloth and shaman sticks, floating dancing marijuana flags with peace symbols, and the smell of the divine herb wafting through the void vortex that we created." Ralph Gleason wrote: "A beautiful girl in an Indian headdress handed me a stock of slow-burning incense and another handed out sprigs of bay leaves. Women and men alike carried flowers and wore ribbons in their hair. There were more clean long-haired males assembled in one place than at any time since the Crusades."

A landmark event in itself, the Be-In also marked a turning-point. Through the rest of 1967, Haight-Ashbury went from being the private revolution described by Bob Stubbs into something much more public. Against a backdrop of growing social and political unrest, opposition to US involvement in Vietnam, and generational conflict, the mainstream media latched onto the hippie phenomena, seizing on the drugs and sex (the new Haight-Ashbury lifestyles rarely included celibacy) aspects with particular relish. Unintentionally, the media reports encouraged legions of disaffected youth from all over the US to travel west. In a bizarre echo of the gold rush, the summer of 1967 (what would become known as the "summer of love") saw Haight-Ashbury's population swell from 7,000 to 75,000, most fresh arrivals having little money and nowhere to stay. Encouraging the invasion was Scott McKenzie's hit record *San Francisco (Be Sure To Wear Flowers In Your Hair)* which promised a city full of "gentle people" where "summer time will be a love-in there."

In *Storming Heaven: LSD and the American Dream*, Jay Stevens outlined the routine for Haight-Ashbury arrivals: "Your first night was usually spent on one of the many communal crash pads, eating sandwiches together with a dozen friendly strangers. Your inhibitions and frequently your virginity were the first things to go, followed by your clothes and your old values—a progressive shedding that that was hastened along by your first acid trip. Within days your past life in Des Moines or Dallas or wherever was as remote as that school outing you took as an adolescent."

Advertising "the only foreign tour within the continental limits of the United States", sightseeing companies began adding hippie-spotting tours of Haight-Ashbury to their itineraries (as had happened with Beats in North Beach). On Haight Street some hippies responded to the busloads of gawping tourists by holding up mirrors, inviting the "straights" to look at themselves. The police, too, began paying more attention to the district. As Haight-Ashbury acquired a reputation as a refuge for underage runaways and draft dodgers, police felt obliged to harass anyone who looked like a drug user, which to them was more or less everybody. By late 1967, drug raids on private houses, including the Grateful Dead's, were common.

It's Free Because It's Yours

In late 1966 around twenty people associated with the Mime Troupe broke away to become a kind of anarchist collective called The Diggers (named after the English seventeenth-century anti-capitalist, agrarian sect). The Diggers used surplus market food to feed the hungry of Haight-Ashbury with free meals in the Panhandle, circumventing legal restrictions by claiming to be having a picnic. In the *Berkeley Barb* in October 1966, George Metevsky described a Digger picnic:

> *In the afternoon, at a little before four, they come down Ashbury, cross Oak and gather around a Eucalyptus tree in the Panhandle. They wear wide eyes, tattered clothes, and talismans around their necks. Some are in their teens, most in their twenties, and a few are closing in on forty. They talk about anything, smile about everything and do what they want to do with the food that they bring to each other. They are THE*

DIGGERS. And everyday at four o'clock they provide anybody with anything to eat.

The first time I noted them I thought it was a picnic. The second time I thought I was hallucinating. The third time I had to stop. And I sat down with them and ate food and discovered that I didn't but I did. I talked to a young girl with bare feet and hair that fell over her shoulders and whose name began with an N.

'Who are the Diggers?'

She smiled: 'I don't know. I'm not a Digger. Are you a Digger?'

'FUCK THE DIGGERS!!!' shouted a kid with a scar and everyone laughed and repeated it.

I asked him whose food it was. He said it was free.

'Yes, but who donated it? Who's laying it on?'

'It's free because it's yours,' came a reply.

Digger food included Digger Bread, easily recognized by a distinctive shape that resulted from its being baked in coffee cans. The Diggers gave away the recipe for the bread (with which they would later be credited with introducing whole wheat to the counterculture) with the stipulation that "you always give it away."

Working from an office and kitchen at the Episcopal All Saints Church on 1350 Waller Street, the Diggers also arranged free "crashpad" accommodation for the growing numbers arriving in Haight-Ashbury, staged numerous events intended to challenge conventional thinking (becoming unwitting role models for the confrontational tactics of the Hippies), and created the free stores which offered furniture, clothing and other items (found, donated, some perhaps stolen) free to anybody who walked in. The Diggers were, according to Dominick Cavallo's *A Fiction of the Past: The Sixties In American History*, "forcing people to perceive the store and its goods as props and the positions of customers and consumers, clerks and owners as roles that they performed without thinking. Once they became conscious that their roles could be changed simply by altering the script, anything was possible."

The Diggers saw Haight-Ashbury as potentially a money-free, non-capitalist mini-society that, by its very nature, was revolutionary. Their numerous broadsides, which could be witty, provocative or scathing, were distributed not just in Haight-Ashbury, but around the city. An early one headed "Money Is An Unnecessary Evil" read: "As part of the city's campaign to stem the causes of violence the San Francisco Diggers announce a 30 day period beginning now during which all responsible citizens are asked to turn in their money. No questions will be asked." At their best, the Diggers' broadsides posed simple yet vexing questions to prompt consideration of the Haight-Ashbury's paradoxes: such as asking why a hippie, supposedly with no belief in money, would beg for a dime when he could ask for an apple.

The Diggers began tilting as much at Haight-Ashbury's own hippie entrepreneurs as the wider capitalist world. The once hip dance promoters were increasingly becoming businessmen (particularly Bill Graham (1931-91), who was on the way to becoming the US's major rock promoter; his events were picketed by The Diggers). With a few exceptions, owners of the new "head shops" along Haight Street were raking profits from hippie customers through posters, books, and marijuana paraphernalia (denied membership of the extant traders' organization, the merchants banded together as Haight Independent Proprietors, or HIP for short). Digger opprobrium was also directed at the local underground bible, *The City of San Francisco Oracle*, the most enduring of a number of publications that the neighborhood created and one that became noted as much for its design as its written content.

The San Francisco Sound

Also from late 1966, the "San Francisco Sound" was an all-encompassing term spreading across the US and beyond to describe the music emanating from Haight-Ashbury, even though each band had its unique style. In the city, dances were rapidly becoming concerts, where the audience would turn up to see a particular band rather than be part of an event. Even light shows, by now a staple part of any rock show, were becoming professionally run affairs with an estimated 500 specialist light show operators in the Bay Area who, at one point, went on strike for higher pay.

Major record companies had begun signing the prominent bands (in an unprecedented step, some insisted on complete control over their releases) and for some TV appearances, touring, and recording became more common than free shows and benefits. The Jefferson Airplane undertook their first nationwide tour during 1966. During an appearance in Iowa, their tour manager recalled the audience slowly warming to the band until "guys ripped off their ties. They went nuts, It was like the turning of America in a way." A year later, the "turning of America" was even more evident as the band had hit singles with "Somebody To Love" and "White Rabbit", the latter an *Alice In Wonderland*-inspired paean to LSD.

Greatly aided by Janis Joplin's voice and charisma, Big Brother and the Holding Company's first album *Cheap Thrills* was released in 1968 and sold a million copies, setting Joplin on course to become one of rock's first superstars as well as one of its first casualties, dying of a drugs overdose in 1970. The Grateful Dead's first album appeared in 1967, as did *Electric Music For The Mind and Body* from Country Joe and the Fish, a Berkeley-based band who appeared at many early events. In 1969, the Woodstock Festival (and film) elevated Country Joe and the Fish's status and provided a breakthrough for another Bay Area band, the then unsigned Santana. In *Buried Alive*, a biography of Joplin, Myra Freidman records: "In the first days of the Haight, there was only a cluster of San Francisco bands... By December of 1966, there would be some 1,500 bands flourishing in the Bay Area."

Although it became the most famous rock festival of the 1960s, Woodstock was not the first. In June 1967 a three-day festival at Monterey, 115 miles south of San Francisco, featured British and American bands (plus Ravi Shankar and Hugh Masekela), including several from Haight-Ashbury. Filmed in documentary style by D. A. Pennebaker (as *Monterey Pop*, released in 1969), Monterey has come to be viewed by many as the seminal rock festival of the early hippie era. Among San Francisco bands at the time, however, there was widespread skepticism over the LA-based music industry's domination of the event. The Grateful Dead's manager Rock Scully remarked: "...backstage the sharks are busy scheming and maneuvering. All those L.A. record company types. Man, are they scary." Many viewing the film today may wonder why the Grateful Dead did not appear at the festival. In fact they did, taking the stage between The Who and Jimi Hendrix after refusing to sign away their film rights.

And while Haight-Ashbury had been a home and inspiration for the core bands of the San Francisco Sound, the area's appeal quickly paled as their success made them hippie celebrities and the focus of fan and police attention. Most departed for the rural spaces of Marin Country. The music once played for free was now big business. Quoted in Gleason's book, the vice president of the Bank of California gleefully predicted: "By the mid-1970s, rock music will be San Francisco's fourth-largest industry led only by construction, finance, insurance and manufacturing."

The Death of Hippie

The first anniversary of the illegalization of LSD, October 7, 1967, was chosen (by the Diggers and others) to mark the failure of Haight-Ashbury's private revolution and advertised with leaflets inviting mourners to attend the funeral of "hippie, devoted son of mass media". The evening before, a wake was held at All Saints Church followed by a climb to the top of Buena Vista Hill from where a procession along Haight Street would begin at sunrise. Around eighty people showed up and a cardboard coffin, complete with symbolic hippie, was carried along the route.

By the end of 1967, Haight-Ashbury was far removed from what Hank Harrison termed "a paradise of sorts... the working psychedelic capital of the Universe" and was a place even cult-leader Charles Manson (who recruited some members of his "family" while resident in Haight-Ashbury) warned his followers to avoid. In his biography of Manson, Ed Sanders wrote: "by the end of the summer of flowers, the streets of the Haight were griseous and filthy, psychedelic weirdburger stands were springing up in mutant profusion."

Where acid had been the drug of choice, and for some a surrogate religion, destructive and addictive substances such as heroin and barbiturates were flooding the neighborhood controlled by organized criminal gangs. A soaring crime rate included murders and frequent street robberies in what Charles Perry called "a heroin-infested slum where one could get knifed for a bag of groceries." The *Oracle* published its final and pessimistic edition in 1968. Dominick Cavallo notes that the progenitors of what became the hippie scene were often from stable family backgrounds but the "new Haight residents were a motley brew of high school dropouts, religious fanatics, naive 'flower children', callous drug dealers, thugs and pimps." And, as one contemporary account put it, "rape was as common as bullshit."

The reluctance of established medical facilities to treat hippies as drug-related problems, venereal disease, and an endless variety of foot ailments (a result of walking barefoot on filthy streets) became rife, encouraged a young doctor, David Smith, a Haight-Ashbury resident while an intern at San Francisco General Hospital, to open the Haight-Ashbury Free Clinic at 558 Clayton Street in 1967. While it was open to all, the Free Clinic's initial purpose was to be hippie-friendly; funding came largely from donations and fundraising events, and staff worked for free. The clinic remains today, treating predominantly low-income patients as do the other clinics which it inspired across the US.

In December 1969, San Francisco hoped to emulate the Woodstock festival (aided by a successful film, the event in upstate New York had stolen San Francisco's thunder and was being viewed as the apotheosis of the peace and love era) with one of its own. The festival was not much more than an idea when Bay Area radio stations leaked news of it, creating a momentum that became unstoppable, and the festival went ahead despite poor organization. Instead of the hoped-for setting of Golden Gate Park, the venue became the uninspiring Altamont Speedway (about thirty miles east of the city) for a day that would include the Jefferson Airplane on a bill topped by the Rolling Stones.

Of Altamont, Ralph Gleason wrote: "In twenty-four hours we created all the problems of our society in one place: congestion, violence, and dehumanisation. The name of the game is money, power and ego." Marred throughout by random violence and aggressively policed by pool-cue-wielding Hell's Angels, the doomed festival was documented by the film, *Gimme Shelter*, including its chilling climax when an audience member appears to raise a gun towards the stage and is promptly set upon by Hell's Angels and fatally stabbed. Far from replicating Woodstock, Altamont became the event that chroniclers of the decade like to take as marking the moment when a dream became a nightmare.

As the 1970s dawned, Haight-Ashbury was in the despondent throes that continued into the mid-1980s. It was only then that the neighborhood began to experience a regeneration. Its dilapidated homes were purchased and restored by a small band of in-comers, aware of the properties' potential and the neighborhood's unique history. The new settlers organized schemes to aid the area's homeless and hungry and to encourage drug dealers to leave its streets. By the 1990s, Haight Street was flourishing as an offbeat shopping strip, with independent record- and bookstores, well-stocked thrift stores, the best tie-dyed T-shirt outlet in the city, and even a few updated versions of hippie-style head shops. So complete was the about turn that rents and property prices escalated and up-market restaurants appeared, as did, to great fuss, a branch of the clothing retailer, The Gap.

The appearance of the latter symbolized Haight-Ashbury's upward mobility. The musicians, poets and painters who might once have colonized the area were, from the mid-1990s, gathered down the hill in the area known as the Lower Haight. Nonetheless, with skateboarding punks, buskers, and independent traders still apparent along Haight Street, reports of the neighborhood's gentrification are exaggerated. In *The Promised Land*, published in 2001, journalist Decca Aitkenhead found Haight-Ashbury "a lifesize souvenir of itself... Red eyed teenagers squat on the pavement, smoking wistfully and talking rubbish."

Looking back to the 1960s, Ralph Gleason's upbeat book ends with a list of gloriously evocative San Francisco band names compiled for a television documentary. Some are instantly recognizable, others existed for a day. Some may be apocryphal, but others almost inspire dancing without the aid of music: the Cleanliness and Godliness Skiffle Band, Gale Garnett & the Gentle Reign, Melvin Q Watchpocket, the Jook Savages, Serpent Power, Weird Herald... Charles Perry's detailed and sober account, published in the 1980s, astutely warns that "one generalizes about the people who passed through Haight-Ashbury at one's peril." He describes the Haight Street cop who gave up the beat to open an occult bookstore and the "fellow who wore a door knocker around his neck (who) wouldn't speak to you unless you knocked first." Of the Diggers and the "serious hippies", Cavallo's scholarly account concludes with an almost touching eulogy: "For a brief interlude they turned their little piece of America on its head."

The Castro: the Rise of Gay San Francisco

The "wide open city" of gold rush-era San Francisco was populated by an almost exclusively male population that grew with unprecedented speed. Most men were single, searching for fortune and adventure, and far from the restraining influence of family, church, and peers. Although written records of the time reveal little about homosexual activity, anecdotal evidence suggests that liaisons between consenting males were commonplace. It is known, though, that the lack of female partners for square dancing led to men taking the female role and indicating as much by wearing a red handkerchief around their arm: a practice revived in the 1970s when gay men often signaled their preferred sexual role using the "hankie code".

Same-sex love between women in early San Francisco was suggested when a hundred-year-old time capsule was unearthed in Washington Square in 1979. Inside, author Laura De Force Gordon had placed a copy of her book, *The Great Geysers of California*, with a handwritten fly-cover note stating: "let it be known that the author of this book was a lover of her own sex." In the 1920s, Elsa Gidlow, author of what would be described as the first published collection of lesbian verse, become part of the city's literary circle while living openly with her female lover at a bucolic retreat near Muir Woods.

Despite being the US's most sexually permissive city with a deserved reputation as a place where anything goes, for gay men and lesbians almost nothing, legally, went in San Francisco until the 1970s. Dancing with same-sex partners and even same-sex touching was unlawful, as was the serving of alcohol to homosexuals (the latter effectively overturned when a lawyer asked a judge to put himself in the bartender's position and point out the homosexuals in the courtroom). Laws against posing as a member of the opposite sex, outlawing drag kings and queens, were circumvented by some drag queens wearing a note declaring "I'm a boy."

Places of entertainment with a strongly gay male or lesbian clientele were frequently the targets for police raids. In 1908 the city's first known gay bar, The Dash, at 574 Pacific Street, was closed, and for decades customers in and around gay-friendly bars and clubs were routinely harassed. Not until 1951, after a series of police corruption scandals (officers had been taking bribes from gay bars in return for not arresting their customers), did the California Supreme Court outlaw the enforced closure of a bar simply because most of its customers were homosexuals.

Rich gays amid the city's upper social strata could, however, effectively buy immunity from blackmail and life-ruining exposure of their sexual preferences. In *The Mayor of Castro Street*, Randy Shilts wrote: "Templeton Crocker, scion of the city's prominent banking family, reportedly headed local gay royalty, throwing lavish parties and surrounding himself with pretty young men. Other famous characters fluttered in and out of the tea dances and private parties where each guest was carefully vouched for. A homosexual septuagenarian fondly recalled decades later how in his youth, no less than the Catholic archbishop had 'gently laid hands' on him."

By the 1930s, discreetly gay-orientated nightclubs were presenting cross-dressing cabaret entertainment. Prominent among them was the Black Cat Club at 710 Montgomery Street, which lasted 15 years. It was here that Jose Sarria (the "Nightingale on Montgomery Street") appeared every Sunday afternoon as a heavily-sequined Madame Butterfly and led a communal rendition of "God save the Nelly Queens". Predating the Black Cat and longer lasting, Finnochio's at 506 Broadway opened in 1936 and stayed in business until 1999, by which time its shows had traveled from the outer limits of permissible entertainment to the almost mainstream. Mona's Club 440, on 440 Broadway, attracted a predominantly female audience for its male impersonators on bills that might offer "'Butch' Minton singing gay songs" and regularly featured Gladys Bentley, a cross-dressing blues singer who came to prominence during the 1920s Harlem Renaissance.

San Francisco's first prominent gay to campaign for political rights, Sarria gained a respectable 5,600 votes running for a seat on the Board of Supervisors in 1961 and, though failing to be elected, raised the prospect of gays being elected to public office. Meanwhile, the Black Cat's lead in refusing to pay police bribes was followed by other gay establishments, which, in 1962, united as the Tavern Guild. The US's first association of gay businesses, the guild provided legal services, bail for anyone arrested for being in or near a gay bar, and published a leaflet advising how to deal with arrest and police harassment.

Bars began notifying each other if a plainclothes cop was spotted and an impending raid would be signaled by a blinking of the house lights, at which point patrons would promptly change their partners so that gay men would be dancing with lesbians by the time the police entered. Arrest (usually for being "an inmate of a disorderly house") was a serious matter as, aside from any formal punishment, the arrested individual's family and place of work were likely to be contacted by the press; exposed lesbian mothers faced the prospect of losing custody of their children on grounds that their sexual urges rendered them unfit parents.

During the Second World War, San Francisco was the embarkation point for military personnel destined for the Pacific theater: a fact which had a tremendous bearing on its gay population. Many gays and lesbians from rural areas who had disguised their sexuality experienced San Francisco's comparative freedoms at a time when the city provided plentiful opportunities for homo and hetero alike to enjoy what might be a final sexual tryst.

The war was the first conflict where sexuality alone would warrant a dishonorable discharge from the US military. Gays and lesbians exposed as such were dispatched from service with discharge papers, necessary for obtaining a civilian job, distinctively colored blue and marked with a large red H to denote "homosexual". Faced with being ostracized (and unemployable) in their home towns, many stayed in San Francisco, as did those who had found same-sex partners during military service and wanted to begin new lives. As anti-Communist hysteria in the 1950s equated homosexuality with political subversion, gays and lesbians forced out of federal government jobs found succor in San Francisco.

In 1955 San Francisco produced what is believed to be the world's first lesbian organization, the Daughters of Bilitis, who published a groundbreaking newsletter, *The Ladder.* Two years earlier, the Mattachine Society, probably the first organization of gay men, relocated from Los Angeles to San Francisco and began issuing the weekly *ONE Magazine.* In contrast to the semi-secrecy that both organizations were forced to operate within, the mid-1960s saw the founding of the San Francisco-based Society for Individual Rights (SIR), determined to function openly and assertively. At a time when police raids were escalating and the Black Cat was forced to close, SIR's newsletter, *Vector*, was on sale at mainstream news outlets, and community events were being staged throughout the city, including sporting competitions, bridge clubs, art classes and dances. The latter were of particular interest to the police who were still seeking to make arrests for same-sex dancing. In a landmark ruling, a city court cleared those arrested during a gay New Year's Eve party and condemned the police action.

SIR opened the US's first gay and lesbian community center in San Francisco in April 1966, a major step in fostering a sense of community and an early version of what would become gay pride. Bolstered by the achievements of the Free Speech Movement in Berkeley, the influence of the sexually adventurous Beats, and the ideas of free love fermenting in Haight-Ashbury, San Francisco's gays and lesbians became increasingly visible and determined. In August 1966 a picket was organized outside Compton's, a Tenderloin cafeteria, following the establishment's banning of gay patrons (a move aimed at the cross-dressers with whom it was popular). The cafeteria became one of the first businesses to feel the brunt of gay anger when a crowd of drag queens smashed its plate glass windows. The action at Compton's was a foretaste of an event three years later in New York's Greenwich Village, when resistance to a police raid on the gay Stonewall Bar led to a two-day battle. Like Compton's, but with much more fanfare and global resonance, Stonewall became a turning point, showing that gays were no longer willing to endure police intimidation and were prepared to stand as a community to defend themselves.

Harvey Milk and the Castro Clone

The economic changes of the 1950s and 1960s saw San Francisco's middle classes vacate established city neighborhoods for new homes in the suburbs. One such neighborhood was the Castro, west of the Mission District and south of Haight-Ashbury, set in one of the valleys typically described by realtors as "sun-filled". Like many of San Francisco's western districts, the Castro had developed after being linked to Downtown by cable car in the late nineteenth century and had seen the building of streets lined with elegant family homes, many in the fashionable Italianate style. By the early 1970s, the affordability

of these homes made the area attractive to single, young professionals drawn to San Francisco by white-collar jobs in the Financial District's new high rises. Equally alluring for some was the city's fast-growing gay and lesbian community. Castro Street, the main commercial strip of the declining neighborhood, was revived by new customers and new gay-owned and gay-friendly shops, bars, and restaurants.

Among the settlers was Harvey Milk (1930-78), who arrived from New York in 1972 and opened a modest camera shop. Quick-witted and charismatic, Milk quickly became prominent in neighborhood politics and made his first unsuccessful bid for public office in 1973. The transformation of the Castro did not go unnoticed by San Francisco's police, many of whom had family links with the area and resented the change. Police brutality against gays became routine and encouraged Milk's attempts to rally local support; as he once proclaimed: "I pay my taxes for police to protect me, not persecute me."

Most established Castro Street businesses lost their antipathy towards gays when the fresh arrivals started spending money, which in some cases prevented bankruptcy. Building supply stores did spectacular trade as old homes were renovated by their new owners. Randy Shilts described how "block after block of high Italianate Edwardian homes burst forth in polychromatic splendour." Castro property values rose sharply, at times doubling every six months. Unable to resist the profits to be made, many long-time residents sold up, creating more housing for gay arrivals. Between 1969 and 1973, an estimated 900 gay men moved to San Francisco. From 1974 to 1979, some 20,000 arrived. A police survey in 1976 suggested that 140,000 out of San Francisco's 700,000 population were gay or lesbian.

Many more came to visit. The air shuttle from Los Angeles was nicknamed the "gay express" for the week-ending LA gays it carried. In *Cities on a Hill*, Frances Fitzgerald noted that "the Castro had become a 'Mecca' (as the press kept putting it) for gay tourists... New Yorkers,

Chicagoans and others would spend their vacations in San Francisco, staying at gay hotels, going to gay restaurants and shopping at gay stores."

Sheer numbers suddenly gave San Francisco's gays and lesbians something that all politicians, regardless of their views on a person's sexual preferences, recognized: voting power. By the mid-1970s, having shed his hippie-style attire for "three-piece suits he bought secondhand from a Castro district dry cleaner", Harvey Milk had established himself as an effective campaigner on many populist issues such as housing and healthcare, appealing to ethnic minorities and crucially gaining endorsements from traditionally anti-gay organizations such as the labor unions and the city's fire-fighters. Running for the Board of Supervisors in 1975, Milk failed to win a seat but polled enough votes to confirm his importance, not least to the new mayor, the liberal George Moscone. Changes in San Francisco were mirrored in state politics when conservative governor Ronald Reagan was succeeded by his political opposite, Jerry Brown. In what would be seen nationally as a groundbreaking legal move, one of Brown's first acts was to repeal California's anti-sodomy laws.

Despite bomb threats, poison pen letters, and opposition from within the gay community as well as the political establishment (one campaign was described in the press as "Harvey Milk versus the Machine"), Milk continued to build support. With San Francisco gays and lesbians galvanized by a homophobic electoral success in Florida that suddenly put gay rights issues in the national spotlight, Milk was elected to the Board of Supervisors in 1977 as one of the first openly gay holders of political office in US history.

By the time of Milk's election, some 25,000 gays lived in the Castro and 250,000 attended the annual (held each June since 1973, commemorating Stonewall) Gay Freedom Day Parade. The streets of the Castro were increasingly dominated by what evolved into a stereotypically gay male look: leather bomber jackets, expensive plaid shirts unbuttoned to reveal tufts of body hair, and new jeans "tight at the ass and suggestively stretched at the crotch." One local clothes shop, All American Boy, according to Randy Shilts was: "the quartermaster depot of the 'Castro clone' look." The uniformity prompted dismay among longer-established residents who believed gays should simply see themselves (and be seen by non-gays) as individuals. But Milk commented "these guy's have been through hell... this is a necessary stage they're going through." Many Castro newcomers had indeed endured lives of sexual repression and were keen to make up for lost time in a neighborhood that promised and delivered an abundance of sex and sexual partners. In describing the feelings of one resident, Randy Shilts put it: "After over thirty years of living with the assumption that he would never experience a moment of passion, much less love, just seeing such a panoply of available partners was enough to set a guy's head spinning."

Whether in its cruise-oriented cafés, bars and restaurants, its gay-run shops, or simply in its very streets, the Castro seemed alive with sexual possibility. Yet while it was the major gay residential area, the Castro was eclipsed by the Folsom Street area south of Market Street (SoMa) for the highest-velocity gay nightlife. Gay venues had flourished in SoMa chiefly because it was a mainly industrial area deserted at night. It was in SoMa in 1962 that San Francisco saw the first of its gay leather bars, The Tool Box, where a strict dress code banned sneakers and sweaters in favor of a more macho leather-and-levi look; one wall was covered by a large mural based on the motorcycle film, *The Wild Ones*.

The Tool Box helped create a SoMa that from the late 1970s was the bacchanalian heart of gay San Francisco. Amid scores of bars and clubs were The Barracks, "a four-storey maze of fantasy sex"; The Cauldron, where patrons wore only their boots; The Slot, which boasted a set of stocks; and The Trench, which offered a free schnapps to uncircumcised customers (subject to inspection) visiting for the weekly "uncut night". Several cowboy bars, such as Rawhide II, also flourished, replaying the gold rush days with all-male square dancing nights competing for attention with the pool table, pinball machine, and bushy mustache contests. All manner of gay sex was on offer and on show at the bars, as it was at the city's gay bathhouses—commonly dimly-lit buildings with many rooms connected by corridors where patrons, having left their clothes in a locker and wearing only a towel (sometimes barely even that), cruised the rooms to observe or participate in diverse sex acts with any number of anonymous partners.

A Fury Unleashed

Elected on the same day as Milk was Dan White, representing the Excelsior district where many constituents feared what was perceived as a takeover of the city by gays and Latinos. While seen as sympathetic to this view, White was also viewed as a relative moderate, hindered by a volatile temper. Significantly and controversially, however, he had addressed his predominately blue-collar conservative constituents with the following words: "There are thousands and thousands of frustrated angry people like yourselves waiting to unleash a fury that can and will eradicate the malignancies which blight our beautiful city... I am not going to be forced out by splinter groups of radicals, social deviates and incorrigibles."

Despite White having been supportive of Milk on some gay-related issues, a feud had developed between them when Milk withdrew his opposition to a psychiatric clinic planned for White's constituency. Citing personal reasons, White resigned from office but was persuaded (by the Police Officers' Association which considered him an ally) to ask the mayor for his job back. Milk, however, had cheered White's resignation and successfully convinced Moscone that re-appointing him would result in the loss of gay support.

On November 27, 1978, gaining entry through an open basement window to avoid the metal detectors at the main entrance, White walked to the mayor's office and, after a short wait, went inside and began a conversation with Moscone. Soon after, White pulled a Smith and Wesson revolver from his jacket, fired two shots into the mayor's body and two more into his head after he fell to the floor. Pausing to empty the revolver and reload it with dumdum bullets (their filed tips causing the bullets to spin around inside a victim's body, ensuring almost certainly fatal internal injuries), White walked toward the supervisors' offices where he found Milk and asked to speak with him. White entered his own former office with Milk, raised the revolver and fired five bullets. Leaving Milk for dead, White dashed from City Hall, met his wife outside St. Mary's Cathedral, and walked with her to a police station to turn himself in. As news of the killings spread across San Francisco, a silent candle-lit vigil to City Hall was arranged for that night, attended by around 50,000 people.

Pleading diminished capacity and using what became known as the "Twinkie defense", claiming that his mind had been unbalanced by the consumption of too much candy, White was convicted in May 1979 of voluntary manslaughter and received a lenient five-year prison sentence. The failure to find White guilty of murder and the relatively short sentence inflamed many San Franciscans, particularly in the Castro from where 5,000 marched on the night of the sentencing to City Hall, where a rock was hurled through the entrance doors and a full-scale riot ensued. Fourteen police cars were overturned and set ablaze in unrest that continued until midnight, causing damage estimated at $400,000.

As calm appeared to have been restored, many of the demonstrators returned to the Castro only to find the police (without formal sanction and with their identity-revealing badges concealed) launching a revenge attack. Entering Castro Street bars in full riot gear and using batons against customers and bystanders, they also at times attacked those fleeing along the street. The main target was the Elephant Walk, a gay bar that had rejected furtiveness and installed large plate glass windows, allowing customers to see out and the public to see in. With a large contingent of the city's media gathered in the Castro following the riot, the police brutality was widely recorded and condemned, as was the earlier violence of the rioters.

Aware of the level of hostility towards him, Milk had foreseen the possibility of assassination and had made several tape recordings to be played in the event of his death. On these, he listed his preferred successors and recorded a speech intended to inspire those who followed him. One of the tapes includes what became a much quoted (and misquoted) prescient line: "If a bullet should enter my brain, let that bullet destroy every closet door."

AIDS: A New Battle

The killing of Milk and Moscone shocked and saddened most of San Francisco. But the gay community, in particular, was about to be confronted with death on a scale greater than anyone might have imagined possible outside of a war zone. In the early 1980s US health officials detected a sharp rise in deaths among otherwise healthy men apparently due to unusual forms of pneumonia and skin cancer. The cause was eventually established as a virus, HIV, which developed inside the victim's body into Acquired Immune Deficiency Syndrome, or AIDS, destroying the sufferer's immune system. Twenty-four cases reported in San Francisco by December 1981 had risen to 118 by the end of 1982, and numbers continued to grow at an alarming pace.

Even more extraordinary was the fact that the virus seemed only to attack white gay men. A 1985 survey suggested that 37 percent of gay men in the city had been exposed to the virus and it was feared that as much as a tenth of the Castro's population might soon die from the disease. Ten percent of all the US's reported AIDS cases were in San Francisco (only New York, with a much larger population, had more) and most of these were in the Castro. With little known about the disease or how it was spread, fear caused some landlords to evict infected tenants; other victims lost their jobs and some were shunned by health workers fearful of becoming infected themselves. This, combined with the reluctance of the federal government (headed by Ronald Reagan and committed to reducing social expenditure) to respond with appropriate urgency, forced the Castro to take a leading role in confronting the epidemic.

Raising funds for organizations such as the Shanti Project, largely volunteer-staffed and providing domestic, social and spiritual help for AIDS sufferers, and raising public awareness with AIDS education initiatives, the Castro spearheaded the national response to the crisis. The neighborhood was helped by San Francisco mayor Dianne Feinstein, who declared the country's first AIDS Awareness Week in 1984, and by the city's media, who led the nation in treating the matter as a public health issue rather than a minority concern. Soon everyone in the Castro either had, or knew someone who had, been directly affected by the disease. It was a period when, as Frances Fitzgerald put it: "a lot of mothers came to San Francisco." The mothers were not coming to admire the Golden Gate Bridge, but to nurse their dying sons.

During 1985 on the annual candle-lit procession to City Hall to mark the murder of Milk and Moscone, a Castro activist called Cleve Jones asked those attending to create placards bearing the names of friends and lovers who had died from AIDS. Jones and others then fixed the placards to a wall of the Federal Building, adjacent to City

Hall and overlooking UN Plaza, where they came to resemble a giant patchwork quilt. The quilt image stayed with Jones when he helped create what became the first panel of the AIDS Memorial Quilt, by 1987 formally organized as the Names Project Foundation.

Inviting lovers, friends, and family to mark the loss of a loved one by making a three-by-six-foot quilt remembering their life, the Names Project sewed each quilt into an ever-growing patchwork. The quilt was carried to Washington DC in October 1987 for the annual gay and lesbian rights march and laid out along the National Mall—becoming a potent signal to the US government of the number of AIDS deaths. At that time it had 1,920 patches; a year later, it had over 8,000. Sent on tour, the quilt contributed to increasing AIDS awareness, inspired local quilts, raised around $3 million and, by October 2001, having become the world's largest community arts project, had 44,000 patches representing 19 percent of AIDS deaths in the US.

As it became established that the HIV virus was transmitted through bodily fluids, the promiscuity of San Francisco's gay population, particularly in the bathhouses, became a major issue. Pressure rose for the bathhouses to be closed or at least the activity within them to be regulated. What might initially be seen as a matter of public health provoked a fierce debate on civil liberties issues. The bathhouses had played a major role in gay history, offering for the first time a chance to explore gay sexuality with negligible fear of arrest, violence, blackmail, or ridicule. Many in the Castro saw closure as marking an end to the freedoms they had fought so hard to acquire. It was also argued that closure (particularly as so much about the virus was still uncertain) would be seen as an attack on the gay community that other cities with less liberal attitudes would follow by imposing harsh anti-gay laws. Some in the Castro even feared that the virus might be a form of germ warfare, perpetrated against them by the FBI or CIA.

A long and painful debate led to the effective end of the bathhouses and the high-risk, health-wise, activities inside them. In many respects, however, San Francisco emerged as a place where the gay community had displayed social responsibility and was not simply promoting a gay agenda. Even the bathhouse owners who had feared a loss of revenue found they made handsome profits by selling the buildings on what was now very valuable land.

The specter of AIDS forced the Castro itself to change. A large majority of residents began practicing safe sex and became less promiscuous. Increasingly aware of their own mortality, they looked inward and re-evaluated their lives and lifestyles. For many, the wildness of pre-AIDS days was something best consigned to the past and they took up tamer forms of entertainment: the Castro Country Club opened to provide an alcohol-free setting for games of Trivial Pursuit, and the long-standing Wednesday night bingo session at the Most Holy Redeemer Church suddenly attracted a large contingent of gay men. Another more visible change on Castro Street was the decline of the clone look: many gay men now simply looked like regular San Franciscans. As Harvey Milk had suggested (although he could not have foreseen the reason), the gay uniform perhaps really was no more than a necessary phase.

An unexpected excuse for a celebration came in 1985 when the Gay Freedom Day parade coincided with the return to the US of two Castro gays who had been among the Americans held hostage following the hijacking of a TWA plane in the Middle East. One of the men, Jack McCarty, had been a Shanti Project volunteer and became an unofficial counselor for the captives as they feared for their lives, unable throughout to explain (fearing execution by his guards) that he could remain calm in the face of death because, as a gay man in San Francisco, he had been forced to accept his own mortality. On their return to the US, McCarty and his lover, Victor Amburgy, stepped from the US Air Force plane arm-in-arm before the national media.

Coupled to the fiction of the San Francisco Giants winning baseball's World Series, the hostage incident was recorded in Armistead Maupin's *Significant Others*, the fifth title in the *Tales From The City* novels that had amusingly documented San Francisco's polysexual make-up since the late 1970s. Finding a balance between humor and the seriousness of AIDS challenged Maupin (b.1944), but *Significant Others* became one of the first works of fiction to deal with the disease as an omnipresent backdrop to San Francisco life.

Queer Capital of the World
Having faced its biggest challenge and endured its greatest losses, the Castro (still the city's gay hub even though gays and lesbians reside all

over the city), emerged as less a place of gay sexual abandonment than a tidy and well-ordered neighborhood of lovingly and expensively preserved homes with a population that enjoyed much higher than average incomes (many gays had well-paid professional jobs and few faced the financial drain of raising a family). By the 1990s, the Castro was also home to an intriguing generational mixture: old-timers remembered the dark days of the 1950s and 1960s; veterans of the 1970s struggles were now settling into middle age; younger arrivals took many hard-won freedoms for granted and bemoaned the neighborhood's lack of nightlife.

While the Castro remained predominantly male, women had established a feminist and lesbian enclave of sorts nearby along Valencia Street, on the western edge of the Mission District. Amid the bookstores, cafés and meeting places, Valencia Street also boasted Good Vibrations, no. 1210, a woman-friendly (in the sense that all customers are welcome, sleaze is absent, and dildos are offered in forms other than big and penis-shaped) sex-aids shop which found space to display what was claimed to be the world's only collection of historic vibrators.

Today's Castro even has children. Some were the fruits of previous heterosexual relationships, some were adopted by gay couples, but most belong to the growing numbers of heterosexual couples who discovered that the Castro has elegant homes, a peaceful mood, good transport links to Downtown, and a strong sense of community: an ideal place, in fact, to raise a family. For offspring of elementary school age, it also has the Harvey Milk Civil Rights Academy, as the former Douglass School was renamed in 1996.

As cozy as the present-day Castro may seem, many gay and gay-related matters, particularly transgender issues, remain the stuff of strong debate and—as evinced by a riot in 1991 that followed the state governor backtracking on an employment rights law—are still liable to provoke a heated uprising. The Castro, too, remains more acutely aware than most of the dangers of complacency in fighting a disease that has not gone away nor been defeated.

The Gay Lesbian and Freedom Day Parade has grown into one of the city's biggest events, albeit one described in the *San Francisco Chronicle* as now "more focused on selling than yelling." Not far behind is the Castro Halloween parade (during the days of police oppression of gay bars, a truce was unofficially observed on Halloween) that grew so big that it, and its vast extravaganza of costumes, was relocated to Civic Center in 1997. And even mainstream guidebooks to San Francisco cover the Castro and offer advice on "where to camp it up in the queer capital of the world."

A Cybernetic Ecology: SoMa, 1985–2001

In 1968 poet and novelist Richard Brautigan "gave" a poem, "All Watched Over By Machines of Loving Grace", to the Diggers who printed it and distributed it throughout the city. Through three short verses, the poem describes a future world where "mammals and computers live together in mutual programing harmony" in "a cybernetic ecology where we are free of our labors and joined back to nature."

Allowing the poem to be freely reproduced by anyone provided they in turn distributed it for free, Brautigan's copyright stipulation was perhaps a foretaste of present-day peer-to-peer file sharing and open source computer software. The poem might also be viewed as part of a thread that began when Allen Ginsberg's epoch-making *Howl* was made possible by IBM (whose machine cost the poet his job, thereby giving him time to write) and continued into the 1990s when San Francisco—particularly the south of Market Street area—set the pace for a cyber-revolution that, despite its impact being distorted by the mood swings of capitalism, is still just beginning.

South of the Slot

The 1851 O'Farrell plan made the south of Market Street district ideal for industrial use. Shipyards and docks were steadily built along First Street and cargo was carried along a network of tracks that converged at the gigantic Southern Pacific Railroad Switchyards. Earlier, however, elegant mansions had made Rincon Hill (located where the elevated I-80 now carries traffic between SoMa and the Bay Bridge) the home of San Francisco's moneyed elite and helped establish the tradition of the higher earners occupying the higher ground. Exclusivity was lost when Second Street was extended south and many residents of means relocated to the newly accessible Nob Hill.

By the time the 1906 fire destroyed the remains of Rincon Hill's mansions, SoMa contained foundries, factories, and warehouses, and was the home of San Francisco's blue-collar workforce. Popularly, the area was known as "South of the Slot" in recognition of the cable car slot that ran along Market Street, the phrase becoming shorthand for the city's class division. Born in 1876 in the district at the corner of Third and Brannan Streets, Jack London used the name for a Jekyll-and-Hyde tale of a sociology professor who crosses Market Street to research the working classes:

> *North of the Slot were the theatres, hotels, and shopping district, the banks and the staid, respectable business houses. South of the Slot were the factories, slums, laundries, machine-shops, boiler works, and the abodes of the working class... The Slot was the metaphor that expressed the class cleavage of Society.*

Unsurprisingly, it was in SoMa that San Francisco's powerful trade union movement grew, driven by a militancy that culminated a city-wide general strike in 1934 and strenuous efforts by the US government to have the waterfront workers' leader, the Australian-born Harry Bridges, deported as a communist. Some of the industrial conflicts feature in the Californian history scenes depicted by Anton Refregiar's WPA murals decorating the interior of the 1940 post office at 99 Mission Street.

The murals and the post office are now absorbed into the Rincon Center, an office and retail space that rose during SoMa's 1980s regeneration, part of the transformation that resulted from the city offering manufacturing companies (those that survived the industrial decline of the early 1970s) financial incentives to leave the city. In their wake, disused factories and warehouses were commonly converted into live-work areas for artists, and rehearsal rooms and performance spaces for music, dance, and drama. Folsom Street, meanwhile, evolved into a nightlife area, first with gay bars and clubs, later with some of the city's leading mainstream nightspots and live music venues. During the 1990s, the construction of the Yerba Buena Center cultural complex was crowned by the opening of the Museum of Modern Art, raising San Francisco's cultural profile and driving up SoMa property values.

Multimedia Gulch

Amid the mixture of new developments, declining factories, low-rent apartments, and alternative art spaces, one section—South Park—still bore the marks of Rincon Hill. With Georgian-style homes modeled on a posh London terrace overlooking a green oval of sycamores and weeping willows, South Park had been laid out by an English developer in the 1850s but had not been completed before the well-to-do snubbed SoMa and its family homes became apartment houses.

Computer-based multimedia businesses, boosted by the rise of personal computing and the advent of the CD-Rom, began moving into former warehouses near South Park in the mid-1980s. The proliferation of programmers and graphic designers, all searching for groundbreaking software applications that would bring massive financial rewards in the fast-expanding market, brought the immediate area a new nickname: Multimedia Gulch.

Describing a declining South Park in the *San Francisco Chronicle* in 1917, Walter J. Thompson, wrote of strolling "...down Third street as far as Bryant and Brannan, where the business signs are made up of strange characters and the air is charged with the jargon of foreign tongues to a bewildering degree." The same description could almost have been applied eighty years on as Multimedia Gulch drew settlers from all over the country and foreigners bearing H1B visas enabling "speciality workers" to live and work in the US: forty percent of such visas at the time went to computer software specialists. The wooden floors and iron-beamed ceilings of the former warehouses were colonized by the casually attired workforce of new informally-run companies for which the nearest thing to a corporate logo might be a handwritten label stuck on a wall near the entrance. A more visible sign of change was the upward rise of South Park, which accumulated a French bistro and scores of homes smartly restored by affluent new occupants, soon to be swapping gossip on how the potential of the CD-Rom was being eclipsed by a thing called the internet.

By 1993, outsiders could read about the emerging cyber scene with the launch of the SoMa-based *Wired*, the first magazine devoted to digital media and eulogizing its potential to change the world. With "dazzling layout and kaleidoscopic typefaces", *Wired* spread a lengthy quote from 1960s media guru Marshall McLuhan across the opening

pages of its first issue and stood in opposition not only to mainstream media but to established computer publications more concerned with selling advertising than defining the future.

Some San Franciscans had tasted cyberspace with SFNet, a local version of what would become the internet. SFNet users could engage in online chats with other users either from their own homes (two thousand subscribers by 1995) or from a café equipped with a terminal where 25¢ bought six minutes of use. An even earlier version of community connectedness appeared in Berkeley during 1972, when the Community Memory Project linked a noisy teletext machine at Leopold Records (a music store known for its message board) to a San Francisco mainframe computer and printed out scores of personal messages, usually to bemused onlookers. By the early 1980s, the Community Memory Project had evolved into coin-operated kiosks (reading was free; sending was cheap) around Berkeley, linking hitchhikers with drivers and carrying lengthy personal observations on topical issues. It was, as one of its founders put it, an "information flea market".

Silicon Suburbia

As the internet grew, Multimedia Gulch became increasingly important to San Francisco's economy, even though much of the action was taking place forty miles south in Silicon Valley, a name created by a journalist in 1971 to describe the sprawling electronics-dominated communities across the San Mateo and Santa Clara valleys, around the city of San Jose and the Stanford University campus at Palo Alto.

Earning over $30 million annually from its patents and charging some of the highest tuition fees in the US, Stanford University also forged the valley's reputation for scientific innovation. In the 1930s, a part-time electronics engineering professor called Frederick Terman encouraged his graduate students to stay in the area and start their own businesses, eager to close the gap between research and commerce. Two who did so, first operating out of a garage (something that became a valley tradition and gave rise to the modern term "out of the garage" to describe a company on the rise) were William Hewlett and David Packard, who rose from developing an automated urinal flusher to head the world's second largest computer company.

Advances in radio and radar raised the valley's reputation through the Second World War, and the ready availability of Stanford graduates encouraged the New York-based business system provider, IBM, to open a $32-million research center at San Jose. IBM's facility pioneered magnetic disk drives and encouraged more technology firms to absorb local farmland. William Shockley (a Nobel Prize winner for co-inventing the transistor) arrived and initially operated his semiconductor firm from a former apricot-drying shed. A group of disgruntled Shockley employees broke away to form Fairchild Semiconductors from which, in turn in 1968, two frustrated staff departed to concentrate on the technology that gave birth to microprocessors and to start a new company called Intel.

The early-1970s success of the valley-based Atari showed that a market existed for home computer games and the now much mythologized Homebrew Computer Club began a few years later in a room adjacent to Stanford University's Linear Accelerator. Among the club's home-computing enthusiasts were those who would create Apple Computers and, in the late 1970s, launch the Apple II with the user-friendly graphical interface that suddenly made computers useable and desirable for a mass market.

As desktop computers became fixtures in the home and office, Silicon Valley firms provided the software and the hardware to run them. Local names such as Cisco Systems and Sun Microsystems (an acronym derived from Stanford University Network) founded in the 1980s soon became globally known, and by the time the internet-based economy boomed in the late 1990s, a new generation of Stanford graduates had created web-based companies such as Yahoo! and Google.

The surge in desktop computing brought rapid expansion to San Jose, and its population soon exceeded that of San Francisco. By engulfing smaller towns and turning farmland into science parks, however, San Jose was a city without a soul in the middle of what *USA Today* called a "tangle of freeways and tiny towns". San Jose had little beyond well-paid jobs to offer the twenty-something explorers of the cyberspace frontier. San Francisco, by contrast, offered plenty and became the preferred home for many new Silicon Valley employees.

Unease that San Francisco was becoming a suburb of Silicon Valley rose during the 1990s when the peninsula's major public transit provider, CalTrans, recorded a doubling of southbound morning traffic. Increasingly congested freeways showed that many more were commuting south to the valley by car: particularly on I-280, easily accessed from SoMa and the neighboring Mission District.

The Rise and Fall of the Cyberhood

A 1998 survey found 35,000 San Franciscans, equal to seven percent of the work force, employed by 379 new technology companies, most of them in the SoMa "cyberhood" which generated annual revenue of $2 billion. The same year, venture capitalists injected $657 million into the city, a year later, $3.3 billion. With start-ups quickly moving to stock market flotation, staff were liable to be offered (and want) stock options as well as wages, which were already 65 percent higher than the Bay Area average. As public relations, marketing, and office administration staff swelled the ranks of designers and programmers, it became common for dotcom companies to double in size every few months, making the search for office space ever more intense. SoMa rents began exceeding those of the Financial District, and landlords, too, began demanding stock options as well as rent.

Residential accommodation was also at a premium. The search for living space spread west from SoMa into the Mission District, a strongly Latino area where landlords began evicting tenants in the rush to turn modest apartments into luxury condos for high-income dotcommers unlikely to worry about paying the city's highest rents or a purchasing price close to a million dollars. Meanwhile, informally dressed dotcom executives dining al fresco outside South Park bistros were liable to have their lunches interrupted by a serving of résumés from recent graduates hoping for a dotcom job. Even non-tech staff such as secretaries and receptionists enjoyed higher wages than those in identical old economy jobs.

As *Wired* continued to expound a utopian cyber future from its SoMa base, its commercial success was exceeded by another San Francisco publication, *The Industry Standard*, founded in 1998 in the old economy heartland of the Financial District. Soon required reading for dotcom entrepreneurs, *The Industry Standard* carried news, views, and endless speculation about start-ups, mergers, takeovers, and stock market flotations, while advertising—worth $140 million in

2000—made the magazine as thick as a small town telephone directory.

Inviting comparisons with the gold rush, the dotcom frenzy brought sudden and sharp change to San Francisco, and the city seemed to be embracing the new at the expense of the old. Gyms, juice bars, and sushi restaurants catering to dotcommers spread through SoMa and into the Mission District, destabilizing the existing community and driving out family-run businesses along with the numerous non-profit organizations that provided free or low-cost community services. Also disappearing were the artists' loft spaces and performance venues.

Across San Francisco, rents doubled between 1995 and 1999, evictions increased four-fold, and many long-time residents were forced out of the city (some opted to live together, enduring overcrowded conditions to pay the raised rents) while the demolition of low-rent projects drastically reduced the city's affordable-housing stock. Even traditionally wealthy areas such as Pacific Heights and the Marina District felt the change with rocketing rents and property prices indicating that merely being rich was no longer enough to live comfortably in San Francisco.

The irony that an industry that promised a new online world free of physical boundaries needed to occupy a few blocks of a single city did not go unnoticed, particularly as evidence mounted of live-work spaces designated for artists being illegally used by those dotcom companies which found the city planning department could be easily duped. A scheme for a 159,000-square-foot office and loft development called Bryant Square in a Mission District residential quarter that involved the loss of fifty artists' studios was just one high-profile plan that inspired the city's biggest protest rallies since the 1970s. The Mission Yuppie Eradication Project was a one-man initiative but captured the zeitgeist by promising to scratch any BMWs, Porsches or SUVs parked (parking itself became a major issue) in the Mission District. The dotcom invasion was creating what the *San Francisco Chronicle* called "the great schism of 1999" as it charted the mayoral election campaign waged that year.

Many who arrived for dotcom jobs were unaware of the resentment that awaited them. But that very resentment was based in part on the newcomers being unaware of the city's traditions for being something other than a place simply to get rich—and certainly not a Silicon Valley suburb. A *San Francisco Chronicle* editorial raged against "20 somethings in $70,000 sport utility vehicles talking to their brokers on cell phones." It was a theme pursued by Paulina Borsook in the (San Francisco-based) online magazine, *Salon.com*, in an article headed: "How The Internet Ruined San Francisco":

> *San Francisco has become a city of 22-year-old Barbie-bunny market-ing girls who don't realize the Web is not the Internet, and guys who have come to San Francisco because the dotcom version of Dutch tulip-mania offers better odds of instant wealth than making partner at Merrill Lynch. The result is a city whose unique history and sensibility is being swamped by twerps with 'tude.*

And of their lack of respect for San Francisco and its neighborhoods, Borsook wrote:

> *Dotcom people just need a place to crash after they work 15 hours a day—sleep is for the weak and sickly. They haven't lived here long enough to know or care about civic issues, for the most part—and for those who subscribe to the prevailing high-tech orthodoxy of libertarianism, there's not much reason for them to care.*

The *Chronicle's* Mike Weiss offered what by local standards might be seen as a serious public health warning: "there may not be any differences between San Francisco and anyplace else in the age of the global economy." He also complained that the city was "in danger of becoming ordinary" before curling into a metaphorical fetal position to moan: "the city misses Herb Caen" (referring to the late columnist). More directly in June 2000, a *Bay Guardian* editorial stated: "It's no secret San Francisco is on sale to the highest bidder," and described a "tidal wave of gentrification" sweeping through SoMa and the Mission District.

The 1999 election was won by the incumbent, Willie Brown, narrowly defeating the anti-growth advocate Tom Ammiano. So dominated by dotcom issues was the campaign that neither Brown's

Africa-American origin—he became the city's first black mayor in 1995—nor the fact that Ammiano was gay, were viewed as important. As the great schism remained, some presciently warned that San Francisco, in its drive to accommodate the e-economy was turning it into a single-industry town: and if the industry were to collapse, then so might the city.

The e-economy entered the new millennium with its stock on the rise, as it had been from the mid-1990s. But by 2001, when the failure of highly capitalized dotcom companies to make a profit was combined with a broad computer industry downturn and wider economic uncertainties, the tech-based economy crashed. Those who had sat on rising paper fortunes suddenly found their stock options worthless, and in San Francisco and Silicon Valley redundancies became common. Increasingly charting close-downs rather than start-ups, *The Industry Standard* had to report its own demise as sharply falling advertising revenue forced its closure in August 2001.

During that same summer, the only thing booming in SoMa were the "pink slip parties", intended to bring newly unemployed dotcommers into contact with those still able to offer jobs (usually non-high capitalization "bootstrapping" companies with a specialist niche) and the opportunity to drown their sorrows in cut-price cocktails. The city became awash with pastel-colored curvy sofas and lava lamps as bankrupt dotcoms auctioned off their furniture; apartments were now findable if still barely affordable; and the San Francisco-Silicon Valley freeways were suddenly less congested.

Proving the decline had set in, the twelve months to November 2001 saw more people leave the Bay Area than arrive in it; 65,000 dotcom jobs disappeared in the year to February 2001, raising the prospect of a shrinking population for the first time since the 1970s and potentially disastrous economic consequences for the city. In South Park, it was not just dotcoms that closed: the highly-regarded Ristorante Ecco shut its doors as disappearing dotcoms left it with too few mouths to feed.

Archive of the Future
The financial bubble had burst, but the "com" in dotcom stood for commercial and it was the e-economy that was damaged, not the cyber

future. Brautigan's cybernetic meadow may have been trampled in the rush to fast dollars but the forest was intact. For all the infrastructural problems that the e-economy saddled San Francisco with, it was in the nature of the city to be at the forefront of a new form of communication, what cyberspace writer Douglas Rushkoff termed "the people's internet".

One indication of a fresh direction had appeared during 1999 when, in a remarkable fusing of the old and new, a former military hospital at the Presidio (1,500 acres of hills, cliff tops and woodlands that originated with the Spanish garrison of 1776) became the site of the world's biggest library. A library without books but with hundreds of computers storing the ever-expanding Internet Archive, co-founder and cyber-guru Brewster Kahle compared it with the Library of Alexandria, the ancient world's great repository of knowledge.

Despite getting less coverage in the financial pages than during the boom years, the annual San Francisco-based Webby Awards (launched in 1996) continue to present prizes for website excellence in categories that include Activism, Commerce, Spiritual, and Weird, and draw more nominations from more countries than ever before. Insightfully perhaps, the 2002 presentation ceremony was themed around an Arthur C Clarke quote: "When it comes to technology, most people overestimate the impact in the short term and underestimate it in the long term."

The internet has also brought a revival of a kind for the Diggers, who have made a chronology, historic documents, and other materials available at The Digger Archive (www.diggers.org). Now, as in Haight-Ashbury in the mid-1960s, they (whoever they are) respond to queries with answers that are frustrating, provocative, and ingenious in equal measure. Also on the site is Dominick Cavallo's 1980s reflections on the Diggers and the new world suggested by Brautigan's poem: "It was the quintessential American Eden: social concord achieved through technological progress, a Digger-world devoid of the rat race, careers and endless quests for status and power."

Such a quintessential American Eden would, of course, be viewed anywhere as a hopelessly idealistic pipedream.

Anywhere, that is, except San Francisco.

Further Reading

Non-Fiction

Adams, Ansel, *An Autobiography*. Boston: Little, Brown, 1985.

Adams, Ben, *San Francisco: An Informal Guide*. Clinton, Mass: Colonial Press, 1961.

Asbury, Herbert, *The Barbary Coast*. New York: Dorset Press, 1989 (first published New York: Alfred A Knopf, 1933).

Atherton, Gertrude, *California: An Intimate History*. Freeport, NY: Books For Libraries Press, 1971 (first published 1914).

– *My San Francisco: A Wayward Biography*. New York: Bobbs-Merril Co., 1946.

Austin, Leonard, *Around the World in San Francisco*. San Francisco: Fearon, 1959.

Bakalinsky, Adah, *Stairway Walks in San Francisco*. San Francisco: Lexikos, 1984.

Bronson, William, *The Sky Shook The Sky Burned*. San Francisco: Chronicle, 1986 (first published Doubleday, Garden City, New York: 1959).

Byrne, Chuck et al, *San Francisco Architecture*. San Francisco: Chronicle Books, 1992.

Caen, Herb, *Baghdad by the Bay*. Sausalito: Comstock Editions, 1988 (first published New York: Doubleday, 1949).

– *One Man's San Francisco*. Sausalito: Comstock Editions, 1978.

Campbell, James, *This Is The Beat Generation: New York, San Francisco, Paris*. London: Secker & Warburg, 1999.

Cavallo, Dominick, *A Fiction of the Past: The Sixties in American History*. New York: St. Martin's Press, 1999.

Cole, Tom, *A Short History of San Francisco*. San Francisco: Don't Call It Frisko Press, 1988.

Corbett, Michael R., *Splendid Survivors: San Francisco's Downtown Architecture*. San Francisco: The Foundation For San Francisco Architectural Heritage, 1979.

Dana, Richard Henry, *Two Years Before The Mast*. Santa Barbara: The Narrative Press, 2001 (first published 1841).

Davis, William Heath, *Seventy Five Years in California*. San Francisco: John Howell, 1929.

Delehanty, Randolph, *San Francisco: The Ultimate Guide*. San Francisco: Chronicle Books, 1989.

Dunlap, Carol, *California People*. Salt Lake City: Peregrine Smith Books, 1982.

Eldredge, Zoeth Skinner, *The Beginnings of San Francisco*. New York: John C. Ranking Company, 1912.

Friedman, Myra, *Buried Alive: A Biography of Janis Joplin*. New York: Harmony Books, 1992 (first published New York: William Morrow & Co., 1973).

Fong-Torres, Shirley, *San Francisco Chinatown*. San Francisco: China Books & Periodicals, 1991.

Forbes, James M., *Café San Francisco*. San Francisco: James M Forbes, 1993.

Foster, Lynn V., *California: The Mission Trail*. New York: Fielding Travel Books, 1988.

Gaddis, Thomas E., *Birdman of Alcatraz*. Bath: Chivers Press, 1983 (first published 1956).

Gleason, Ralph J., *The Jefferson Airplane and the San Francisco Sound*. New York: Ballantine Books: New York, 1969.

Goins, David Lance, *The Free Speech Movement: Coming of Age in the 1960s*. Berkeley: Ten Speed Press, 1993.

Genthe, Arnold and John Kuo Wei Tchen, *Genthe's Photographs of San Francisco's Chinatown*. New York: Dover, 1984.

Gentry, Curt, *The Madams of San Francisco*. Sausalito: Comstock Editions, 1977 (first published New York: New American Library, 1964).

Gesensway, Deborah and Mindy Roseman, *Beyond Words: Images from America's Concentration Camps*. Ithaca: Cornell University Press, 1987.

Gordon, Mark, *Once Upon A City*. San Francisco: Don't Call It Frisko Press, 1988.

Hansen, Gladys, *San Francisco Almanac*. San Rafael: Presidio Press, 1980 (first published 1975).

Harrison, Hank, *The Grateful Dead*. London: Star Books, 1975 (first published 1973).

Hart, James D., *A Companion to California*. Berkeley and Los Angeles: University of California Press, 1987.

Herron, Don, *The Literary World of San Francisco and its Environs*. San Francisco: City Lights Books, 1985.

Jackson, Donald Dale, *Gold Dust: The California Gold Rush and the Forty-niners*. London: George Allen & Unwin, 1980.

Johnson, Diane, *The Life of Dashiell Hammett*. London: Picador, 1985 (first published New York: Random House, 983).

Kroeber, A.L., *Handbook of the Indians of California*. New York, Dover Press, 1976 (first published 1925).

Lai, Him Mark et al, *Island: Poetry and History of Chinese Immigrants on Angel Island, 1910-1940*. Seattle: University of Washington Press, 1991.

Lee, Martin A. and Bruce Shlain, *Acid Dreams: The Complete Social History of LSD, the CIA, the Sixties and Beyond*. New York: Grove/Atlantic, 1985.

Marinacci, Mike, *Mysterious California: Strange Places and Eerie Phenomena in the Golden State*. Los Angeles: Panpipes Press, 1988.

Martin, Don and Betty, *The Best of San Francisco*. San Francisco: Chronicle Books, 1990.

McClure, Michael, *Scratching the Beat Surface*. New York: Penguin, 1994.

McDowell, Jack (ed.), *San Francisco*. Menlo Park: Sunset Books, 1969.

Milner, Clyde A. et al (eds.) *The Oxford History of the American West*. Oxford: Oxford University Press, 1994.

Miles, Barry, *Ginsberg: A Biography*. London & New York: Simon & Schuster, 1989.

Neville, Amelia Ransome, *The Fantastic City*. Cambridge, Mass: The Riverside Press, 1933.

Nicosia, Gerald, *Memory Babe, A Critical Biography of Jack Kerouac*. New York: Grove Press, 1983.

Nopy, Gary (ed.), *Distant Horizon: Documents from the Nineteenth Century American West*. Omaha: University of Nebraska Press, 1999.

Nordhoff, Charles, *Nordhoff's West Coast*. London & New York: KPI, 1987 (first published 1874-5).

Patterson Doss, Margot, *San Francisco At Your Feet*. New York: Grove Press, 1974 (first published 1964).

Perry, Charles, *The Haight-Ashbury*. New York: Random House, 1984.

Pitcher, Don, *Berkeley Inside/Out*. Berkeley: HeyDay Books, 1989.

Richards, Rand, *Historic San Francisco*. San Francisco: Heritage House, 1991.

Sanders, Ed, *The Family*. New York: Avon Books, 1972.

Schumcher, Michael, *Dharma Lion—A Biography of Allen Ginsberg*. New York: St. Martin's Press, 1992.

Scully, Rock, with Dalton, David, *Living with the Dead*. New York: Cooper Square Press, 2001 (first published 1996).

Senkewicz, Robert M., *Vigilantes in Gold Rush San Francisco*. Stanford: Stanford University Press, 1985.

Shilts, Randy, *And the Band Played On*. New York: St. Martin's Press, 1987.

Shilts, Randy, *The Mayor of Castro Street*. New York: St. Martin's Press, 1982.

Siefkin, David, *Meet Me at the St. Francis*. San Francisco: St. Francis Hotel Corp., 1979.

Slick, Grace, with Cagan, Andrea, *Somebody to Love?* New York: Warner Books Inc., 1998.

Soulé, Frank et al, *The Annals of San Francisco*. New York: D. Appleton & Co., 1855.

Stevens, Jay, *Storming Heaven: LSD and the American Dream*. New York: Atlantic Monthly Press, 1987.

Swanberg, W.A., *Citizen Hearst: A Biography of William Randolph Hearst*. New York: Collier Books, 1986 (first published 1961).

Twain, Mark, *Roughing It*. New York: New American Library, 1994 (first published 1872).

Waldhorn, Judith Lynch and Sally B. Woodbridge, *Victoria's Legacy: Tours of San Francisco Bay Area Architecture*. San Francisco: 101 Productions, 1978.

Ward, Geoffrey C., *The West: Illustrated History*. Boston: Little, Brown, 1996.

Wolfe, Tom, *The Electric Kool-Aid Acid Test*. New York: Bantam Doubleday, 1999 (first published New York: Bantam, 1969).

Fiction and Poetry

Atherton, Gertrude, *Rezanov*. Kingston, Ontario: Limestone Press, 1998 (first published 1906).

Bierce, Ambrose, *The Devil's Dictionary*. Oxford: Oxford University Press, 1998 (first published New York: Albert & Charles Boni, 1911).

– *The Complete Short Stories of Ambrose Bierce* Lincoln, NE: University of Nebraska Press, 1985.

Far, Sui Sin, *Mrs. Spring Fragrance and Other Writings*. Champagne, Ill: University of Illinois Press, 1995.

Gibson, William, *Virtual Light*. New York: Bantam Doubleday Dell, 1993.

– *All Tomorrow's Parties*. New York: Putnam Publishing Group, 1999

Ginsberg, Allen, *Howl and Other Poems*. San Francisco: City Lights Books, 1956.

– *Reality Sandwiches*. San Francisco: City Lights Books, 1963.

Gores, Joe, *Hammett*. New York: Harper Collins, 1982 (first published New York: Putnam Publishing Group, 1975).

Hall, Austin and Homer Eon Flint, *The Blind Spot*. London: Greenhill, 1987 (first published in book form, Philadelphia, PA: Prime Press, 1951).

Hammett, Dashiell, *The Maltese Falcon*. Mattituck, NY: Amereon, 2000 (first published New York: Alfred A. Knopf, 1930).

Harte, Bret, *The Luck of Roaring Camp and Other Writings*. New York: Penguin, 2001.

Kerouac, Jack, *Dharma Bums*. London & New York: Penguin, 1991 (first published New York: Penguin, 1958).

– *On The Road*. London & New York: Penguin, 1991 (first published New York: Viking, 1958).

Lee, Gus, *China Boy*. New York: EP Dutton, 1991.

London, Jack, *Martin Eden*. London & New York: Penguin, 1994 (first published New York: Macmillan, 1909).

– *The Strength of the Strong* (collection including *South of the Slot*). Mattituck, NY: Amereon, 1976 (first published New York: Macmillan, 1914).

Maupin, Armistead, *28 Barbary Lane: Tales of the City Omnibus*. New York: Harper Collins, 1990.

Norris, Frank, *McTeague: A Story of San Francisco*. New York: Vintage Books/The Library of America, 1990 (first published New York: Double & McClure, 1899).

– *The Octopus: A Story of California.* New York: Penguin, 1994 (first published New York: Doubleday, Page, 1901)

Seth, Vikram, *The Golden Gate.* Boston and London: Faber & Faber, 1986.

Snow, Jade Wong, *Fifth Chinese Daughter.* Seattle: University of Washington Presse, 1989 (first published New York: Harper, 1950).

Tan, Amy, *The Joy Luck Club.* New York: Prentice Hall, 1994 (first published New York: Putnam Publishing Group, 1989).

Web Sites

Many more websites than I can possibly name made researching this book a lot less frustrating than it might otherwise have been. I'd especially like to recommend and thank the following:

www.sfmuseum.org

An already comprehensive but ever expanding online museum, curated by former city archivist Gladys Hansen.

www.zpub.com/sf/history

A multitude of newspaper and magazines clippings from times past, a message board packed with San Francisco lore, and the full text of some revealing and long out-of-print San Francisco books.

www.ci.sf.ca.us

Scrutinizing the city budget and filing a complaint against the police are just two of many possibilities at this official city and county government site. Feel free to email the mayor with your ideas for improving San Francisco: damayor@sfgov.org

www.sfgate.com and www.sfexaminer.com

Online editions of the city's daily newspapers, the *Chronicle* and the *Examiner* respectively.

www.sfbg.com and www.sfweekly.com

The weekly alternative reads from the *Bay Area Guardian* and *SF Weekly*, respectively.

www.diggers.org
They appeared in Haight-Ashbury in the 1960s and they are still around, with many pages of archive material and contemporary Digger wisdom.

www.sfvisitor.org
Useful if predictable, and somewhat bizarrely designed, tourist-aimed site of the Convention & Visitors Bureau.

Neighborhood sites
Each has local historical and contemporary information, and useful links:
The Castro: www.castroonline.com
Chinatown: www.sfchinatown.com
and www.sanfranciscochinatown.com
Haight-Ashbury: www.haightashbury.org
Mission District: www.sfmission.com
North Beach: www.sfnorthbeach.com
The Richmond & Sunset: www.outsidelands.org
Russian Hill: www.rhn.org

Listen to San Francisco
Most San Francisco radio stations make their broadcasts available online. Get a list at www.radioguide.com/cities/sf.html. For a taste of Bay Area radical radio, albeit one under threat from market forces, tune into www.kpfa.org.

Other interesting and (usually) self-explanatory sites
www.bart.gov
www.carneval.com
www.citylights.com
www.countryjoe.com
www.goldengatebridge.org
www.gracecom.org
www.hippiemuseum.org
www.mistersf.com
www.nps.gov/alcatraz

www.saintjohncoltrane.com
www.sfheart.com
www.sfheritage.org
www.sfmoma.org
www.sfmuni.org
www.sfstation.com
www.shapingsf.org
www.vesuvio.com
www.webbyawards.com

✳

Index of Literary & Historical Names

✳

Index of Places and Landmarks

*